TAKE THE
YOUNG
STRANGER BY
THE HAND

THE CHICAGO SERIES ON SEXUALITY,
HISTORY, AND SOCIETY
a series edited by John C. Fout

Also in the series:

*Improper Advances: Rape and Heterosexual Conflict
in Ontario, 1880–1929*
by Karen Dubinsky

*A Prescription for Murder: The Victorian Serial
Killings of Thomas Neill Cream*
by Angus McLaren

*The Language of Sex: Five Voices from
Northern France around 1200*
by John W. Baldwin

*Crossing over the Line: Legislating Morality
and the Mann Act*
by David J. Langum

Sexual Nature/Sexual Culture
edited by Paul R. Abramson and Steven D. Pinkerton

*Love Between Women: Early Christian Responses
to Female Homoeroticism*
by Bernadette J. Brooten

*Trials of Masculinity: Studies in the Policing
of Sexual Boundaries, 1870–1930*
by Angus McLaren

The Invention of Sodomy in Christian Theology
by Mark D. Jordan

*Sites of Desire/Economies of Pleasure:
Sexualities in Asia and the Pacific*
edited by Lenore Manderson and Margaret Jolly

Sex and the Gender Revolution, vol. 1
*Heterosexuality and the Third Gender
in Enlightenment London*
by Randolph Trumbach

John Donald
Gustav-Wrathall

TAKE THE
YOUNG
STRANGER BY
THE HAND

Same-Sex Relations and the YMCA

The University of Chicago Press

Chicago & London

JOHN DONALD GUSTAV-WRATHALL is an independent scholar.

The University of Chicago Press, Chicago 60637
The University of Chicago Press, Ltd., London
© 1998 by John Donald Gustav-Wrathall
All rights reserved. Published 1998
Printed in the United States of America
08 07 06 05 04 03 02 01 00 99   1 2 3 4 5
ISBN: 0-226-90784-8 (cloth)

Library of Congress Cataloging-in-Publication Data
Gustav-Wrathall, John Donald.
    Take the young stranger by the hand : same-sex relations and the YMCA /
John Donald Gustav-Wrathall.
        p.   cm. — (The Chicago series on sexuality, history, and society)
    Includes bibliographical references and index.
    ISBN 0-226-90784-8 (cloth : alk. paper)
    1. Young Men's Christian associations—United States—Membership.
2. Male Friendship—United States—History.   3. Gay men—United
States—History.   I. Series.
    BV1090.G88   1998
    267′.3973—dc21   98-9904
                                                                              CIP

⊗ The paper used in this publication meets the minimum requirements of
the American National Standard for Information Sciences—Permanence of
Paper for Printed Library Materials, ANSI Z39.48–1992.

To my husband and special friend,

Göran Gustav-Wrathall

CONTENTS

ILLUSTRATIONS

PREFACE

As this manuscript about the Young Men's Christian Association goes to press, another Christian men's movement is making the headlines. In the summer of 1997, the "Promise Keepers" organized a "million man march" on Washington, DC. Despite its insistence that it is simply a self-help organization that teaches men responsibility, self-control, and faith in Christ, the organization has been dogged by controversy, criticized for having an ulterior right-wing political agenda. The philosophical basis for the Promise Keepers movement is the claim that traditional family values have declined because men have failed in their responsibilities as husbands and fathers. If men had not "abdicated" their benevolent but authoritarian role as *pater familias*, women would not be seeking work outside the home or demanding positions of leadership in society, children would not be growing up in single-parent families, and gay men and lesbians wouldn't be demanding equal treatment and the right to marry. Men must take back their lost positions of leadership and control—in the family and in society. Once they are at the reins of government and the home again, they can make America the Christian society it was meant to be. Although the Promise Keepers organization was formed only in recent years, Christian men's movements seeking to win America for Christ are not new. Indeed, young men's Christian associations or societies are as old as the Republic, and trace their roots to evangelical men's movements in eighteenth-century England.

But while Christian men's movements have been a part of the American social landscape for over two centuries, twentieth-century movements like the Promise Keepers have a different emphasis than their eighteenth- and nineteenth-century predecessors. Promise Keepers emphasizes male leadership in the home to a much greater extent than any previous movement like it. In the twentieth century, Christian manhood has come to be defined by the roles of husband and father. A man becomes virtuous and wins the approval of (a presumably male) God by asserting himself as head of the home. This is a departure from nineteenth-century Christian men's movements, which defined Christian manhood on the basis of character that was inherent in a man—regardless of his other roles. This book is a narrative about the most successful of the Christian men's movements—the Young Men's Christian Association. The YMCA began in 1848, in an era when Christian manhood was defined in terms of individual character. But it survived and thrived in the twentieth century by adopting a more family-oriented focus, a focus fueled by the desire to undermine feminism and to stamp out homosexuality. This book documents that transformation of focus, and how the YMCA came to adopt its new definitions of Christian manhood. Though the YMCA never quite had the rancorous edge that peeks around the corners of modern Christian-right movements like Promise Keepers, it has used similar rhetoric, sought out similar constituencies, and used similar tactics to promote its agenda. An understanding of the history of the YMCA one hundred years ago may lend insight into some of the issues and struggles that trouble our own time.

ACKNOWLEDGMENTS

Many people and many relationships have played a role in the completion of this book. I am especially grateful to Clarke A. Chambers, who led me to pursue this topic in the first place seven years ago, and whose intellectual guidance and support were invaluable. I am also in debt to all the other members of the Ph.D. committee at the University of Minnesota who oversaw the dissertation on which this book is based: Sara Evans, Jacquelyn Zita, Roland Delattre, and Martin Marty (who served as an outside, nonvoting member). Rudy Vecoli, my advisor, deserves special thanks for providing both feedback and encouragement from the beginning. Steven Ruggles was not a committee member, but offered me crucial information and advice about the quantitative aspects of my research. Matt Sobek also helped with the "quant," and Jim Brown provided necessary technical assistance in the tabulation of machine-readable data.

It is impossible for me to thank deeply enough the wonderful staff of the YMCA of the USA Archives, Andrea Hinding, Dagmar Getz, and David Carmichael. Their advice, ideas, feedback, and encouragement have been invaluable. They offered more time, care, enthusiasm, and insight to the project than anyone else I worked with. Their knowledge of the YMCA's history and familiarity with its records were a tremendous resource. I am also deeply thankful to Jim Kepner and Jean Tretter, of the International Gay and Lesbian Archives, West Hollywood, California, who treated me as a friend, and went out of their way to offer me leads and connect me with oral history narrators in my search for material about some of the more hidden aspects of YMCA social life. The entire staff of the Chicago Historical Society Archives were friendly and responsive, and made my research there efficient, useful, and pleasant.

Special thanks are also due to Allan Bérubé for advising me in the early stages of my research on cruising, for pointing me to critical source material, and helping me connect with oral history narrators. Martin Marty's advice and feedback, especially on the religious history aspects of my material, have been encouraging, interesting, and useful. Susan Armeny of the *Journal of American History*, in the editorial work she did with me on "Provenance as Text: Reading the Silences around Sexuality in Manuscript Collections" (June 1993), helped to crystallize and clarify some key insights that have contributed to the overall development of this research project. And I am deeply indebted to Tom Cook for bringing the 1912 Portland sex scandal to my attention, and for sharing data with me.

In the final stages of this project, I have been most thankful for the cheery enthusiasm of Doug Mitchell and Matt Howard, at the University of Chicago Press, whose encouragement has been a beacon to me. John Fout, the series editor, provided critical feedback without which this book's arguments and presentation of evidence would be much weaker. Thanks are also due to the many readers, editors, and staff at the University of Chicago Press who must here remain nameless, but who have each, in their own way, made a contribution.

Finally, I would like to thank my husband and friend, Göran Gustav-Wrathall, for letting me bounce ideas off him and for his patience in helping me get through. Many people helped directly and indirectly by giving me the personal support and community without which any major undertaking is impossible. Thanks especially to Jerie Smith, Peg Pfab, and David Selzer of (respectively) Lutheran Campus Ministry, United Ministries in Higher Education, and the University Episcopal Center at the University of Minnesota, who supported me personally and spiritually. I also wish to thank a bunch of radical faeries, especially Mumsy, Steve, Willow, Vi, Blossom, Wolf, Sparkle, Viva, Trav and David, Burly, Kuki, Rocky, Heron, Hummingbird, White Ash, and Patrick, for encouraging me, giving me spirit, and making it all worthwhile. And last of all, thanks to Robert "Eddie" Robinson and members of the Twin Cities Community Gospel Choir, who have lifted me up, helped me find peace of mind and some "higher ground," and reminded me that God will always take care of me.

INTRODUCTION

Most Americans take the Young Men's Christian Association (YMCA) for granted. It has become an unremarkable feature of our social landscape. Most Americans have taken a swimming lesson, or attended a concert, or participated in a youth summer camp, or worked out at a YMCA at least once. The ubiquity and the blandness of the YMCA make it a particularly interesting subject of study to the historian, perhaps offering to illuminate best what mainstream America likes to take for granted about itself. The Y's ubiquity has been due to one-hundred-fifty years of relentless outreach. Its blandness has been achieved through studied avoidance of controversy. Above all, the YMCA has earnestly striven to be useful. Nevertheless, closer scrutiny of the YMCA reveals anything but blandness. Within the strife, fears, scandals, hopes, and triumphs of the YMCA is an irony-filled and sometimes tragic story about young men trying to build meaningful community amidst wrenching change.

When young men in Boston and Montreal followed the example of George Williams and J. Christopher Smith of London by founding their own Young Men's Christian Associations in 1851, they intended the YMCA to be a place of spiritual refuge in the city. YMCAs sponsored Bible studies and prayer circles, but also provided early employment bureaus and housing registers. YMCAs did this because they believed that a stable situation and respectable housing were necessary to undergird a life of high spiritual and moral standards. The earliest YMCAs were essentially Christian support groups. They provided not merely intellectual nurture and practical assistance but emotional community. They offered young men the love and friendship of other young men. It is no coincidence that the unofficial anthem of the YMCA early became "Blest Be the Tie That Binds."

The YMCA was driven by a potent spiritual mission. Its leaders saw it as the most powerful evangelical force of the modern age. It would transcend the religious sectarianism that had divided young men for centuries and forge them into a unified force of righteousness. Under its influence, Christian young men would make America a leader of nations and prepare the world for Christ's Second Coming. This mission from God, combined with an ethos linking young men to other young men in love, inspired more than the incidental participation that one expects in most young men's clubs. Men gave their lives to this organization and to each other.

This book examines the emotional underpinnings of the YMCA, and the changes that took place in that organization's and the broader society's views of same-sex love and sexuality. Because of various taboos regarding same-sex love, and because the meanings attached to certain expressions of same-sex love have changed in the last century, such an examination almost always proves controversial. Many will deny that the exercise has any value. This book is probably not for those who are invested in denying gay people a rightful place in society, or who are incapable of viewing homosexuality as anything but sickness or moral perversion. Since such attitudes toward same-sex love usually assume the form of an article of faith, and since propositions of faith can rarely be altered by mundane facts or historical arguments, my, and most readers', time would be wasted on strenuous arguments aimed at such a readership. For those who are not invested in denying gay people a rightful place in society, or history, the endeavor may create greater understanding. Toward the goal of greater understanding and, I hope, the compassion without which understanding is mostly useless, it is worthwhile to wade through the historical evidence.

This book will focus on the passionate commitments that young men of the YMCA made to each other. Many of these commitments were exclusive, life-long, and emotionally intimate. Through the course of the nineteenth century between one-fifth and one-third of YMCA leaders were life-long bachelors who gave their lives to YMCA service. Some of the most revered YMCA leaders of the nineteenth century—Robert R. McBurney, Robert Weidensall, and Sumner F. Dudley, to name just three—were life-long bachelors known for their intense love for young men. YMCA men allowed themselves to become interdependent, and they supported each other through the most difficult challenges they had to face in life: career uncertainty, crises of faith, illness, and death. Many YMCA leaders were single, but they were never alone. The spiritual community created by the YMCA meant that men prayed together, studied together, and worked together, but also ate together, traveled together, and lived together. When some men, reflecting on their careers, used the metaphor of being "married" to the YMCA, there were ways in which this was true. It certainly appears true that in the context of the YMCA men could provide one another more constant and more fulfilling companionship than many nineteenth-century marriages. An obvious analogy to the kind of life commitment made by many YMCA leaders in the nineteenth century is to be found among the many women reformers of the same era—like Jane Addams, Lillian Wald, and Vida Scudder—who similarly remained unmarried and who sustained intense, nurturing relationships with other women in movements with a mission to help other women.

In the past twenty years, as gay and lesbian historians have challenged the silence that has surrounded our lives, and have looked to the past for understanding of modern lesbian and gay communities and identities, a debate has been sparked about the lives of these nineteenth-century women reformers.[1] This debate seems relevant to an analysis of the life commitments of many YMCA leaders. Were "Boston marriages"—the name given to the long-term, intense commitments that some women in these movements made to each other—actually lesbian relationships? The answer to this question remains disputed partly because of a lack of data. We simply do not know whether there was a sexual dimension to these relationships. Even if these relationships had been sexual, it is unlikely that individuals would have left evidence of this for the historical record. But it is also contested largely because historians cannot seem to agree on precisely what they mean by "lesbian relationship." Some historians have argued that a lesbian is a woman who lives a "women-centered life," bypassing altogether the question of sex. Other historians, both lesbian and heterosexual, have argued that redefining lesbianism in such a way as to allow for a sexless relationship reifies the term in a way that is not very meaningful to most people or helpful to lesbians who value the sexual dimension of their relationships.[2] Similarly, in the YMCA there is no question that much of the YMCA leadership consisted of men living lives that were emotionally as well as socially and economically "men-centered." Were a significant number of them gay? This is a question that is very difficult to answer, but nevertheless meaningful for those of us today who are struggling for justice and social equality for sexual minorities.

I find the "women-centered women" analysis valuable because focusing too narrowly on sex does injustice to the complexity of the human drives and emotions that draw people together, even when there is a sexual dimension to their relationship. Many modern gay men and lesbians became aware of their attraction to members of the same sex and acted on it by seeking out community and intense friendship with members of the same sex long before they acted on it sexually, if they ever acted on it sexually. Because modern gay and lesbian relationships include economic interdependence and emotional intensity, modern gays and lesbians recognize an affinity with nineteenth-century individuals who structured their lives around intense emotions and economic interdependence with members of the same sex. To the extent that these kinds of relationships in the nineteenth century were atypical of society's mainstream, to the extent that they clearly broke with a dominant pattern of heterosexual marriage and family-building, we recognize that affinity even more acutely. It would probably delight most gays and lesbians to somehow prove that these relationships, like ours, also included a sexual element. But even if this cannot be proven, it seems significant that individuals in another era of history departed from the marital, heterosexual norm to create social and emotional alternatives.

Living a men-centered life in the YMCA could meet unique emotional needs that heterosexual marriage could not. Whether these men experienced their relationships and their attractions to other men in the same way as modern gay or bisexual men is virtually impossible to prove. But it is significant that they created a way of life for themselves with which many modern gay and bisexual men can recognize an affinity. They created a social alternative for themselves in which emotional needs recognized as unique to gay and bisexual men could have been met. By the early twentieth century, that social alternative was effectively demolished. A number of dramatic changes in the YMCA's program, mission, and demographic makeup eliminated the men-centered-men ethos that dominated the organization in the nineteenth century. Some of those changes were expressly made for the purpose of combating or preventing homosexuality, a goal that increasingly became a priority in the organization after the 1890s as a result of the YMCA's role in early sex education.

The story of how the YMCA went from celebrating to suppressing men whose emotional center was other men is also the story of how the YMCA acquired most of the characteristics that we today recognize as typical of the organization. It is the story of how "the Association," as nineteenth-century

YMCA members and leaders called it, evolved from an evangelical mission-driven movement into a social service organization that sold memberships. It is also the story of how physical education and the gymnasium grew from minor attractions into the defining features of the organization. Finally, it is the story of why the Young *Men's* Christian Association now admits women as members on an equal basis with men, and why the primary membership-selling technique of most modern YMCAs is (heterosexual) family-oriented marketing and (heterosexual) family memberships.

In the 1880s, in its drive to be useful to young men, but also out of a need to build a more stable membership basis, the YMCA embarked on an ambitious physical education program. YMCA leaders conceived the physical program as requiring a major sex education component. The Association sought to build the whole man, to shape a Christian "super man" who would be morally clean and physically fit to face the perils of the modern age. YMCA leaders envisioned modern science as a key component of this campaign to create the Christian super man. They coined the term "scientific man-making" to describe their strategy of moral and physical reform. YMCA physical education leaders studied the bodybuilding techniques of the German, Swedish, and American physical culture movements, and then simplified them to make them accessible to every man. They brought in medical experts to apply the most recent scientific knowledge to their physical and sex education programs. All of this they sought to harmonize with traditional evangelicalism. YMCA leaders believed that they should bring Jesus Christ into the gymnasium and the doctor's office.

In the process, however, the YMCA came to view men's bodies and men's relationships in increasingly sexual terms. The YMCA's sex education program, which was heavily influenced by new ideas from the American medical and psychiatric professions, scrutinized men's sexuality and boyhood sexual development. YMCA sex education leaders called for increased vigilance over men's relationships. The YMCA popularized modern medical and psychiatric views of sexuality two or three decades before the American public at large would be reading and discussing popularized Freudian psychology. It also raised warnings against homosexuality decades before the American psychiatric profession persuaded the United States Army to institute a psychiatric screening program that would expose millions of Americans during World War II to the new sexual categories of "heterosexual" and "homosexual."[3] In the process, it subverted some of its own most valuable traditions. It undermined the tradition of the bachelor YMCA secretary which provided the backbone of the YMCA's dynamic leadership. It ruined the tradition of pietistic, intense same-sex friendship which had been the YMCA's primary outreach tool in the nineteenth century. But there is a grander irony in the story of same-sex relationships and the YMCA. The more closely the Young Men's Christian Association sought to guide and control the sex lives of its constituents through evangelism and education, the more it found itself confronted with uncontrolled and, in the eyes of the Association, disturbing sexual deviance. The very institutions established to help the YMCA shape men's physical and sex lives, the gymnasium and the dormitory, became sites of rampant same-sex sexual activity.

Like most Americans in the decades covered by this study, YMCA leaders and educators found the possibility of ethical sexual relationships between men inconceivable. So as sex between men became increasingly conceivable, the YMCA found it difficult to honor any kind of passionate commitment between men. Instead, it became obsessed with male physical self-mastery and "family values." The existence of nineteenth- and twentieth-century sex radicalism and sexual utopianism as (albeit marginal) alternatives in American culture proves that more passion-affirming sexual ethics were possible.[4] But the civic and religious powers with which the YMCA was (and still is) firmly aligned demanded that men's passions be channeled into the patriarchal families that undergirded social order. Perhaps the greatest tragedy of this story is that so much of the dynamism and power of the early YMCA flowed from the passionate commitments between men which were later denigrated and neglected as the YMCA sought to prove its heterosexuality.

THE THREADS OF this story are complex, so I have chosen a thematic rather than strictly chronological approach. Chapter 1 will provide a brief overview of the YMCA's history. It will document how physical and sex education went from being a marginal, tentative concern of the Young Men's Christian Association to being a major program emphasis with solid support from national leaders of the Association. Most of the rest of the story hinges on that transformation. Chapter 2 examines the history of intense friendship in the organization. Young men in the YMCA of the nineteenth century formed an intimate emotional community. Promotion of friendship became the organization's primary evangelistic tool. With growing awareness of the new ideas about sex promoted by the physical department, passionate male friendship was cast under suspicion and openly questioned. Chapter 3 documents the fact that a disproportionate number of secretaries in the nineteenth-century YMCA were life-long bachelors. ("Secretary" was the term used to refer to the employed general executive of a YMCA.) The life-long bachelor secretaries were part of a leadership corps that was overwhelmingly made up of young, single men. After the turn of the century, however, the YMCA displayed growing uneasiness with "celibate" leaders. Hiring policies, pro-marriage rhetoric, and programs that marginalized the unmarried virtually eliminated the bachelor secretary phenomenon by the 1920s.

Chapter 4 documents the institutionalization of the "Y wife." In the nineteenth century, wives of YMCA leaders were largely ignored and invisible. After the turn of the century, however, the organization sought to integrate wives into its social fabric. The YMCA socialized the wives of secretaries to play a particular kind of role that would allow the secretaries to be married and still maintain an all-encompassing commitment to other men. It created a unique culture (perhaps shared by families of ordained clergy) in which women had to accept "YMCA widowhood." Chapter 5 moves from a consideration of secretaries' wives to the role of women in the YMCA in general. In the nineteenth century, international policies barred women from Association membership. A minority sought to include women, but their arguments were rejected. The majority believed that segregated single-sex organizations could more effectively meet the needs of men and women, and the YWCA was promoted as women's alternative to YMCA membership. But in the twentieth century, fear of homosexuality and the new stress on marriage severely weakened this consensus. The result was a complete reversal of the YMCA's membership policy in 1933, despite appeals to tradition and strenuous protests from the YWCA. Chapters 6 and 7 are devoted to a study of the evolution of a same-sex cruising scene on YMCA premises, and its implications for how the YMCA viewed men's relationships.[5] Chapter 6 shows how the YMCA's new building and physical education programs, which were intended to shape and control men's sexuality, created an environment conducive to same-sex sexual encounters on YMCA premises. Chapter 7 examines the history of same-sex cruising at YMCAs, particularly focusing on a devastating sex scandal at the Portland, Oregon, YMCA in 1912. It will be argued that the YMCA cruising scene flourished partly because of an incomplete understanding among Association leaders of male relationships and sexuality. The YMCA's inability to positively integrate homoerotic yearnings, indeed its active warfare against such yearnings after about 1900, created weaknesses in the moral fabric of the organization which made YMCA staffs and traditional supporters ineffective in the YMCA's program of sexual vigilance. Many YMCA men may have used cruising in an attempt to make sense of longings they could no longer express in the organization in a socially acceptable manner.

chapter 1

FROM URBAN PIETISM TO
SEX EDUCATION

Most Americans today have experienced the YMCA as a provider of swimming lessons, day care, summer camping for
youth, or as a family health club. To those who primarily
know the YMCA for these services and who are unacquainted
with its history it is unclear how the YMCA is a Christian
organization. YMCAs actually began their existence in the
1840s and 1850s as men's Bible study and prayer groups in the
British Isles and the northeastern United States and Canada.
YMCAs were known throughout most of the nineteenth century for their evangelical emphasis. In the twentieth century,
the emphasis on physical fitness and "family values" grew
dramatically and the evangelical emphasis declined. These
changes occasioned conflict and accusations that the organization was losing its spiritual foundation, though the growing
emphasis on fitness originated from a desire to be loyal to
the established churches and the sincere belief that faith and
science could and should be harmonized. Contrary to what
many today might suppose, the decline of the YMCA's evangelical posture and the growing emphasis on fitness also led
to an increase in homophobia.

The first YMCA was founded in 1844 in London.[1] Its founder was George Williams, a clerk in a large dry-goods establishment. Williams and his friend and roommate J. Christopher Smith were concerned about the demoralizing working and living conditions of the young men employed at the company. They lived in crowded, poorly maintained, company-owned lodgings. Williams and Smith feared that in the sordid environment where they worked, men's morals and spiritual life would suffer. The informal group organized by Williams and Smith first met in the men's private quarters. It eventually received financial support and a meeting space from the establishment that employed them. Early YMCA meetings were mostly prayer groups and Bible studies whose focus was to win converts to Christ and encourage young men to live moral lives. The early organizations eventually sponsored lectures aimed at improving the intellectual lives of young men. The YMCA became very popular in London, and soon expanded to other parts of England, Wales, Scotland, and Ireland.

The London YMCA was founded during a period of urbanization and industrialization in North America. At the time, United States and Canadian cities were attracting large immigrant populations and an influx of migrants from North American farms, villages, and small towns. The vast majority of urban newcomers were single young men. The YMCA found fertile ground among North Americans who feared that the growing numbers of unattached, unchurched young men in American cities posed a threat to society. The YMCA spread to North America in 1851, through the intermediary of United States and Canadian tourists in London who were impressed by the achievements of the British Association. Associations were founded through two separate initiatives in Boston and Montreal in 1851 (fig. 1). The evangelistic spirit of the Boston Association led its members to actively promote the YMCA in other cities, leading to the rapid establishment of associations all over North America in the 1850s. In 1854, United States and Canadian associations formed a confederation for mutual support, the sharing of information, and to assist new associations in their growth and development. In 1855, largely through the organizational energies of North American YMCA leaders, a World Alliance of Young Men's Christian Associations convened in Paris. North American YMCAs continued to spread and grow until the outbreak of the U.S. Civil War in 1861.[2]

The war had a mixed effect on YMCAs in the United States. It cut off YMCAs in the South from northern and Canadian associations. It depleted the membership of all United States and Confederate States associations as young men were sent off to war. Many YMCAs disappeared or were disbanded. But some northern associations were energized through their participation in the YMCA's Christian Commission, which provided Bibles,

1. (a) St. Helen's Baptist Church, Montreal, (b) Old Smith Chapel, Boston. The first meeting places of YMCAs in North America were churches. Photos courtesy of the YMCA of the USA Archives, St. Paul, Minnesota.

supplies, and a variety of social services to Union troops.[3] After the war, the North American Confederation of YMCAs underwent a dramatic reorganization. The YMCA created an International Committee to oversee the growth and development of new associations and to coordinate relations between existing North American associations. The International Committee was permanently established in New York City. In 1868 Robert Weidensall (1836–1922), one of the YMCA's great bachelor secretaries, and Richard Cary Morse (1841–1926), who remained single until the age of forty-two, were hired as the first full-time employees of the International Committee. (Their numbers grew in future years as the role of the International Committee expanded.) In 1868 and 1869, the Association of YMCAs of the United States and British Provinces established membership policies that became binding on local associations for the purposes of representation at North American conventions.[4] Women were barred from membership. Young men who were not members of evangelical churches were not allowed voting privileges. The term "evangelical" was defined, though it was left to local associations to figure out which churches fit the definition.[5] In general there was agreement that the term excluded Unitarians, Catholics, and Mormons. Following the model of the Boston YMCA, YMCAs adopted a two-tier membership system: active, voting membership for evangelical men, and associate membership for nonevangelicals. Most YMCAs adopted a third tier of auxiliary membership for women, who were encouraged to support the Association by keeping its quarters clean and helping it raise money.

Although the North American YMCA still officially possessed a confederated structure and local associations were still supposed to have great freedom in shaping their policies, the post–Civil War reforms had the effect of centralizing power considerably, and promoting greater uniformity among YMCAs throughout North America. I have chosen 1868 as the starting point for this study, because that is the year that North American YMCAs established some of the structures and policies that gave them their distinctive characteristics for the rest of the nineteenth century. The polity and governance structure that evolved in the post–Civil War years remained essentially unchanged until the twentieth century. In 1912, Canadian YMCAs separated from United States YMCAs to form their own national council.[6] In 1922, YMCAs in the United States reorganized their constitution. They dissolved the International Committee, and returned many formerly centralized functions to the control of local associations. The new national deliberative body became the National Council. Conventions continued to be held, but their primary role was educational and inspirational.[7] Thus, for most of the era covered in this study, YMCA policy and programs were directed by the International Committee, and were under more centralized control than they ever were before or have been since.

One of the innovations of the post–Civil War era was the practice of hiring "secretaries" to oversee local associations and to assist the International Committee. Prior to that time, associations were almost completely run by volunteers. Volunteers still played a crucial role, but hired secretaries became a class of professional leaders on whom associations depended. Secretaries took the initiative in developing and executing programs and shaping the spirit of individual associations. Robert R. McBurney (1837–1898) another of the YMCA's great bachelor leaders, and the general secretary of the New York YMCA from the mid-1860s until his death thirty years later, was perhaps the most charismatic and dynamic general secretary in North America. He used the prominence of the New York Association and its geographic proximity to the International Committee to promote an activist vision of the general secretary throughout the YMCA. Robert Weidensall, the International Committee's field secretary, and John B. Brandt, general secretary of the Indianapolis YMCA, organized a North American association of general secretaries for the purpose of promoting secretarial leadership in 1872. Weidensall vigorously promoted YMCA secretarial training. He played a pivotal role in the foundation of the Western Secretarial Institute in 1886. In 1885, the YMCA created the School for Christian Workers (later called the YMCA Training School, and ultimately Springfield College) in Springfield, Massachusetts, for the purpose of training YMCA secretaries.

YMCA membership before and after the Civil War was largely recruited from the ranks of the urban, white middle classes, mostly upwardly mobile clerks, bankers, lawyers, doctors, and merchants. YMCA rhetoric always upheld an ideal of brotherhood in Christ which was supposed to transcend race, class, or geography. But brotherhood with African Americans was weakened by northern white men's desire to avoid political controversy before the Civil War and to heal the breach with white southerners after the war. The YMCA's version of interracial brotherhood was segregated "Colored," "Chinese," and "Indian" associations, which were generally underfunded and understaffed. They were the last to acquire buildings, and were generally the least developed associations in North America.[8] The YMCA did outreach to working-class men in the nineteenth century primarily through "railroad work," the brainchild of Robert Weidensall. After the turn of the century the YMCA developed "industrial work" as well. Though middle-class YMCA leaders often had a genuine concern for the welfare of working-class young men, the railroad and industrial branches were both well known for their procapital bias. Their programming generally consisted of organizing Bible studies, lectures, and prayer groups and providing work-ers with minimal conveniences. YMCAs sought to make workers good and pious, not to help them win a better piece of the industrial pie. The YMCA also created rural and "county work," also pioneered by Robert Weidensall. But rural associations did not have as much financial support as the urban associations, and always remained relatively underdeveloped. The most successful area of specialized work in the YMCA was that area which best catered to the growing middle class: "college work." Robert Weidensall established early college associations in the 1870s, and recruited Luther Wishard as international college work secretary in the 1880s. College work became one of the fastest growing programs in the twentieth century. Other departments that grew dramatically in support and appeal also catered to the YMCA's predominantly white, middle-class, urban constituency: physi-cal work and boys' work.[9]

With the creation of a centralized, activist International Committee and with the employment of a professional secretarial leadership class, the YMCA steadily unified its mission and program. Antebellum North Ameri-can YMCAs were notorious for the chaotic diversity of their programs. Bible study and prayer groups were the most common program staple. But many associations enthusiastically provided a plethora of social services, from sewing classes for young girls to Sunday-morning reading classes to bread-lines. YMCAs frequently organized ad hoc crisis relief projects in response to earthquakes in San Francisco, yellow fever epidemics in New Orleans, fires in Chicago, and of course, the Civil War. YMCAs pioneered numerous educational programs and organized libraries. Many YMCAs also spon-sored tent meetings and revivals. After the Civil War, the International Com-mittee reined in the expansive tendencies of local associations and encour-aged them to focus on work "for young men only."

One of the problems the International Committee faced was that unbridled evangelistic activity of local YMCAs was treading on the toes of established churches. Even though revivalistic evangelism was popular among early North American YMCAs from the 1860s through the 1880s, the interna-tional leadership recognized that revivalism risked alienating the YMCA's most valued supporters, the Protestant churches. It could take the YMCA down a path similar to that of early Methodism or the Salvation Army— from evangelistic/reform society to sect. Focusing on young men only and making church membership a requirement for active membership allevi-ated the worry of the churches that the YMCA might become a competitor. The committee sought to curb YMCA revivalism in favor of religious activi-ties that would supplement rather than replace membership in established churches. But as long as the YMCA focused primarily on religious work, it still seemed to be duplicating the work of the church. The "Fourfold Program," the notion that the unique niche of the YMCA was to develop the "whole man," "spiritual, mental, social, and physical," was the vehicle chosen by the national organization to steer clear of offending the churches. Emphasizing a mission of overall spiritual, social, moral, mental, and physical welfare of young men allowed the YMCA to fill a niche that seemed to harmonize with the churches rather than compete with them. The Fourfold Program was eventually collapsed into "the Triangle" of "mind, body, and spirit." (The YMCA still uses a triangle as its emblem to symbolize this trinity of the spiritual, intellectual, and physical.)[10] Under this program emphasis, the YMCA's physical department eventually grew to be the YMCA's most important form of outreach.

A significant program emphasis within the YMCA's physical education regime was sex education. In some sense, concern about sexual morality had always been a force in the YMCA. Fear that a large population of unrestrained single young men would lead to widespread sexual immorality was an important motivating factor in organizing YMCAs in the first place. But early YMCA leaders believed that men could best be fortified against the temptations of the city by indirect, spiritual means. YMCAs generally avoided talking about sex prior to the 1880s. Rather, they elevated spiritual practices like prayer and scripture study and believed that simply leading young men to Jesus Christ was enough to reform their moral life. Thus, the YMCA officially eschewed the kind of activism engaged in by temperance unions and sexual purity societies even as it expressed sympathy with their goals. True, the confederated structure gave local chapters leeway to try political activism or sexual purity educational work if they wanted. And as the fourfold mission of the YMCA developed, some associations adopted the position that moral purity needed to be cultivated through sex education and legislation. Out of this conviction, the New York YMCA launched the New York Society for the Suppression of Vice and later its own White Cross League, and YMCA sex education was born. Yet, despite the fervor with which the New York YMCA promoted sexual purity, and despite the leading role of the New York Y in the North American movement, the International Committee distanced itself from such activism. Sex education remained a marginal concern of the Association as a whole until YMCA "physical work" came into its own.

When YMCA physical education began to flourish in the late 1880s, it contributed a new philosophy and a physical education elite tutored by the American medical establishment. The physical education regime gave sex education a new anointing. Like most other Victorians, YMCA leaders conceived of health—the ultimate goal of physical education—in broad, holistic terms. Adequate attention to health and fitness required attention to sexual habits and behavior.[11] Under the guidance of the physical education program, sex education went from being a marginal concern to one of the YMCA's most prominent programs, with widespread support from local and national leaders. The integration of sex education into the YMCA's general curricula profoundly affected the YMCA's social and spiritual life. But before discussing this transformation it is first necessary to describe the YMCA's journey from evangelical pietism, silence about sexuality, and ambivalence about the body to fervent promotion of physical and sex education.

THE "OLD ASCETICISM"

Physical work did not come easily to the YMCA. The conception of physical work that came to predominate in the YMCA by the early 1900s included physical exercise, sports activities, and sex education. In the 1860s, the widespread acceptance of such a program by YMCA leaders seemed extremely improbable. First, most evangelicals considered attention to physical concerns and bodily health a distraction from higher, more spiritual pursuits. In some quarters, there was even an attitude that spiritual attainments were made possible only by the mortification of the flesh. Finally, even if YMCA leaders could be convinced of the necessity for physical education, there was intense discomfort with and resistance to open discussion of sexuality. Looking back, twentieth-century YMCA leaders described nineteenth-century YMCA attitudes as "the old asceticism."[12] This generalization was not completely accurate; some of the resistance was inspired not necessarily by asceticism, but by old-fashioned pietism. Many early YMCA leaders simply sought to maintain a pure focus on prayer, Bible study, and teaching about Christ; physical work was not bad per se, but a distraction. But asceticism did have a hold on the organization. As physical work spread, some YMCA leaders condemned it and fiercely resisted it. In the early YMCA Christian pietism and asceticism combined, creating an ethos in which physical work seemed alien, inappropriate, and possibly threatening. That the YMCA eventually adopted a program that combined physical exercise and sex education seemed miraculous.

Nineteenth-century YMCA leaders practiced a form of Protestant asceticism despite conscious efforts to curb it. Many YMCA leaders bore abuse of their own bodies as a badge of honor. Correspondence of numerous secretaries with the International Committee showed that YMCA secretaries regularly overworked themselves, deprived themselves of sleep and food, and drove themselves to nervous breakdowns. There were voices of moderation on the International Committee, although those who called for physical moderation were often the most unrepentant work addicts themselves. Despite what they told each other about the necessity of caring for themselves, many of these men believed at some level that the spirit could be elevated only to the extent that the flesh was mortified.

Robert Weidensall, one of the worst offenders, saw the asceticism of St. Paul as a model for all Christians:

> It is most interesting and profitable to learn from Paul's own testimony, not only how unevenly, indeed, unsatisfactorily the needs of his body were met, but also how joyfully he maintained a constant, blessed contentment with the help of the Lord. . . . Paul experienced in his own life during his ministry more bodily suffering of every kind than any other man. On the other hand, however, his soul was filled with constant and rapturous joy by the glorious presence and the inspiring and heavenly comfort of Jesus Christ and the Holy Spirit.[13]

Denial of one's material needs was considered a form of virtue. John V. Farwell recalled of Dwight L. Moody,

> [He] never would take a salary, as it would hamper him as a free hand. He spent all his accumulations in business on his mission work, and was discovered sleeping on benches and eating crackers and cheese in the YMCA union prayer meeting room. It was then that I urged him again to take a salary, which he refused, on the basis that he had only one source for orders in his ministry.[14]

R. C. Morse complained in numerous letters about secretaries who, "over burdened with work, [had] broken down under its pressure."[15] At one time or another, Weidensall, McBurney, Ober, Wishard, Boardman, and other international secretaries all experienced physical or nervous breakdowns as a result of their overwork.[16]

Among YMCA leaders there was entrenched opposition to "amusements," an aspect of Victorian culture that has been well documented and has recently received renewed scholarly interest.[17] Throughout the first decades of their existence, YMCAs debated whether to allow cardplaying, billiards, dancing, and theatergoing, and generally came down against them. Similarly, conservatives condemned gymnasiums as a form of pernicious amusement. Samuel M. Sayford, a YMCA college work evangelist, declared: "The prevalent cry for recreation is a snare of the devil, and puts in peril the Christian man or woman who gives heed to it. . . . It is putting young men and young women into college to train for athletic sports and to become adepts in the practices of 'swell society.'"[18] Some YMCA leaders described bodybuilding as a waste of time that detracted from other, more noble pursuits. H. L. Chamberlain of the San Francisco YMCA complained: "The reluctance of christian [sic] young men to engage in earnest and instructive mental discipline is a matter of profound regret, when it is considered how much time is given to the cultivation of the powers of the body."[19] Another anonymous critic complained that the gym instructor employed by the San Francisco YMCA "was not the best [influence] on the young men of the Gymnasium; . . . he was now conducting a Dancing Academy, and some of the young men had been induced to neglect their religious duties for the purpose of attending the dancing classes."[20] George J. Fisher, an early physical work leader, believed George Williams, the founder of the YMCA, to have been "alarmed" at the development of physical work.[21] Some YMCA leaders never fully understood or accepted physical education. Even some eventual supporters of the YMCA's physical program warned that "a start . . . made to become a perfect man" could result in "a perfect animal."[22]

L. L. Doggett described the opposition that early physical work encountered at the Boston YMCA:

> At that time the idea of a man being both a gymnast and a Christian was deemed almost ridiculous. Many of those who frequented the exercising hall were not men of elevated character. There is evidence that some were of dissolute habits. Indeed, the attitude of the Associations throughout the country at this time toward the gymnasium was very dubious.[23]

Only after the late 1880s did the gymnasium begin to win general acceptance in the Boston YMCA.

Whenever philosophical controversies broke out, debates over the role of gymnasiums inevitably sprang up. One of the most divisive controversies in the YMCA before 1900, the Kansas-Sudan controversy, was profoundly colored by the old asceticism. In the early 1890s the YMCA's state committee in Kansas, under the leadership of Weidensall protégé George S. Fisher, had assumed a strong revivalistic orientation. The state committee grew until it had the largest budget and largest personnel of any state or provincial committee in North America. It was not only promoting general evangelism in the state, but launched an independent foreign mission in sub-Saharan Africa. This was in direct violation of the International Committee pact with the churches not to engage in foreign mission work without their permission and cooperation. As the International Committee began to tighten the reins on Kansas and sought, mainly through persuasion, to pull it into line, Kansas leaders characterized the International Committee as a tool of Satan trying to institute a new "popery." Charles Helmick, a member of the

Kansas committee's Sudan mission expedition, called Cephas Brainerd, the chair of YMCA's International Committee in New York, "unchristian" and McBurney a liar. He added: "Be certain the Devil did not start the Kansas Mission. We are not quite so certain as to his share in your work."[24]

Its opposition to physical work was one aspect of the Kansas committee's dissatisfaction with the broader YMCA movement. Frank M. Gates, a member of the Kansas committee, belittled physical concerns in general. His argument against physical education employed a theological posture in which things physical were generally debased: "I cannot believe that the Lord left the right hand of God and spent those unspeakable years of fleshly degradation and suffering that the young men of Kansas might have better digestion, be brighter social stars, or that their intellects be broadened." Heaven was idealized as a perfect realm of spirit uncorrupted by fleshly concerns, while physical concerns were viewed as frivolous and unbecoming of Christian men. Not only did he find the YMCA's Fourfold Program irrelevant, but he also attacked the conservative rationale of using the gymnasium as a lure for "higher" more "spiritual" programming. He claimed that in Kansas at least "there had scarcely been a conversion . . . from the gymnasium and yet of their immense membership it is liberal to estimate that not one out of twenty joined for anything else than the gymnasium privileges."[25]

Hostility to the physical program in the Kansas movement was accompanied by a general hostility toward any form of physical comfort. W. A. Holmes, who had been active in the leadership of the Kansas associations and at one time a Kansas-Sudan movement supporter, described Kansas state workers as

> monks without the monastery, divinely led, fed, clothed, taught men, who felt sorry for those who did not enjoy such divine favor, alleging that those who did not were unregenerate or at least living on a very low plane, feeling it their duty to bring all men, especially Association men, to embrace their doctrine.[26]

George S. Fisher demanded "the giving up of costly homes, useless jewelry and expensive raiment and food, and all unnecessary things, by whatever name they may be called, for the purpose of [spreading the Joyful Message], and indeed the absolute surrender and offering up of soul, body and property to this end."[27] Fisher condemned large urban associations for spending vast sums of money on enormous dormitory and gymnasium buildings. According to Fisher, such buildings might take up entire city blocks and literally house thousands. He demanded that associations buy simpler, less expensive buildings whose focus would be on evangelism. He also argued that YMCA secretaries should be paid according to need rather than ability or the status of their position. In this, he indirectly criticized the fact that general secretaries of large urban associations like Chicago or New York, for instance, received much more than secretaries of smaller, rural associations. Need-based salaries, he argued, would discourage sinful "pride." [28] Other Kansas people attacked the entire notion of paid secretaries. A paid workforce was turning the Association away from "prayer" and toward "worldliness." [29] The Kansas committee's condemnations of worldliness made International Committee members particularly defensive if only because they themselves came from a spiritual tradition that distrusted the world, the flesh, and mammon.

The International Committee dismissed the Kansas committee as religious fanatics, seeking to downplay a critique that threatened the entire financial and social foundation of their organization. They were particularly sensitive to charges of mammon-worship, because of the warm relationship eastern YMCA leaders had established with American business. The criticisms of the Kansas YMCA were so shrill because by the early 1890s it was clear that the majority of associations in the United States and Canada were beginning to embrace physical work. At the same time, their discomfort with physical work was understood by eastern secretaries, if only because such discomfort had prevailed throughout the Association a generation earlier. The Kansas YMCA expressed doubts that had been voiced before and would be voiced later in eastern YMCAs as well.

Physical work, as it was conceived by pioneers in the field, included everything that related to the healthy functioning of the body—not just bodybuilding, aerobics, or sports. Thus, sex education was seen as a natural and integral component of any complete program for the promotion of male physical health. If the old asceticism was an obstacle to the acquisition of gymnasiums and the establishment of bodybuilding, sports, and exercise programs, it also posed unique problems for the institution of scientific sex education.

The primary obstacle to early sex education was the general discomfort on the part of YMCA secretaries before the 1890s with straightforward talk about sex. The issue of sexuality elicited complex reactions. Even though most YMCA leaders agreed that control of sexual behavior was important, open discussions of sexuality caused fear, anxiety, and discomfort. When YMCA leaders of this era did speak about sex, it was almost always through euphemism. The preferred term for the sexual vices was simply "immorality." A typical catalog of sins might run: "lying, gambling, stealing, drunkenness, and immorality." Arguably, lying, gambling, stealing, and drunkenness are all forms of immorality, so the last item on the list appears redundant unless one knows it to stand for that last form of immorality that has so far gone unnamed—sexual immorality. "I do not think he is guilty of any immorality nor has he any questionable habits," wrote Walter T. Hart of one young man about whom he was concerned.[30] From other YMCA correspondence, it is evident that the term "questionable habits" referred to such things as drinking, gambling, theatergoing, dance-hall attendance, and so on. For instance, L. Wilbur Messer wrote a letter to J. F. Oates expressing concern about a group of YMCA members who had been seen regularly frequenting a saloon. "Perhaps we should do something," he wrote, "to advise these members that we know of their practices and request that they change their *habits*."[31] If "questionable habits" referred to the majority of namable vices that concerned YMCA leaders, the term "immorality" was a stronger term intended to cover those vices that they felt less comfortable naming.

Samuel M. Sayford toured the country delivering what was popularly referred to as his "Confidential Talk" or his talk "For Young Men Only"—for all intents and purposes an antimasturbation talk. Sayford was in high demand, especially on American college campuses, and he received many requests to "come give us your Confidential Talk," although none of the letters begging his assistance openly discussed the subject matter of the talk. Newspapers gave some indication of the content of Sayford's morality talks, although even they tended to focus on the "safer" kinds of immorality—cards, theatergoing, drinking, and tobacco use. The strongest notice appeared in the *Boston Globe* in an article entitled "Personal Purity":

> MR. SAYFORD speaks frankly on the nature of true manhood, and with homely and simple directness shows the limitations of the body and the consequences of its abuse. These are matters which few of our public teachers have the courage to discuss, and it is only by the learning which comes from painful experience that most of us arrive at a position of safety.[32]

A Philadelphia article was more typical. It described his talk proclaiming the "great need for real men." The article described in detail and even quoted lengthy excerpts from Sayford's discussion of tobacco, cards, the theater, and even "profanity," but declined to go further regarding his discussion of "more serious sins, which he called ruinous." The article noted only that he "dealt with them plainly, making a strong plea against immorality."[33] Another euphemistic way of referring to the content of Sayford's talk was to note that he preached "the necessity of a high standard of Christian character."[34]

Speaking euphemistically about sex was not simply another kind of discourse about sex. Euphemism was by definition ambiguous, and occasionally caused confusion. The potential for misunderstanding was revealed in one letter of a YMCA secretary: "I had heard general rumors for quite a while but *this I understood* to be a recent specific moral lapse of a sexual sort which his Bible class had taken up and which I understood to have resulted in his giving up the class. Perhaps your letter referred to the same thing."[35] He sought to clarify the exact nature of this man's moral failing, because although the euphemistic references to immorality in "general rumors" and in the letter he had received led him to assume a "moral lapse of a sexual sort," he was not entirely sure. The letter does demonstrate the tendency of Victorians to assume that when a sin was discussed euphemistically it almost certainly was a sexual sin. But it also shows that euphemism could leave uncertainty in the mind of a listener or reader. One could always choose to put a different, nonsexual interpretation on euphemistic discourse, or one might wrongly sexualize a discourse that was not so intended.

The use of euphemism put a special aura around sex. Sexual sin was in a league all its own. It was the worst—or at least the most embarrassing—type of sin one could commit. Other kinds of evildoing—drunkenness, theft, disorderly conduct, business dishonesty, Sabbath-breaking, even murder—did not require the kind of verbal tiptoeing that adultery, fornication, masturbation, or sodomy universally invoked. Consider, for example, Chicago general secretary L. W. Messer's request to investigate a report of inebriation at a YMCA camp:

> A letter from Lake Geneva reports that three of the West Side athletes were drunk at the camp Saturday night. . . . If it is true, such members should be disciplined promptly, as the report will be widespread among Associations, on account of the representative character of the gathering. If the statement is false, we should run it down and disprove it. Please make an impartial investigation at once.[36]

In this case, although alcohol abuse was clearly an embarrassment to the Association, YMCA leaders could still deal with it noneuphemistically.

Though sexual immorality was seldom mentioned in public, it was always considered the most *serious* sin. Sexual immorality was the sin "worse than death" and the "unpardonable sin." The editor of *Association Men* castigated sexual immorality in the strongest possible language. In the following editorial, it is unclear what provoked the commentary, although it is possible that the writer was responding to a particular incident:

> A sickness of heart comes to a fraternity when a leader falls into immorality and goes out into the darkness of isolation that is worse than death, and by his own act closes the door to any further return behind him. Honorable death would seem sweet, and an unsullied name held in cherished memory as compared with the fall of a leader into gross and continued immorality. . . . Society may be responsible for the toleration of the business, and yet society will not reaccept, and the moral sense of the community forbids, that a leader who has gone down into the

rot and reek of sensuality may come back to Christian work, though he pass through the purging hell of repentance. He may regain his self-control and gain forgiveness, but his work is over. The man's name is blemished, his wife is worse than widowed and his children orphaned.[37]

One reason such a serious sin was rarely discussed in public was because knowledge about sex was itself considered dangerous. It was carefully guarded with meticulously constructed ignorance. The following editorial was a tirade against "slumming," though its principles were generalized to all forms of knowledge about "immorality":

> It is the ages-old story of familiarity with vice until it fascinates and the filth that clings to and defiles the imagination until it corrupts morals and contaminates the life. This is the perversion that comes from the study of personal impurity until the mind and the person is impure. . . . It is better not to try to know so much about nastiness. It is enough for us to learn from hearsay and have a horror of all salaciousness without acquaintance with its dirty details.[38]

It is significant that open discussion of sexuality was generally taboo except when discussing the evangelization of nonwhite peoples. In this, the International Committee behaved just like the Kansas-Sudan movement. Kansas YMCA leaders justified the urgent need to send out missionaries to sub-Saharan Africa immediately. By raising images of "the sweeping destruction of the social sin," and the fact of the natives living "as nearly naked as they well can be," they were sure to unleash shocking images of promiscuity and sexual abandon.[39] But Richard C. Morse of the International Committee did not use any less sexually explicit imagery to describe the "heathens" of India, when he expressed concern about "the orgies, obscenities & infinite degradations of a heathenism & a Pantheon—the abominations of which had been but feebly pictured to us," and suggested them as a justification for European militarism and colonialism that he otherwise found repulsive.[40] The projection of anxieties about sexuality applied as well to domestic subjects of evangelization, as evidenced in YMCA missionary Charles Conrad Hamilton's extreme discomfort in socializing with lumbermen during his YMCA mission work in Wisconsin, or in YMCA foreign secretary Frank H. Wood's refusal to take passage for India with working-class sailors.[41] Both professed disgust at these men's sexual habits and profanity, and acted as if unmitigated contact would leave them contaminated. The fact that sexual immorality could be openly discussed in descriptions of the "other" suggest that sexuality occupied a special place in the Victorian imagination. Open discussion of sexual sin was most useful in conjuring lurid and frightening images of the working class, people of color, and the colonized third world.

THE ADVENT OF "PHYSICAL WORK"

Given the widespread discomfort with gymnasiums and physicality and given the complexity of attitudes toward sex, it seems amazing that the YMCA ever developed the kind of physical program it did. But the YMCA eventually abandoned the old asceticism and came to embrace the gymnasium so completely that the YMCA today is identified more with physical education and health than with any other program. The silence, euphemism, and halting discourse about sexual purity were replaced with "scientific" approaches to sex, and a "sex hygiene" program that was thoroughly integrated into the YMCA's physical work. This astounding transformation was nothing less than a complete revolution of YMCA attitudes and emphasis. It requires some explanation.

Institutional considerations were critical. The YMCA needed to find a program emphasis that did not compete with the churches. Physical education and the philosophy of developing "the whole man" into a "balanced Christian" was one way of achieving this. Secondly, as associations began to adopt physical work, they found it to be extremely popular. The gymnasium brought in more new members than any previous outreach program. Psychological and social factors likely played a role in this. Men in American cities feared that "civilization" was sapping them of vitality. The gymnasium was seen as a source of salvation. Sex was linked to fears about race survival and individual salvation, contributing to the growing appeal of sex hygiene work. But the most important factor was the successful adaptation of physical culture to the Christian philosophy and ethos of the YMCA by men like Luther Halsey Gulick and Robert J. Roberts (figs. 2 and 3). Without Gulick's leadership and ingenuity as a physical education philosopher and program builder, it seems unlikely that YMCA leaders would have adopted physical work as wholeheartedly as they ultimately did. By the turn of the century, the official line of the YMCA could be summarized in the words of Major D. Whittle of the Chicago YMCA in 1898: "The former distinction between spiritual and secular agencies is no longer pressed. The earnest desire is to develop thoroughly rounded manly character. All agencies that tend to this result are now regarded as spiritual in the best sense." [42]

Although the YMCA eventually came to view physical work as having spiritual value, some observers of the YMCA believe that more mundane considerations were initially at work. Sociologist Mayer N. Zald has argued that while revivalism helped to promote organizational loyalty and enthusiasm, it was not a very stable source of income. Growing reliance on a dues-paying membership that paid for gymnasium privileges, and the use of low-cost residences as a source of supplementary income, helped to stabilize the organization financially. In providing these resources to urban young men,

2. Luther Halsey Gulick. Courtesy of the YMCA of the USA Archives, St. Paul, Minnesota.

the YMCA filled an important urban economic niche. By 1900, YMCA physical work had begun to surpass religious work in sheer numbers of men served in most cities.[43] This helps to explain why some YMCAs invested in gymnasiums long before the organization had developed a philosophical rationale to reconcile physical work with its traditional Christian mission. Yet, the transformation that ultimate took place could not have been accomplished solely on the force of economic considerations. Physical work in the 1860s floundered precisely because of confusion and doubt among YMCA leaders across the country about the value of physical education. Only as

3. Robert J. Roberts. Courtesy of the YMCA of the USA Archives, St. Paul, Minnesota.

the YMCA gradually developed a philosophy integrating physical and spiritual concerns did the new physical work become truly compelling and gain widespread support.

YMCA leaders did not consciously set out to develop a new concept of Christianity. The first argument in favor of building gyms was that young men were attracted to them and they could be used as a lure to expose young men to Christianity. The argument that YMCA gyms attracted young men to Christianity continued its usefulness as a rationale well into the 1930s and

1940s. In 1921, for instance, *Physical Training* was still publishing articles like "Moral and Religious Opportunities in the Physical Department."[44] But this rationale weakened under the growing evidence that the vast majority of men who participated in the YMCA's physical program were satisfied with associate membership and were not participating in any of the YMCA's Christian programs. "Our statistics tell us," wrote YMCA physical director R. C. Cubbon in 1912, "that 70 per cent of the membership are attracted by other than religious appeal."[45]

Men like Robert J. Roberts, physical director of the Boston Association, and Luther Gulick, who trained physical directors at Springfield College, deserve the credit for developing a philosophy that made the physical program comprehensible and acceptable within a Christian framework. This philosophy justified physical development as a positive spiritual good in itself. These early philosophers of the YMCA's physical work acknowledged their indebtedness to already existing German and American physical culture movements.[46] Their claim to fame was the integration of new health-oriented and body-centered philosophies into a Christian theological framework and the popularization and mainstreaming of physical culture for the general American public. Roberts and Gulick created a bodybuilding program that could be adapted to the work schedules and skills of average men.[47]

Gulick and Roberts made the most of the fact that YMCAs had already begun justifying the existence of their physical programs simply by adding the word "physical" to the list of attributes ("spiritual, intellectual, and social") that YMCAs already claimed to develop in young men. The New York YMCA was the first to adopt what was later called the Fourfold Program in 1866. The first gymnasium constructed specifically for a YMCA was built in 1869 during McBurney's general secretaryship at New York's 23rd Street branch.[48] Luther Gulick's mind-body-spirit philosophy developed out of his commitment to the Fourfold Program, which became popular in the late 1880s. But as an 1888 circular demonstrated, he still saw the need to subordinate the physical program to spiritual concerns:

> The chief work of the gymnasium instructor is to reach young men through the Physical Department. The spiritual work of the Association is its most prominent aim, and the one to which all others must bend. The gymnasium instructor must be an earnest soul winner. . . . While the correct view of Association work is that it is a fourfold job—viz., the physical, social, intellectual, and spiritual welfare of young men—the spiritual objective stands out far beyond the others, which are merely a means of reaching this greater goal.[49]

In the early 1890s, however, Gulick began to emphasize the "unity and symmetry" of body, mind, and spirit rather than a hierarchy of spirit over mind over body. "An Association should work," he declared in 1891, "for the whole aim, that is, perfect Christian manhood. For one man to work for the more distinctly spiritual, another for the intellectual, and a third for the physical, each ignoring the work of the others, would be a curious anomaly."[50] Jesus Christ himself, Gulick declared, "spent his time working for man as a whole. He worked for man physically as well as spiritually."[51] Gulick reminded YMCA members "why every Christian worker should take systematic physical exercise," even citing scripture to prove that physical culture had a biblical basis:

1. Because his body is an essential and eternal part of him, and must be developed if he is to become a perfect man.—1 Cor. 13.
2. Because the health of his body affects his mental and spiritual condition, and these affect the amount and quality of work he can do in the world.—Prov. 17:22.
3. Because Christ's work is for the whole man (1 Cor. 6:20) and the Christian stands as the exemplar of that work to the community.—2 Cor. 3:2.
4. Because he cannot tell others to "do as I preach, not as I practice."—1 Cor. 11:31.
5. Because it will add a score of years to his work for the Master at the time of life when his experience qualifies him for the best work of his life.—Prov. 3:1, 2.[52]

One of Gulick's final statements on the matter asserted that "the different lines of work that were undertaken were done for the purpose of getting men under religious influence. We now conceive of the religious life as including everything there is in man—body, mind, and spirit in one complete whole."[53]

Gulick himself displayed a remarkable adaptability, and an ability to experiment and grow beyond the limits he had set for himself. Biographer Ethel Dorgan noted that Gulick once took up smoking and drinking wine "as an experiment." "He concluded that smoking had nothing to do with morals but was a matter of taste." Gulick was also one of the first to reject medical paranoia about the supposed effects of masturbation.[54] In raising his daughters, he for a time refused to allow them to play with dolls in the belief that it promoted an unhealthy view of gender, though he later revised his views and concluded that doll play was a manifestation of an irrepressible "mother instinct."[55] Gulick appeared to embrace many contradictions. On the one hand, he occasionally seemed obsessed with rules and self-control; on the other, he frequently showed evidence of favoring spontaneity over order, principles over rules, and experimentation over legalism. At times, he appeared to favor sexual repression; at other times, he displayed rational moderation in the realm of human sexual behavior. He was an advocate of eugenics and a believer in social Darwinism who also upheld altruism, service, and self-sacrifice as the highest form of religion. There were definite elements in him of legalism, repression, conservatism, racism, and male supremacy; but to characterize him solely in this way does not do justice to the ways in which he grew toward the end of his life.

Gulick built a strong following among YMCA physical directors and among American physical educators generally. His philosophy promised status to physical directors, who were now entrusted with a crucial role in the progress of society. Indeed, the establishment of physical and health programs in American colleges and high schools in the nineteenth century was largely made possible by wide dissemination and acceptance of these new ideas about the relationship between body, mind, and spirit. These views of physical education were promoted institutionally through the YMCA's training school in Springfield, Massachusetts (founded in 1885), and through official YMCA publications like *Young Men's Era* and *Association Men*. Gulick and his successors in the YMCA, George J. Fisher, Martin I. Foss, and John Brown, Jr., also promoted their social hygiene–oriented vision of physical work through official magazines of the YMCA's physical department published out of the Springfield Training School which were specifically aimed at forming YMCA physical directors: *The Triangle*, *Physical Education*, and *Physical Training*.[56] Long after Gulick left Springfield Training School and the YMCA, he continued to have an intellectual influence on it, and was frequently consulted whenever the YMCA was in need of official interpretations of its physical program. And Springfield continued to have an impact on American physical education generally, as the school trained not only YMCA physical directors but future college and high school physical educators as well.

Even with the nominal acceptance of the mind-body-spirit ideology, disagreement still existed over its meaning, and YMCA leaders found it necessary to justify the physical program. A 1912 article by physical director George J. Fisher, for example, assured YMCA constituents that physical work secretaries were "religious leaders," and men "of sterling Christian character," and that their influence could not help but wear off on the young men with whom they worked. He promoted YMCA physical work as a form of "Christian character making" and athletics as a "moral force."[57] Other YMCA leaders made similar exaggerated claims as a way to win over opponents of the physical work: "The Physical Department Curriculum of today so pulsates with religious education that it is scarcely possible to dissociate the terms physical and religious."[58] The elaboration of a theology of physical education began to convince some of the opponents of physical work. Even Samuel Sayford, a prominent YMCA evangelist and student work leader from Massachusetts who initially opposed physical work in the

1880s, eventually became convinced of the importance of developing the "whole man." Although he had initially suspected athletics of encouraging worldliness, he eventually conceded that at least YMCA "athletic sports" and "physical development" were "free from the brutal exhibition of the ring, and the demoralizing influence of gambling."[59] After the 1930s, physical education became more or less an unquestioned aspect of the YMCA program, without any need to continue rationalizing it.

Luther Gulick conceived of physical education in much broader terms than mere gymnastic training. It was also to include attention to diet, bathing, sleep, clothing, and sexual development. Gulick criticized the "athletic clubs" for focusing too narrowly on physical exercise, claiming that YMCA physical departments were promoting a rounded "scientific knowledge" of "anatomy, physiology, hygiene, effects of exercise, philosophy of gymnastic systems, and so forth."[60] *The Triangle, Physical Education,* and *Physical Training* dealt with a plethora of topics, including material that one would expect in a physical education magazine, such as discussions of team sports rules and descriptions of how certain physical exercises could build up specific parts of the body. But they also covered topics like biblical rationales for physical exercise, Christian defenses of the mind-body-spirit philosophy, essays on diseases of the heart, lungs, liver, and kidneys, studies of bone growth, essays on diet, sleep, and bathing, discussions of sexually transmitted diseases, and debates about how best to approach sex education. Most articles fell into one of four categories: physical exercise and team sports, Christian philosophy of the physical program, biological and medical scientific treatises, and sex hygiene. Thus, YMCA physical education laid the groundwork for YMCA sex education work. Indeed, the holistic manner in which YMCA physical education leaders conceptualized physical work demanded it. Sex education was a natural outgrowth of the YMCA's physical work.

SEX EDUCATION

The earliest YMCA forays into sex education began in the mid-1880s with its participation in the White Cross movement and its publication of pamphlets promoting sexual purity. But it was the growth of the YMCA's physical program that led the organization to develop sex education as a major program focus by the early twentieth century. Increasingly after 1900 sex education in the YMCA was not isolated in or confined to specialized courses on sex, with limited constituencies. It became a consistent program emphasis in the YMCA's physical work, and in all YMCA educational settings that focused on "developing manhood" and "character-building." By the 1920s and the 1930s, as many YMCAs began to do "mixed work," that is, work involving young women and young men in gender-integrated programming, sex education and "marriage preparation" accounted almost entirely for the educational content of this programming. Promoting "normal" relations between the sexes and readying young people for wedded union were the most compelling rationales in the 1920s for shifting from the YMCA's traditional single-sex focus to gender-integrated programming in the first place.

Some historians have suggested that medical and psychiatric conceptions of sexuality around the turn of the century entered public consciousness primarily through marital and sex-advice manuals that proliferated in the 1920s.[61] Freudian psychology and new medical discourses about homosexuality would not, according to these historians, have become common knowledge outside the medical and psychiatric professions until a generation or two after they were invented and disseminated among American physicians. But a study of YMCA physical and educational work from 1885 to 1920 suggests that YMCA programming was a major vehicle for disseminating the latest medical and psychiatric "knowledge" about sexuality almost as soon as they became available to American physicians. The YMCA's physical program, under the national leadership of Dr. Luther Halsey Gulick, was the driving force in mainstreaming and popularizing medical knowledge about sexuality for broad YMCA constituencies.

Sex education work in the YMCA began in 1885 when the New York Association—the largest and most influential Association in the country—founded its own White Cross League. The White Cross movement was a popular vehicle of sexual purity work. White Cross leagues were fraternities of young men who pledged to remain sexually abstinent until marriage, and faithful to their spouses within marriage. The New York Association had already been a sexual purity activist organization since 1868, when it organized the New York Society for the Suppression of Vice. Under the leadership of a young new YMCA member by the name of Anthony Comstock, the society secured New York State legislation banning obscene literature. The New York Society later successfully lobbied for national legislation similar to that in New York, and was actively involved in local campaigns against vice. The YMCA not only presented petitions to city councils and made legislative efforts, but assisted police in tracking down and arresting violators of the antiobscenity legislation they had helped to write.[62] Despite the opposition of influential YMCA leaders, including Robert Weidensall and some leading general secretaries, the New York YMCA White Cross chapter grew rapidly. Weidensall and the other leaders did not object to the idea of White Cross work per se, but believed that sex education was a type of "moral reform" on a par with abolition or temperance. It might coincide with YMCA aims but would divert energy and resources from the task of winning young men to Christ. They believed that if the YMCA focused on the primary objective of making young men into Christians, sexual purity would come afterward as a natural fruit of the Holy Spirit.[63]

This early resistance to sex education gave way in the 1880s as the YMCA embraced physical work. By the 1890s the International Committee was actively publishing and distributing sex education pamphlets across the United States and Canada. It developed YMCA sex education through its physical program, in physical work publications, and in its international training schools.[64] The 1892 *Hand-Book*, published by the International Committee as a definitive guide to local associations—a sort of bible of YMCA procedure—stressed the importance of including sex education work as an integral component of YMCA physical work.[65] "Sex education and ideals" were included as an important emphasis in physical education in subsequent handbooks as well.[66] Sexuality came to occupy a privileged place in YMCA physical education discourse. It was one of the areas that, in the minds of virtually all YMCA leaders, simultaneously embraced concerns about physical health and moral/spiritual health. In some sense, sex education was a microcosm of the new YMCA philosophy, demonstrating that mind, body, and spirit were inseparable.

Through the physical department, Gulick and other physical directors focused attention and concern on sexuality and sexual development more openly than ever before in the YMCA. Physical department publications included instructions on how to identify venereal diseases in the examining room, reports from "vigilance committees" and "social hygiene societies," and debates about sex education and prostitution. Gulick devoted at least half of his book, *The Dynamic of Manhood* (1917) to a discussion of sex. He discussed his beliefs about its evolutionary origins, the role it should play in society, how it contributed to manhood and womanhood, how children developed sexually, what were the causes of sexual abnormality or perversion, the most effective means to prevent masturbation and the consumption of pornography, and how to deal with bad sexual habits.

Gulick was not only concerned about the prevention of sexual abnormality or perversion, but saw the physical and spiritual encompassing the promotion of proper gender roles as well. Physical education would make healthy, happy mothers and housewives out of women, and strong but gentle, protective, independent, and intelligent fathers out of men. Men would play a more active role in the rearing of children; women, in order to be suitable companions to their husbands, would be better educated and more interested in society and politics. Children's sexual development had to be carefully watched, lest masturbation or premature sexual experimentation spoil them for marriage. But Gulick encouraged parents to talk openly with their children about sex. Parents should teach children why masturbation, pornography, prostitution, and free sex were wrong so as to prepare them morally to resist temptation and to take the allure out of sexual sin by demystifying it. Men were also counseled about how to repair the spiritual damage done by previous sexual mishaps—mainly through sheer self-control. He also advised men to "marry early." Twenty or twenty-one was the ideal age for marriage, according to Gulick, an astounding view in light of the fact that most white, middle-class men of this era married in their late twenties. But Gulick went so far as to suggest that the community's interest in preventing the sexual ruin of youth justified their economic support of young couples who were not yet financially independent.[67]

YMCA physical work literature equated sin and sickness. Ill health could be caused by sin, but failure to maintain oneself in top physical health was itself a sin. By his own account, Luther Gulick began his journey with physical work with the realization of "the relation of good bodies to good morals."[68] YMCA leaders spoke about sex hygiene and physical health in terms traditionally reserved for purely spiritual purposes. The mission statement of the Waterbury, Connecticut, YMCA physical department policy, for instance, proclaimed its aim to be young men's "physiological salvation."[69] Another *Association Men* article warned against "temptations to neglect our physical well being," declaring that "we have a moral obligation not only to ourselves but to our family and country to live right lives physically, as well as morally, mentally, and socially."[70] "True morality," George J. Fisher asserted, "rests upon a sound muscular and nervous system."[71] "Bodily care," he taught, "is a religious duty."[72]

If ill health was sin, then physical directors became the new priests of physical strength and good health. "His examination room is a holy place where men's lives and habits stand revealed before him for correction," declared a 1912 *Association Men* editorial, "All life is his to touch and influence."[73] An anonymous article in *Association Men* called "Revelations of the Examining Room" offered a model of the new spiritual relationship between the young man and the physician. The article described how the staff of "a western Association" had examined seventy-four men and found that "only 34.6 per cent were normal, although the Association was very liberal in the use of the term normal." (Obviously, the term "normal" was not being used here in the statistical sense.) Of the "abnormal" cases, "35 per cent had some deformity of the generative organs." The young men were in danger of "chronic invalidism or premature death," from which the examiners were able to "save" them through advice on how to "[right] their physical habits." The young men were also counseled about their spiritual lives, as a discussion of their physical habits "led naturally to talks about . . . mental culture and religious experience." The author, himself one of the examiners, recounted how he "received [a] young man's confession of Jesus Christ in the bicycle room one afternoon [and] took him to the altar myself." The author called this sort of physical work "scientific man-making." He declared, "It is leading men to the sources of power, physical and spiritual."[74]

Sex education became established as a key fixture in the YMCA's physical department, even as the physical department was becoming the most important program in the YMCA. By 1910, the physical work was dwarfing all other YMCA programs in terms of sheer numbers of participants. In the 1910 *Year Book*, associations reported 258,855 members using the physical department and 159,027 members enrolled in gym classes. By comparison, associations reported 60,163 students in Bible classes, 15,139 men serving on religious work committees, and 56,232 enrolled in educational classes. The physical department had specific strategies for overseeing and shaping the sexuality of members, beyond distributing sex education pamphlets or discussing sexuality in health classes. The 1892 *Hand-Book* stressed the importance of one-on-one interviews between the physical director and individual members during physical exams, held in the privacy of the physical director's office. It specified that physical exams and accompanying interviews "should be made compulsory upon every new member." The *Hand-Book* exhorted that during the physical exam, the physical director "has an unusual opportunity to become acquainted with men, to correct evil habits of life, and to gain an influence over them that he can use for their welfare. . . . The busiest physical directors find time for the most numerous and thorough examinations."[75] YMCA physical directors were encouraged to discuss sex hygiene and masturbation with men during the physical exam. In 1910, the same year that associations reported only 60,163 men enrolled in religious classes, 66,590 men received physical exams. Between 1900 and 1940, YMCAs in the United States and Canada gave about four million physical exams to young men involved in their physical education programs (fig. 4). The importance of sex education as a major program emphasis in the YMCA's physical work received additional impetus in 1915 when John R. Mott became general secretary of the YMCA, since Mott maintained a special interest in sex hygiene throughout his YMCA career.[76]

The prevailing philosophy of sex education as it developed in the YMCA's physical department was shaped by men who were trained in the American

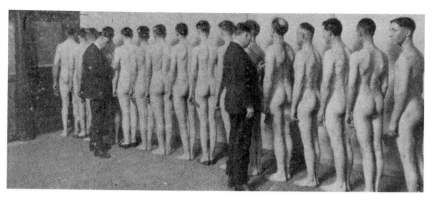

4. The above photo, published in the January 1922 issue of the YMCA publication *Physical Training*, portrays a typical physical examination at the Lincoln, Nebraska, YMCA in which "20 to 50 men are examined" each week. Courtesy of the YMCA of the USA Archives, St. Paul, Minnesota.

medical profession. Although the vast majority of YMCA physical directors across the country were not doctors, trained medical doctors created the YMCA's physical education curriculum. Doctors created the YMCA's physical work philosophy. Doctors trained physical directors at the YMCA's training schools and summer camps. Doctors wrote the handbooks for YMCA physical directors and filled the pages of YMCA physical education periodicals with articles discussing every aspect of YMCA physical work. Doctors set the standards for YMCA physical work.[77] As the YMCA physical directorship was still in its formative stages, some expressed the belief that medical training should be a prerequisite for YMCA physical directors. This requirement was wisely rejected, if only because at the turn of the century YMCAs were suffering from a shortage of physical work staff. Such a steep requirement would have made the task of finding qualified physical directors virtually impossible. But the centralization of YMCA physical work training and standards under the leadership of trained medical doctors guaranteed that the medical profession would have a disproportionate say in the development of YMCA physical work. The YMCA physical department took pride in its "scientific man-making," and strove to incorporate the most up-to-date scientific and medical knowledge about human physiology and health into its programs and curriculum. Thus, the YMCA became one of the earliest disseminators of medical discourse about sexuality to a broad, general audience.

The view of sexuality promoted by the YMCA's medical elite was progressive, holistic, and eugenic. It was progressive in that it stressed the importance of widening healthy discussion of sex, speaking frankly about it to the young, and promoting public dialog about the public policy and personal implications of sex problems. It was holistic in that it viewed sex as permeating every human drive, desire, and activity. Sex was the basis for community life, for religion and spirituality, for maternal love and masculine self-sacrifice; it was the driving force in all of society and in life itself. Most important, sex had a "normal" path of development that could easily be disrupted by the wrong kind of upbringing, or by childhood or adolescent mishaps—premature sexual experience, exposure to pornography, or inadequate parental gender roles. Boys had to be protected sexually from men. Boys needed to interact with girls in order to learn how to develop healthy relationships with them early on. "Sex perversion" was the tragic outcome of a failure to properly lead a boy to manhood and masculinity. YMCA sex education generally focused on the positive, but it also nurtured an awareness that young boys needed to be steered between the Scylla of heterosexual promiscuity and the Charybdis of homosexuality. Finally, it was eugenic in that individual sexuality was connected to the health and survival of the race as a whole.[78] Sex was seen as a natural, animal instinct that was fundamentally good, though it needed to be harnessed for the greatest collective welfare. Sexual desire was a valid motivation for marriage, though it should not be the sole motivation. No marriage, however, could ultimately succeed without it as the basic bond between a man and a woman. This view of sex was already coming into shape by around 1900 and was fully developed by about 1915. One of the definitive statements of this perspective was published in 1917, in Luther Gulick's *The Dynamic of Manhood*.[79]

Some historians have drawn attention to discontinuities between late-nineteenth-century medical discourses about sexuality and social purity discourses.[80] The former increasingly viewed sexuality as an animal drive that required healthy outlets, and came to see sexual development and "normal" sexual expression as vital to healthy human development. The latter focused on promoting male self-restraint and ending the double standard by encouraging men to be chaste. C. Howard Hopkins, in his *History of the YMCA,* recognized these two distinct approaches to sex education coexisting in the YMCA, referring to them as "the new approaches to sex" and "the older ascetic attitude."[81] Similarly, Elmer Johnson, a historian of the YMCA's physical education work, distinguished between early purity work of the YMCA, which he characterized somewhat negatively, and early-twentieth-century sex education, which he saw as healthier and more realistic about human needs.[82] Although Johnson's perspective, that of a progressive YMCA physical educator in the 1970s, naturally inclined him to emphasize the discontinuity between "purity" and "sex education," there is little evidence that YMCA leaders around the turn of the century were troubled by apparent inconsistencies between the two approaches.

Despite some YMCA rhetoric that put the body on a par with spirit and mind, YMCA sex hygiene was generally conceived of in terms of controlling sexuality rather than liberating it. Despite his espousal of a more body-positive view of Christianity, Luther Gulick "stated that Judaism first taught two truths, namely that real religion is being true inwardly and outwardly, and of necessity has a basis in sexual purity."[83] YMCA physical director George J. Fisher combined the mind-body-spirit philosophy with a form of Christian eugenics whose aim was not the liberation of the body, but rather its ultimate mastery: "Bodily energy must be reckoned with if mental ability and spiritual power are desired. . . . The body may often be the block to higher powers. It likewise may be the secret of a higher experience. . . . Most sins are physical. Much temptation may find its source in bodily ills. Much failure is due to lack of bodily energy."[84] The effect of this kind of ideology was to focus ever more energy and attention on the body as the field on which the battle for race survival had to be fought. "The Association will lead in the new eugenics," Fisher asserted. "It will teach men the sacredness and responsibility of parenthood. It will develop in men a Christian race conscience and will thus help to raise the standard of life through heredity."[85]

The International Committee published and distributed pamphlets from both "purity" and "sex education" perspectives simultaneously from about 1899 until the 1910s. Before 1899, International Committee literature consisted solely of purity literature. After 1899, the International Committee distributed both purity literature and more modern sex education literature, which grew in volume. After the 1910s, purity titles were phased out. In 1914, Max J. Exner, a YMCA physical director, medical doctor, and one of the YMCA's leading sex educators from the turn of the century through the 1920s, wrote a pamphlet entitled *Physician's Answer*. Its primary purpose was to dispel the notion that new ideas about sex implied that chastity was unhealthy. Although Exner's thinking about sexuality was clearly influenced by new medical and psychiatric views, the centerpiece of *Physician's Answer* was a statement signed by over three hundred physicians "that continence is essential to the highest physical, mental, and moral efficiency." Exner's position on chastity was not essentially different from that of Orrin G. Cocks, whose sex education writing for the YMCA reflected a more traditional "purity" sensibility. Cocks had clearly not been influenced by modern medical and psychiatric views.[86] A 1928 *Association Men* editorial by Karl Reiland showed that YMCA sex educators were still discussing potential contradictions between modern ideas of sex and the traditional defense of purity. They insisted that continence was consistent with the highest moral good as well as physical health. "You hear of sex instinct, self-expression, repression, normal function and natural imperative," he noted, but insisted, "No power of instinct is able to overcome and subdue the mind unless the mind wills it, or is too weak to resist it."[87] Reiland did not question the reality of the sex drive; nor did he see it as an excuse for capitulation. This was and ever would be the position universally held by YMCA sex educators. That YMCA leaders saw a basic continuity between earlier purity work and later sex education work is graphically demonstrated in book and pamphlet catalogs published by the International Committee and the Association Press from the late 1880s on. The earliest sex education pamphlets were written from a purity perspective, but were listed under books and pamphlets associated with Physical Education; in later catalogs sex education pamphlets were listed side by side with the older purity literature.[88]

The growing importance of sex education as a YMCA program emphasis is evidenced in YMCA book and pamphlet catalogs and Association Press publications. The first YMCA publication addressing sex appeared in 1892. *A Handbook for Young Men on Personal Purity* by Dr. Charles D. Scudder was published by the New York Association's White Cross Committee, and was listed in the International Committee pamphlet catalog under the physical work section. In 1899, the International Committee began to distribute two pamphlets by Sylvanus Stall: *What a Young Man Ought to Know* and *What a Young Husband Ought to Know*. In 1901 they began to distribute *What a Man of Forty-five Ought to Know* and *What a Young Boy Ought to Know*, by the same author. The growing list of sex education titles after 1907 included Lyman E. Sperry's *Confidential Talks with Young Men*, H. Northcote's *Christianity and the Sex Problem*, and numerous works of Dr. Winfield S. Hall (*Reproduction and Sex Hygiene; Youth, Its Education, Regimen, and Hygiene; Developing into Manhood;* and *Life's Beginnings*). Popular books by Max Exner included *Rational Sex Life for Men* and the above mentioned *Physician's Answer*. The International Committee also began to distribute works on sex education pedagogy, like F. N. Seerley's *Suggested Methods for Instruction in Sexual Hygiene* (1913). The year 1918 was a significant year for YMCA sex education because of the key role played by the Association in providing social services for the United States armed forces during World War I, and the emphasis on keeping troops "fit to fight" and free of venereal diseases. Starting in 1918, sex education earned its own section in book and pamphlet catalogs, and the flood of new titles included works that were clearly aimed at "the fighting men": *Better Than a Fortune, Friend or Enemy* (by Max Exner), and *Nurse and the Knight*.[89]

Perhaps more important than the pamphlets distributed by the International Committee and books published by the Association Press which were specifically devoted to sex education, were books of a more general nature devoting significant attention to sex problems. One example of this type of educational material was *Life Problems: Studies in the Native Interests of Young Men*, by L. L. Doggett, William H. Ball, H. M. Burr, and William Knowles Cooper, and published by the International Committee in 1905. The booklet was intended as a study guide for young men's groups, and covered issues related to "livelihood," "social and family relationships," and "service." The third of four sections was entitled "Problems of Physical Temptation," in which various dimensions of sexuality were explored—physical, social, and spiritual. This section also included a general discussion of "health" and the effects of "stimulants and narcotics." This approach was typical of the YMCA's approach to sex education: sex was treated as one facet of the "whole man" and sex education was integrated into a broad program of character development. Thus, it was hard to participate in any significant YMCA program without being exposed to discussions of and education about sex.

Sex education discourse modified some of the harsher aspects of purity discourse to take some pressure off youth and ease the transition to adulthood. But both discourses emphasized the importance of chastity before marriage, the end of the double standard, and the belief that sex was good as long as it was reserved for marriage. Both saw the proper use of sex as fundamental to civilization. Both stigmatized and condemned various forms of nonmarital sexuality—masturbation, extramarital sex, prostitution, and homosexuality. The main difference between them was that modern sex educators claimed a more scientific approach to sexuality. YMCA sex educators also sought to take some of the terror and danger out of sex. They tended to emphasize its centrality in human life and its goodness. They sought to demystify sex through plain and rational talk. They had confidence that more talk about sex would promote intelligent sexual behavior.

Another major difference, however, was that early-twentieth-century sex educators drew more explicit attention to homosexuality. Marriage became increasingly important as evidence of "normal" sexual development and healthy maturity. Singleness became increasingly suspect and problematic. The YMCA's progressive emphasis on education and dialog about sexuality, especially aimed at youth, guaranteed that ever larger numbers of young people would be exposed to medical discourses about homosexuality.[90] Furthermore, modern sex education increasingly used the authority of science to buttress its claims, building the argument that traditional moral precepts were supported not only by revelation but by empirical, medically tested facts. Violation of the laws of sexual morality would not only make God angry, but result in loss of health, vitality, and race vigor.[91]

One need look no further than the YMCA's physical department for the source of YMCA secretarial attitudes regarding homosexuality, the importance of "treating the family as a unit," and the promotion of "normal" relations between the sexes. As early as 1905, the YMCA's character-building studies, *Life Problems*, included an entire section on "sex perversion." The lesson was placed immediately after a section entitled "Sex and Life," which discussed—quite literally—the birds and the bees, apparently intending sex perversion to be discussed in contrast with God's intention for nature. Lesson IV of part 3, "Sex and Manhood," promoted discussion of what it meant to be "a manly man." Young men were asked to describe "the characteristics of a manly man" and then to contrast them with "the characteristics of the unsexed." The discussion leader was then called upon to "state some results of sex perversion." Considerable time was to be devoted to this discussion, as the leader was instructed to go into depth discussing "the effects of sex perversion upon the physical nature," its effect on "the mind," and its effect on "the character."[92] By the 1920s, sex education literature used in the YMCA was regularly contrasting "normal" sexual desire and behavior with "perverted" or "abnormal" homosexual character. In 1923, the Association Press published a sex education guide by A. Herbert Gray entitled *Men, Women and God: A Discussion of Sex Questions from the Christian Point of View,* which matter-of-factly contrasted "the great majority" of "normal" men and women with "the girls who 'have no use for men' and . . . the queer men who 'don't like girls.'"[93] Young men who were homosexually inclined were advised that "companionships with other men are insufficient for any man. Instincts in your being which may not be denied demand something else. . . . The other sex should . . . be necessary to your completeness and happiness."[94]

In the 1920s YMCA leaders also increasingly expressed fear of the deleterious effects of keeping young men and young women segregated in YMCA and YWCA activities. These new concerns clearly drew upon conceptions of normal versus abnormal sexuality propagated by the physical department. Dr. Max Exner, in a series of sex education articles published in *Association Men* in 1926, repeatedly used the term "normal" to describe "attraction toward the other sex," which he contrasted with "beastly" "perversions" that "man has . . . developed" "in his departure from the natural to the artificial." What is significant about his article is that its primary purpose was to discourage petting and premarital sex between young men and young women. But Exner clearly felt torn between wanting to discourage

heterosexual promiscuity, and the fear that excessive restraint on heterosexual desire might lead to homosexuality. He sought to walk a fine line,
balancing between sex perversion "in one direction" and "lust" for the opposite sex "in another direction." In this diatribe against petting, Exner
found it necessary to "say a word by way of encouragement of friendships
and companionships between the sexes," which were based upon "the most
deep-seated native impulses of every normal individual." He underlined
that "sex companionship is necessary for normal growth of the personality"
and condemned the YMCA's traditional practice of separating the sexes.
Only when it was abundantly clear that he was a fervent promoter of heterosexuality, did he go on to warn against the dangers of petting.[95]

"Knowledge" of homosexuality was also manifested in the early twentieth century in paranoid warnings against deviants. In the March 1906 issue of *Association Men*, an editorial piece entitled "The Dormitory: Some
Real Questions" worried about "unnameable immoralities" among men in
the dorms, and asserted that these problems "must be met bravely and
squarely, not by rules, but by a man who can look beneath the surface and is
unafraid."[96] Another similar warning appeared in the June 1909 *Association Men*:

> Just now, look out for the ladylike man who volunteers for camp leadership or for
> a place in boys' service—the soft-spoken, lisping, lackadaisical man who has
> picked out the fairest-faced boy for his 'special friend' to coddle and treat to soda
> water and ice cream. Ten to one, the man is bad, rotten bad. Fire him![97]

Although such warnings were aimed at protecting the Association, those
who began to speak increasingly about the dangers of homosexuality had
little idea what impact such concerns would have on the ethos, mission, and
dynamics of the organization as a whole.

CONCLUSION

From the mid- through the late nineteenth century, YMCA supporters
found it difficult to justify gymnasiums on any basis other than as a lure to
bring young men onto the premises of the YMCA, where they could then be
exposed to religious influences. Conceptions of the problematic relationship between body and spirit made it difficult to see anything inherently
redeeming in mere physical activity. The earliest promoters of the physical
work emphasized its missionizing potential. But it was hard to justify in-
vesting significant energy and money in the gymnasium at the expense of

other programs, and YMCA physical work before the 1880s was usually neglected. Scattered YMCAs acquired gymnasiums, but no unified philosophy
governed their management. The quality of physical education leadership
was not very high and most YMCAs did not even bother to hire physical
directors.

Many of the classes of men whom the YMCA saw as objects of missionary
concern were considered to be in need of redemption precisely because
their lives were supposed to be dominated by physical rather than spiritual
concerns. Images of sexual immorality among working-class Americans,
foreigners, and racial "others" abroad had always been one of the most effective means of rallying support for evangelism. The working-class's pursuit of various forms of physical leisure, from prostitution to billiards, hor-
rified YMCA leaders. The perception that working-class youths would not
enter a YMCA to join a Bible class but would enter a YMCA to use its gymnastic equipment was the primary reason why the missionary argument in
favor of physical education worked.

Some historians have argued that the rapid pace of industrialization and
urbanization in the late nineteenth century produced a profound dis-ease
on the part of white, male, middle-class Americans. Some have claimed
there was a crisis of masculinity caused by declining male authority in the
home. Others have countered that the term "crisis" is inappropriate since it
implies a dilemma of relatively short duration, while white, middle-class
American men have claimed to experience spiritual distress and dis-ease as
a rather constant feature of modern, urban society.[98] Whatever the case,
YMCA physical education leaders themselves claimed to be responding to
some kind of a crisis in the modern, urban West. They feared emasculation
and enervation caused by the decrease in physical labor and the increase in
mental labor occasioned by the transition from farm life to city life. YMCA
physical education leaders promulgated a philosophy, current among contemporary physical culturists, that men could preserve their manhood by
reinvigorating their bodies through physical exercise and bodybuilding.
They began to view the YMCA's physical program as a form of redemption.

In articles like "Vitality and Modern Life," Luther Gulick echoed other
physicians of his day who were concerned about the enervation of Western
civilization. Like other contemporaries, he made a case for physical education in the "urban, machine age" because of decreasing physical activity
and increasing "neural" activity.[99] "City life," wrote George M. Martin,
an *Association Men* contributor, "is 'playing hob' with vitality."[100] YMCA
physical director James H. McCurdy argued that the decrease in "muscle
work" in American city life would weaken the "race."[101] The image of the
robust farm boy was, of course, itself a myth, and corresponded more to

men's sense of lost patriarchal control than to reality. In fact, John Brown, Jr., M.D., built a case for spreading physical culture to rural areas on the grounds that even country men risked losing their masculinity without the new emphasis on health: "Too often the country lad is by no means as robust, sturdy, and blooming as we are apt to picture him. On Riverside Drive and even on the Bowery we meet 'pictures of health,' and see many sallow and anemic on the country lane." [102] Given that many middle-class men believed their masculinity at risk, physical culture became a means by which the YMCA could sell masculinity to a larger constituency.[103] By rationalizing physical culture within a Protestant Christian framework, the YMCA baptized it. They made it acceptable to the YMCA's traditional religion-based constituency even as they expanded that constituency by responding to anxieties that were widespread among white, Protestant men in urban America.

There has been some debate among historians over whether Victorians were, according to the general stereotype, sexually repressive. Some have argued that Victorians harbored deep ambivalence about pleasure in general and sexual pleasure in particular. A classic statement of this viewpoint can be found in Steven Marcus's *The Other Victorians*.[104] Marcus argued that Victorians created a dark sexual "underworld" in which pornography and prostitution thrived, because they found it culturally impossible to create healthier, more open outlets for the expression of sexual desire. Others have argued that Victorians enjoyed sex, but that they repressed public expression of it in order to heighten private romance and protect youth from knowledge for which they were unprepared. Revisionist interpretations include Peter Gay's *The Bourgeois Experience*, Ellen Rothman's *Hands and Hearts,* and Karen Lystra's *Searching the Heart*.[105] Steven Seidman has criticized the revisionists, arguing that some of them have misused nineteenth-century sources to make it appear as if there were more of a publicly sex-positive culture than there actually was. Even if Victorians enjoyed sex privately, without supportive public expressions and cultural affirmation, such private attitudes would remain problematic.[106] I would argue that revisionists usually base their arguments on middle-class married couples—a very privileged segment of society—and ignore the ways in which Victorian sexual morality was used to control youth, harass the working class, lynch and dispossess blacks, and, later, torture homosexuals. Adequate understanding of how Victorian sexuality was used socially both inside and outside the inner sanctum of the married, middle-class bedroom requires an account of public cultural expressions of sexuality.

The history of YMCA physical work suggests that ascetic attitudes played a very important role in Victorian culture, but that they were not necessarily an obstacle to the adoption of scientific ideas about health and sex. The YMCA was a prototypical Victorian institution, even by the narrowest definition of that word. It was founded in England, spread to the northeastern United States and eastern Canada, was solidly Protestant, and drew the bulk of its membership and financial support from the urban business classes. Shunning controversy, the YMCA reflected the values of the middle classes it sought as its primary constituency. Harmonizing physicality and spirituality was not easy for the men of the YMCA. Attempts to do so occasioned discomfort, protest, and resistance. But neither was the old asceticism completely incompatible with the new preoccupations. Concern about controlling sexuality was shared by the old pietistic ascetics and the new proponents of scientific man-making. If more "old-fashioned" YMCA leaders eventually acquiesced in the new program, it was because physical and sex hygiene work addressed anxieties that they all shared.

The growing emphasis on the redemptive powers of physical education after the 1880s and 1890s drew sex education from the periphery of the organization to its center. The old silence and euphemism about sex, the old asceticism that inspired nineteenth-century leaders, the hostility to the physical, were transformed into an urgent mission to shape the physical and sexual lives and identities of YMCA members. In the name of preserving sexual morality, YMCA members after the turn of the century were educated about the sex drive, warned against singleness, and taught to recognize "perversity." This new knowledge would have fateful consequences for the organization as a whole.

It is the effects of the new emphasis on body and sexuality to which I will turn in the rest of this book. This programmatic shift would have a profound impact on the pietistic men's movement that was founded in London in 1844 and spread to North America in 1851. In some sense, the YMCA of Luther Gulick and his followers sought a cure for the discomforts and problems of urban modernity that was radically at odds with the program undertaken by the YMCA of Robert Weidensall. Gulick envisioned a Y where spirituality was based on individual physical achievement, self-mastery, and heterosexual "family values," while Weidensall's Association envisioned communal interdependence, emotional and spiritual support, and male-male love.

chapter 2

INTENSE FRIENDSHIP

Begetting union in the hearts of the young, union in the essential, [the YMCA]
forgets minor distinctions, and drawing neither from the moorings of faith, nor
the Church, it liberalizes in the right way. Then, too, its pulse beats in union
with the warm young life of the land, quickened as it is by many a new throb
in the present day, the day of life and of action, and its tongue untaught in the
dialect of the schools, bursts out in the free spiritual language which rushes
from the heart, leaps from the lips, beams from the eye and speaks in every
tone and feature. In all this it is specially fitted to the ardor of our youth.
—Robert Weidensall, 1870

Your love and zeal
Lit in men's hearts
The fires that never die
—Luther D. Wishard

There was an exuberance in the early YMCA, an excitement
and a passion that have been captured in expressions like
those cited above. It is evident that the primary force behind
the creation of the Young Men's Christian Association in North
America was that young men simply liked being together.
They enjoyed and were energized by each other. As L. L.
Doggett, an early YMCA leader and historian put it in his 1896
history of the YMCA, one of the primary aims of the organization was to satisfy "the craving of young men for companion-

ship with each other."[1] Historians have begun to document the importance of "male romantic friendship" in the culture of nineteenth-century young men and adolescents. This phenomenon appears to have been particularly strong in religious settings.[2] The Young Men's Christian Association institutionalized intense friendship, and harnessed it to sustain and nurture the organization. By promoting same-sex bonding, it encouraged conversions leading to organizational growth. Intense friendship created cohesion among its leaders, and won its members' ardent loyalty to this tightly knit set of charismatic pioneers. But in the 1880s, when the organization shifted from a purely spiritual mission to a mission that encompassed physical culture and vigilance against sexual immorality, trouble entered paradise. The emphasis on friendship was too important a part of the organization not to survive into the twentieth century. But after 1900, YMCA leaders began to qualify the stress on friendship with warnings against excess and concern about homosexuality.[3]

Examination of YMCA correspondence and publications confirms that emotional bonds between young men in the YMCA were intense, that friendship was a celebrated and central dynamic of the organization.[4] In focusing on the intense nature of this bonding, I am not suggesting that the YMCA was a "homosexual" organization. I am suggesting that homoeroticism and intense homosocial bonds are a more important part of male culture than has previously been imagined. They play an important role in creating cohesion in an all-male group. As the YMCA integrated into its program a broad sex education curriculum that stigmatized homosexuality, it weakened the dynamic that had historically made the Association most effective as an evangelistic organization. It was difficult, if not impossible, to sustain intense friendships while attacking homosexuality.

FRIENDSHIP AND CONVERSION

In the YMCA, same-sex romantic friendship was the primary vehicle of Christian evangelism and the key to the Association's success among young, white, middle-class men in the nineteenth century. Male solidarity and intense, emotional community provided the context for conversion. In institutionalizing what came to be called "personal work," the YMCA sought to capture the energy of one-on-one male-male bonds. In doing so, Association leaders gave romantic male friendship the YMCA's institutional blessing.[5]

Conversion stories are everywhere in YMCA literature and personal correspondence, sermons, essays, and periodicals. They appear to be a paradigm for YMCA experience. In some sense, conversion stories were a handbook for evangelism, since they told young men how conversion could be achieved. The published conversion stories of prominent YMCA leaders like George Williams are particularly instructive, since they were obviously intended as models for young men. Samuel M. Sayford, who served as state secretary of the Massachusetts YMCA and later as a traveling YMCA college evangelist, published his own conversion story with the admonition "It is a good illustration of the naturalness and ease with which personal work can be done, and I trust its recital may prove an incentive to many to go and do likewise."[6] Conversion stories ritualized young men's entry into fellowship and instructed them about the meaning of life together. Conversion stories also clearly demonstrated the central role of intimate friendship in the process of winning souls for Christ.

Conversion stories often featured an intimate pairing, a relationship between two men in which one either helped bring about the conversion of the other, or in which both found spiritual enlightenment together. Men became specially bonded by the conversion experience, often for life. George Williams, the founder of the YMCA in 1844, found such a soul mate in his roommate, J. Christopher Smith. The nature of their relationship was captured in a late-nineteenth-century inside account of the origins of the YMCA by Laurence L. Doggett:

> The loneliness, temptation and irreligion of his surroundings led him to pour out his heart in prayer that he might find a fellow-worker among the young men. . . . Christopher Smith became George Williams' room-mate. The intimate relations, the Christian fellowship of these two young men will never be known, but the power of their lives exerted an influence which is to-day felt throughout the world. Through their efforts several young men in the establishment became Christians.[7]

Doggett's history, originally published in 1896, relied on interviews with Smith's brother Norton, also a friend of George Williams. But Doggett's florid account of this relationship suggested that in 1896 Doggett also personally identified with this situation. The popularity of Doggett's history—it was widely read in YMCA circles—suggests that many other YMCA men also related to this story and found it inspiring. Other YMCA conversion stories from the 1840s through the 1870s featured similar pairings leading young men to conversion, or providing the model for a chain of conversions. Some Chicago YMCA correspondence revealed a tendency to treat such male pairs as couples and a desire to keep them from being separated in their evangelical work. In 1876 a Mr. Elsing and a Mr. Kerr wrote as a couple to Dwight Moody, then of the Chicago YMCA, to discuss their sense of call, and Moody assumed that they should be kept together in whatever YMCA work they might pursue.[8]

Conversion not only cemented loyalties between men within the organization but helped consolidate men's commitment to the organization itself. Robert R. McBurney, general secretary of the New York YMCA for over a quarter of a century, made his decision to give his life to YMCA work as the result of his role as a YMCA officer in the conversion of a young man in 1862.[9] The warmth of his relationships with young men in his charge was widely known to be one of McBurney's defining characteristics. "His heart and hand were more engaged in that part of the Association work that consists, not so much in the appointment of committees, in the organizing of workers and conventions, and in the construction of buildings, as in the hand-to-hand work wrought out in personal intercourse . . . and in all these quiet, spiritual, personal activities which grow out of the life blood of the Association work."[10] Robert Weidensall, the YMCA's first international traveling field secretary, also claimed to have been drawn to YMCA work by similarly rich emotional experiences.[11]

The autobiography of Richard C. Morse, *My Life with Young Men*, powerfully illustrates how intense friendship could commit young men to the Association for life. Morse came from an illustrious line of distinguished pastors. His grandfather Jedediah Morse founded numerous religious associations, including the first United States Foreign Missionary Society and the American Bible Society. Both his grandfather and his father (also a pastor) pioneered religious journalism in America and founded one of the earliest ecumenical societies, the Evangelical Alliance. Given his heritage, Richard felt considerable pressure to enter the same calling. Morse, however, "knowing the strong desire [his] father felt in this direction," was afraid to disappoint him should he fail as a minister. Morse's fear of failure in the realm of church ministry paralyzed him for many years, as he "seriously distrusted [his] qualification for the calling." He put off announcing his intent to enter into the ministry, "an inclination . . . cherished from boyhood," and as a young adult continued to struggle spiritually. "My Christian life for some years was not a very happy one."[12] Significantly, Morse experienced a change in preparatory school and later in college as he began to form intimate friendships with his schoolmates. He attributed his progress in the spiritual realm to his friends:

> For whatever genuine progress was made in this direction I was deeply indebted
> to the happy friendships begun [in preparatory school] . . . especially with my

roommate Henry Stebbins. . . . In the growing intimacies of our college life, we confirmed one another in our vocational choice, and in the obligations and privileges of the calling for which we were seeking preparation and qualification.[13]

Morse never did enter a congregation-based pastorate. But by the time he abandoned once and for all his cherished childhood dreams and the burden of his heritage, he had been drawn into another communion: the YMCA. Here, more than ever before, Morse was energized by an all-male fellowship united in a common purpose. But he felt particularly drawn to Robert R. McBurney, with whom he shared "unbroken brotherly fellowship."

> Beginning with this period I became intimately associated with McBurney, a fellowship growing in intimacy and tenderness until the end of his life on earth. I was more incessantly with him during these two years than afterward, because I was more uninterruptedly in New York. We took our meals together morning, noon, and night. All my problems were his, and all his were mine. There was a sympathy and intercourse that grew out of both likeness and unlikeness of dispositions, tastes, and opinions.

McBurney and Morse eventually shared the same quarters, living together for a period of five years at the 23rd Street and 4th Avenue Y. Just as Morse "received spiritual impulse" from his friend Henry Stebbins in college, now in the YMCA he experienced a heightened intensity in his prayer life with "a new emphasis on communion."[14] It is clear that for Morse, as for many others in the YMCA, male-male love had the effect of intensifying his spiritual life, helping to resolve his anxieties about succeeding in a career, and granting him a sense of purpose. Almost two decades after the death of McBurney, Morse expressed a longing for him "at every thought of what he was in our lives and what he is yet to be!"[15]

Warm one-on-one relationships fostered the evolution of entire communities of loving men. The relationship between Morse and McBurney was recognized and celebrated by other members and leaders of the YMCA. Indeed, they drew men closer to each other through their example of mutual commitment. Morris K. Jessup recognized the intensity of the relationship between McBurney and Morse:

> Mr. Morse is one of those [truly consecrated], Mr. McBurney is another, and I couple the names of these two men together in my heart, and I say truly with Mr. Brainerd, I love them both. . . . God bless them both! I can't separate one from the other, hardly. Although we are all here to-day to honor Mr. Morse, yet these two men are so inseparably connected in my heart and in my past twenty-five years experience with them that I look upon them as brothers, both of them, and I say to them now, as I have said to them often, that I love them both.[16]

As Robert R. McBurney described it, YMCAs maintained their vitality because young men wanted to belong to a "society of young men whose sentiments are love."[17] Some sense of intimacy seemed almost a prerequisite for the formation of a YMCA. Robert Weidensall recalled his participation in an early association, where "some persons . . . wanted to hasten the organization of an Association, but it was the general sentiment that the prayer meeting should be continued until we could know each other better, as we were then strangers to each other."[18]

Friendship could also, however, be viewed with ambivalence. Association with the wrong type of friends could prove an obstacle to conversion. Samuel M. Sayford told a story of a young man whose ministry was ruined after giving in to "youthful lusts" with a roommate. He warned that "a personal worker should avoid . . . dangerous companionships as he would a leper."[19] While personal friendship was the most effective way to save the wayward, young men received the contradictory warning that it was wisest to confine one's relationships to the converted and to avoid companionship that could become a snare. All-male socialization that occurred in the urban context was seen as the greatest threat to traditional Christian values: "One of the tragic circumstances connected with the younger boys is the fact that they almost invariably travel in pairs and that one of the two is a person of a good deal lower standard of morality and conduct than the other. If these two could be separated one of them might be saved to society."[20] One YMCA leader worried that young men entering college might "even fall into bad habits and bad associates, unless some means are brought to bear for arresting that tendency. The work of the Association is just the means to gather in all who would naturally belong to it, and give them the aid of good associates and good influences from the start."[21]

Usually in evidence in conversion stories was a background of erotic anxiety, resulting in extraordinary emotional intensity. I suspect that mutual, frank acknowledgment of temptation was a form of sublimated erotic intimacy between young men. Sexual tension was usually spoken or written of in a highly coded language, usually in terms of "temptation" or the lure of "immorality." The bright accounts of salvation in Jesus Christ were almost always painted melodramatically against the somber background of the magnetic sinfulness from which young men were redeemed. One dramatic illustration of this appears in the biography of George Alonzo Hall, who served as one of the first field secretaries for the YMCA's International Committee and as the general secretary for the State of New York. Hall was described by George A. Warburton, another YMCA international secretary, as "full of intense passion" for other young men, but with a "nature . . .

peculiarly sensitive, almost morbid in its introspection," "full of self-loathing." Hall's diary included numerous entries like this one:

> To-day I have sinned against my God, I can hardly realize it, yet while in the full possession of my faculties. I wantonly sinned against God. Oh! how can I believe it, yet it is true! And now through the unaccountable goodness of my God I am forgiven. Father, if it can be in accordance with thy holy will, rather than let me commit this again, oh, take me out of the world.

Warburton saw these internal struggles as having "fitted him to enter so fully into the life of boys," as being intimately connected to "that passionate devotion . . . to individual young men, which was, after all, the keynote of his life." Hall's life was described as a series of intense "bonds of personal friendship and love." Hall was known to travel miles out of his way "to help a repentant wanderer," to spend with him a "night of agony, of prayer, of confession, and the morning of joyous restoration."[22]

Doggett's account of George Williams's story recalled the "immoral" "life among the young men" and "the loneliness, temptation and irreligion of his surroundings." Williams's surroundings intensified this "loneliness" and "temptation" through "overcrowded" living conditions, and extremely long work hours that left the men desperate for some sort of release. His response was an anxious flight from sin: "In the Holmes Drapery House there was a little dark room where the wrapping paper was kept, into which Williams used to slip off alone, when he was tempted, and pour out his soul in prayer to God. He says: 'Instead of spending my Sunday afternoons in pleasure as formerly, when the light came, I began to go to Sunday School.'"[23] YMCA evangelist Samuel M. Sayford himself appears to have had a gift for persuading men that he had "felt personally their temptations and has still their tendencies," a gift that was one of the keys to his success as an evangelist and a social purity preacher.[24] A key to his appeal was the intimate talks he held both in group and one-on-one settings about "temptation" and "immorality."

The bedroom was frequently mentioned in conversion stories with a fascinating ambivalence. In Doggett's account of the George Williams story, the men's dormitories were sordid, crowded, and "badly ventilated," a place where young strangers to the city could become "debauched," "degraded," and "debased" under the immoral influence of "old stagers" and "veterans in sin." On the other hand the bedroom could also become the site of conversion to God and a place where the bonds of Christian fellowship were initiated, sealed, and renewed. George Williams and his roommate J. Christopher Smith began their ministry by establishing "bedroom prayer meetings." [25] In either case the bedroom was an enclosed space, shut off from the view of others. The reader was left only to imagine what debauched excesses the "novice in sin" might be led into behind its doors; at the same time the reader could "never know" the "intimate relations" of Christian love that were enacted within its walls. Many conversion stories enshrined the bedroom with a romantic aura as the site of some of the most significant spiritual exchanges. The climax of Samuel M. Sayford's conversion story, as told in his book *Personal Work*, recounted how, upon seeing the man he most credited with bringing him to Christ, "we were both eager to get to his room in the hotel," where they knelt together in emotional prayers of thanks. [26]

There are clues that physical proximity and intimacy were a significant part of the bonds that held these men together. In an interview with Norton Smith, the brother of Christopher Smith, Doggett learned that not only were Smith and Williams roommates, they were bed mates: "He and George Williams slept in the same bed. I was one of the four who occupied the same bedroom." Norton recalled that fifteen to twenty men gathered in their bedroom for the early prayer meetings. That they were not uncomfortable with the physical intimacy required under these circumstances was evident from simple remarks like that of an acquaintance of Williams who recalled Williams walking alone with him "pressing my arm and addressing me familiarly, as [he was] in the habit of doing." [27]

YMCA leaders recognized early the effectiveness of friendship for missionary work and capitalized on it by consciously encouraging what they called "personal work." Personal work was promoted through YMCA talks and literature, though "special training classes for this purpose have become common," noted Sayford in his book *Personal Work* (1899). [28] Advancing personal work as a program rather than allowing it to happen spontaneously, of course, risked defeating its purpose. Potential converts would unlikely enter the fellowship unless they really believed that their friendship was valued as more than just a means to an end. YMCA leaders warned against an approach to personal work that appeared stilted and insincere: "The wise worker will choose and use the way most likely to admit him into the confidence of the person approached. The need of naturalness cannot be too strongly emphasized. A mechanical effort to do personal work is readily detected, and is always to be deprecated." [29] Yet, the YMCA specialized in providing a setting where male friendship was celebrated and enjoyed for its own sake. Richard C. Morse, the general secretary of the YMCA in North America from 1872 to 1915, in a pamphlet entitled "The Young Men's Christian Association as It Is," saw male friendship as a sign of God's grace. But friendship was also viewed as a divine gift and as a good in itself, aside from any redemptive purpose that God might work through it.[30] The YMCA's de facto anthem, "Blest Be the Tie That Binds," was one of the many reminders that intense love between men in the YMCA fellowship was justifiable on the grounds that Jesus commanded his disciples to "love one another" and to become "one." The promotion of personal work, far from degrading friendship into a crude evangelistic tool, romanticized it and gave it institutional blessing.

For Robert Weidensall, the promotion of personal work was simply the acknowledgment that "it takes a young man to exert any influence with a young man."[31] YMCA leaders encouraged young men to see God working in their already existing friendships and to find out for themselves the best way to apply the principles of personal work. In *Personal Work*, Sayford gave guidelines that would likely intensify homosocial interaction. He advised young men to "work, as a rule, with persons of your own age, or younger, and with persons of your own sex." They should "seek an opportunity to converse with the person alone," "be patient," and "carry him in your heart."[32]

The YMCA's ethos of intense friendship made its evangelistic outreach to young, white, middle-class men extremely effective but made its outreach to other classes extremely ineffective. Since a key element of this intense friendship was identification, the networks in which it thrived and through which conversions proliferated tended to be class- and race-homogeneous. This is also why the issue of including women in the YMCA was so emotionally charged and so intensely resisted. The result was that efforts at Christian proselytizing of working-class men, immigrant men, or African American men by the great white, middle-class constituency of the YMCA were always feeble and never as successful.

Dwight L. Moody's early Sunday school work under YMCA auspices was considered remarkable because it crossed class lines. Even then, his work was rife with class tension. "There were many poor families who resented Mr. Moody's efforts to get their children into his Sunday School," recalled John V. Farwell. He recounted a number of stories of brothers or young male friends who "knew of [Moody's] work among the Catholic poor, and hated him for it." Middle-class YMCA workers were shocked by the brutality of working-class culture and life. "One day the worst of these boys came in and took his seat with his hat on, and instantly another planted a stunning blow on his face, sprawling him on the floor, with the remark, 'I'll teach you not to enter Moody's Sunday School with your hat on.'"[33] Moody may have been successful partly because he was willing to get his hands dirty and reacted to violence with his own imposing physical presence.

This is not to say that the intense friendship between personal evangelist and beloved convert never crossed class lines. In a journal describing his mission work in the lumber camps of northern Wisconsin, Charles Conrad Hamilton described a close relationship with one convert that included all the elements of intimacy described above, as well as an overt element of physical admiration: "He is a fine tall broad-shouldered man, and it looked very picturesque with him walking in front of the cutter with his gun and mackinaws, etc." His relationship with this man gave him a heightened sense of connection to the divine. After praying for and talking with "Mr. C.," he wrote in his journal, "Somehow I've felt the power of God present with me today more than I have for a long time. My soul had been so refreshed." [34]

But this example of cross-class friendship was the exception rather than the rule. Hamilton's journal offers many more examples of class tension and hostility than of close friendship. "It is much harder to get hold of and deal with these men," Hamilton commented. Hamilton and his missionary companion typically received raillery and ill will from the lumbermen. Usually the best the missionaries could get was deference, rarely true friendship.

> [The foreman] came into the cook's shanty and danced about and swore pretty hard. He said to the cook, "The Y.M.C.A. boys have gone off. I saw the cutter on the ice!" . . . The cook said, "They haven't gone, for one of them is in here." The foreman was very much taken aback, and Mr. T. heard him go and apologize for his behavior to the cook sometime after.

If the lumbermen found Hamilton's faith laughable, Hamilton found the male culture in the camps repulsive:

> At dinner I sat at the same table with some fellows who, as far as I could make out, all got drunk last night. I never want to take up my abode in these "civilized" parts unless I see it is the Lord's will. . . . In less than 10 minutes, while the brakemen were playing cards, between three of them the name of God and Jesus Christ were blasphemed 54 times. [35]

Besides the fact that middle-class and working-class men had to relate to each other across disparate cultures, the emphasis on personal friendship networks as a means of conversion had the effect of reinforcing a consciousness of middle-class separateness. Samuel M. Sayford recounted:

> Accosting [a janitor], I said, "This is a fine building you have to care for." "Yes," was his reply, "and they're a fine lot of gentlemen in it." "It must make your work all the more pleasant," I said, "to have such men to work for. I trust you are a Christian." "No," came the ready reply, "I've had no one to help me in that way; you see, I'm only a janitor." [36]

Although the janitor's words have been filtered through Sayford's storytelling, it is possible to read a thin layer of sarcasm and class mistrust in his comment "they're a fine lot of gentlemen" and in his matter-of-fact response that he had not joined their ranks because "you see, I'm only a janitor."

MALE-MALE LOVE AND THE YMCA SECRETARY

If intense male friendship was a key element in the phenomenon of conversion in the nineteenth-century YMCA, and if it played a central role in recruiting new membership and creating solidarity, it was an even more potent factor in the relationships between career YMCA secretaries. YMCA leaders expressed a longing love for young men. It was a love that—as I will discuss in greater depth in the following chapter—motivated a significant percentage of them to forego wives and children to devote their entire energies to the organization. They sustained intense, lifelong relationships with one another. As they grew older, they drew younger men into the fellowship and they trained them into leadership, sustaining a tradition and an environment of all-male affection. Correspondence and autobiographical writings of career YMCA secretaries are rich with expressions of this affection. And while secretaries most often expressed this love in spiritual terms, documentary sources reveal an awareness of the embodied nature of male-male affection, a longing for physical proximity, admiration of one another's virility, and a delight in physical touch.

One critic of gay studies scholarship has recently suggested that intense expressions of male-male love in Christian fraternities cannot be classed as "homoerotic" and that they are more appropriately interpreted within the framework of Christian "agape."[37] It seems unnecessary, however, to view homoeroticism and Christian agape as mutually exclusive. There is no reason why an intense love that included elements of physical longing and attraction could not be expressed in the language of Christian devotion. My own experience as a gay man who once served as a Mormon missionary, participated in evangelical and fundamentalist Christian organizations, and lived in a Roman Catholic monastic order has taught me that such sublimation can create the very fabric of spiritual life in intense religious fraternities. Prayer, Christian symbolism of eternal union in heaven, and the language of agape were a perfect means of expressing an attraction that these men experienced as intense and that could not be openly expressed physically or even acknowledged to oneself.

Typical of the relationships that energized YMCA leaders was that between Robert Weidensall and John Lake. Lake and Weidensall worked together for several years as county work secretaries, coordinating YMCA outreach in rural areas. In the time they spent together, they developed an intense and close relationship until Lake left county work in 1904 to do YMCA mission work in China. In 1905, Weidensall went on a world tour visiting YMCAs in Asia and Europe. When he arrived in Canton, he was met by Lake, who stayed by his side virtually until he left again. Weidensall wrote of their parting, "John Lake could hardly give me up—and it was a great strain upon me to part from him, possibly for all time. . . . He went with me to the steamer and there we parted."

After Weidensall's departure from Canton, but before he had left China, Lake sent him a love poem. The poem celebrated the "joy" Lake felt "To grasp your hand, strong, rugged hand, / Look in your face, frank, noble, grand, / And hear the tones that win—command—/ Affection so." Reflecting on the growth of their "love" over the years, he "wondered how you've gripped my heart / . . . wondered why my pulse would start / Whene'er I saw you." Their bond was "no device, no art," but was due to Weidensall's charisma, his power "to radiate / The things that win men's hearts." Lake was saddened by the need to be separated from his friend but was able to release him with the thought that the union he "craved" with him would be found once again in heaven. He also consoled himself with the thought that just as Weidensall's presence "gives me strength," he would go on to "make many brave."[38] Far from being embarrassed by such an effusion of intense emotion, Weidensall clearly cherished the poem, quoting it in full in a prominent place in the memoirs of his world travels.

In writing of his relationship with Lake, Weidensall commented, "Lake was in many respects a real Timothy to me." He thus drew a comparison between their relationship and the relationship between Saint Paul and his close disciple and missionary companion Timothy. This was typical of the imagery Weidensall used to describe his relationships with other men in the YMCA. Weidensall, in an 1876 letter to Cephas Brainerd, indirectly compared his relationships to young men to the relationships between Jesus and the twelve apostles, Ignatius of Loyola and the first Jesuits, and John Wesley and the first Methodists. Like Jesus, Loyola, Wesley, and Paul, Weidensall was an itinerant preacher and organizer who remained single to his death.[39] Furthermore, in Weidensall's words, like Jesus, Loyola, and Wesley, he "gathered around him[self] young men and trained them."[40] In the last years of his life, Weidensall devoted himself to the volunteer extension work that, as he defined it in a letter of 1898, involved "selecting a band of young men—hand-picked young men—spirit called young men" and personally disciplining them. His emphasis was on a close relationship between the trainer and the disciples: they were to remain in intense contact for an extended time, and the group was to consist of not more than twelve, perhaps as few as two or three.[41]

These relationships, which Weidensall described using imagery from the Bible and from church history, were full of emotional intensity. Many of these relationships involved traveling together as YMCA missionaries and organizers. "It is not that I do not love thee!" J. W. Dean wrote to Weidensall, describing a thought that "came to me on my pillow the morning, before day-dawn." "Our last winter's roaming and foraging together served to endear thee to me."[42] Another YMCA secretary wrote to Weidensall of his love for another secretary, "He and I have been like brothers ever since we were thrown together . . . and I pray God that nothing but death shall ever be able to separate the friendship we have one for the other. The way he has stood by me . . . has made a few men very jealous, and I have been surprised to find how some men have been mean enough to seek to break off the friendship."[43] John Boardman, a YMCA county worker, described his love for Weidensall and his growing relationship with John Lake: "I spent all of one day with [Lake] and how our tongues did fly. We walked and talked all day. . . . We were not long in getting close to each others [sic] hearts. . . . [Lake] was kind enough to say he liked me better the more he saw me and talked with me."[44] Weidensall later wrote Boardman, "My heart goes out to you as it does to few people . . . I feel closer to you than to any other living person."[45]

The friendship of these men had an embodied element: a delight in one another's physical proximity, an awareness of each other's bodies, a sort of excitement that overtook them at the prospect of spending time together. This embodiment was celebrated in Lake's poem to Weidensall, as he celebrated his joy "To grasp your hand, strong rugged hand, / Look in your face, frank, noble, grand, / And hear the tones than win—command—/ Affection so." In a number of letters, secretaries teased Luther D. Wishard about his baldness, but in a way that celebrated his physical presence: "Yes, we have had some mosquitoes out our way. I was in hopes you would give them a chance to try their gimlets upon your bald head. I have had my share and was anxious that you should have the same experience."[46] As Wishard was preparing for a trip to China, a missionary friend of his wrote eagerly to him regarding their anticipated reunion:

O how glad I was to get the good news. I stood on my head, cracked my heels together, saying, "In the morning by de Bright Light," & carried on high generally (all this is metaphorical). A great joy has reigned in my heart ever since. "I'm going to see Wish, bald-headed, fat-bellied Wish" is the refrain that soothes my thought & sweetens my dreams. . . . Well, Wish, when I think of your coming I get all on the *qui vive*. Won't we have a jolly time singing, talking over the times when "I were down to Griggstown," "walk to where I live," knock-knees, &c. &c.?[47]

Secretaries remembered moments of physical proximity and shared emotional intimacy as life-changing, spiritual events. Luther Wishard recalled the effects of spending a freezing night in the Berkshires with C. K. Ober:

> [Ober and I] had met at Williams [College] in January 1882 and our hearts were knit together from the first; I may say literally we froze together for we did; it was a bitter night in the Berkshires and the fires in the hotel had burned low; but as we sat together in my room until the small hours of the morning our hearts burned and were fused into a comradeship which I shall enjoy forever. . . . Few men have known Ober as intimately as I have.[48]

Ober and Wishard saw their relationship in continuity with a tradition of male love, united through a mutual commitment to missions. Together they made a pilgrimage to the site at Williams College where a group of men had made a mutual pledge under a haystack to give themselves to foreign mission work. After visiting the site, Wishard imagined that in heaven "the Men of the Haystack are keeping eternal tryst."[49]

Wishard's reference to the "eternal tryst" of the men of the Haystack movement was not the only time that YMCA men shared metaphorical trysts together. R. C. Morse described the relationship between YMCA members and Jesus Christ as "our tryst with Him . . . in all the earth."[50] At a celebration of R. C. Morse's service to the YMCA, John F. Moore described Morse as "the groom and . . . the Young Men's Christian Association [as] the bride."[51] Luther Wishard frequently referred throughout his memoirs to places where men shared spiritual experiences together as "trysting" places.

The intensity of the relationships between YMCA men was often expressed in Christian religious symbolism. Just as John Lake "craved" the final union he would have with Weidensall in heaven, the theme of union in heaven was echoed repeatedly in letters of other YMCA secretaries who shared close bonds with each other. Luther D. Wishard, a disciple of Weidensall in the college YMCA work, wrote him that "the Hanover freshman, the Princeton senior, the college secretary, loves you with eternal love and anticipates your fellowship as one of the sweetest joys of immortality." In another letter Wishard wrote Weidensall that the love that they had for one another "savors of heaven."[52] Writing about prayer or actually praying together were other common ways of expressing love for each other. Charles Conrad Hamilton used prayer to shorten the distance between him and his friend Alex: "Tho' we may be absent in body, and some hundreds of miles apart, yet we will always be present in spirit, bearing each other up before the 'throne of grace.' 'Blest be the tie that binds.'"[53] John R. Boardman recalled in a letter to Robert Weidensall that one of his "happiest" recent experiences "was the hour we talked and prayed about you."[54] Weidensall in turn wrote Boardman on New Year's Eve:

> Oh how I would love to spend this last hour of this year and the first hour of the New Year with you together with the Master, the Holy Spirit, & the Father. . . . I stopped writing for a while to commune with the Lord and make known to him my heart's desire—Oh how I would have enjoyed your presence in this short time of thanksgiving and prayer.[55]

This poignant letter interwove Weidensall's passionate expressions of love for Boardman, Lake, and Wishard, his intense desire to see all young men gathered together under the banner of Christ, and his struggle with loneliness and concern about his "infirmities." The letter illustrates the diffuse homoeroticism that motivated Weidensall to devote his life to the service of young men, his particular attachment to the men closest to him, his intense longings and desires, the tension that accompanied his loneliness, and his reliance on religious language and imagery to assuage his longing in some measure. Throughout the letter, expressions of a burning love for the Master Jesus Christ overlap with expressions of burning love for young men in such a way that the two are indistinguishable, just as Lake had written in his poem of the noble act of "winning men," "the fragrant deeds that ever prove / A burning zeal for Him above, / The song, the sacrifice, the *love*."[56]

THE HEROIC SECRETARY

Not only did male love serve as the primary means of achieving conversion, it came to be seen a prerequisite for YMCA leadership. Jacob T. Bowne, a respected YMCA secretary and one of the founders of the YMCA's Springfield Training School, noted that the Association general secretary "must have intense love for young men as a class, love that will be magnetic."[57] This expectation fostered an environment where affection by YMCA secretaries for the young men in their care was considered natural. It was common for YMCA leaders to express a generalized love for young men in passionate terms: "My heart burns to rescue & save young men."[58] But it was also expected that this love should flow both ways, and it did in the form of a devotion to YMCA leaders that sometimes took the form of hero worship. This hero worship was celebrated by YMCA leaders as natural and even desirable. An *Association Men* article could unselfconsciously note as the moral of one anecdote: "As for the young man: first of all he worships God, but next he almost worships that . . . secretary."[59] Like personal work, the rhetorical celebration of relationships between secretaries and members was another means by which the YMCA openly acknowledged and institutionally reinforced passionate male-male bonds.

Jacob T. Bowne's vision of the secretarial role was one that would, if successful, nurture a very classical homoerotic tension in the organization. Indeed, he conceived of an organization that required homoerotic tension in order to function. According to Bowne, not only should a general secretary have "intense love" for young men, but he must also "be a man whom nature has endowed with far more than ordinary ability as a leader and organizer. He must also be a young man of irreproachable Christian character."[60] Furthermore, as the YMCA's 1892 *Hand-Book,* edited by Bowne, makes clear, physical beauty was also expected of the ideal YMCA secretary: "Good personal presence is an advantage. Any serious defect or peculiarity of body, limb, or feature will prove an embarrassment. . . . An aptitude for athletic and manly sports will largely increase his influence with young men."[61] Bowne's "heroic" secretary would be admirable in every way, physically and spiritually. Bowne believed in "natural" leaders and in a form of leadership based on inherent qualities that would attract young men to the secretaries.

The "magnetism" that drew secretary and young man together was similar to the affectionate ties that in classical Greek philosophy bound (a male) teacher and (a male) student. While in ancient Greece a sexual bond often existed between teacher and student, more often (especially toward the latter period of what we commonly regard as the classical era) teachers who were considered truly virtuous would exercise discipline over their passions, and sexual desire in the relationship would properly go unrequited.[62] As we will see below, by the 1920s, YMCA publications issued explicit warnings against homosexual temptation between the secretary and the young man who accepted his leadership. In Bowne's day such expectations were simply implied in the requirement of "irreproachable Christian character." An interesting irony of balancing homoerotic attraction against the virtues of self-control is that it not only heightened the erotic tension in the relationship, but made self-control/repression an attractive quality in a potential friend. The main difference between Bowne's vision of YMCA leadership and the teacher-student relationships of classical antiquity was that Bowne's ideal, and the models of leadership held up in the YMCA generally, were intended for egalitarian social networks and relationships, and tended to reinforce an ethos of mutual admiration.

The model of leadership Bowne described was acknowledged and celebrated as the pattern for many YMCA relationships, as in the relationship between David Sinclair, the secretary of the Cleveland YMCA, and Edwin L. Shuey, its president for many years:

> When the lad [Edwin L. Shuey] came home from college for his first holiday vacation, the secretary [David Sinclair] captured him utterly. From that moment dated the friendship which this slight volume is written to celebrate—at first (though there was but seven years' difference in their ages) the spontaneous enthusiasm of an aspiring boy for a man of evident power, but ere many years had gone by, a gripping, true-steel affection which bound together indivisible comrades, one in every ideal and purpose and almost in every work.[63]

Doggett, an associate of Bowne, observed that Bowne modeled this kind of relationship in his personal behavior.[64] YMCA leaders all insisted on an ideology of leadership training in which a virtuous leader gathers dynamic youth about him and personally disciplines them. It was fervently promoted in formalized leadership training courses not only by Bowne, but by Robert Weidensall and Charles K. Ober, the two other YMCA leaders who more than anyone else devoted themselves to YMCA leadership development. Samuel M. Sayford preached a popular sermon, "The Need of Moral Heroism in Christian Life," and did not discourage the hero worship of which he was the frequently the object in many YMCA revival settings.[65]

Wishard's autobiography offers an example of how hero worship attracted young men to the YMCA. Wishard first became acquainted with the YMCA at the University of Indiana at Bloomington, though he did not actually join until after he transferred to Hanover College. The YMCA made a powerful impression on the youthful Wishard. Its leaders loomed larger than life in his mind. When he was selected by the Hanover YMCA to represent them at the YMCA's international convention, he doubted his worthiness but could hardly refuse the excitement or the honor of the position. His account of his early college and YMCA careers conveys an image of an impressionable, shy, naive boy, lacking self-confidence and feeling extremely vulnerable away from the shelter of his protective father and warm, small-town community. Every acknowledgment he received from other YMCA men deeply impressed and astonished him.

His account of his trip east and his interactions with YMCA leaders conveys a tone of awe that men of such magnitude could show concern for him:

> I shall never forget my attendance at the noonday prayer meeting of the Boston Association and the open-handed and hearted greeting of the General Secretary, L. P. Rowland. It was not the cold stare of him of Queen City [Boston]. Dear old Rowland had a passion for young men and that passion shone and burned until his sun went down to rise upon the land of Eternal youth.

Wishard particularly identified with Thane Miller, since he, like Wishard, was blind: "Thane Miller, the blind man, was chosen President the following day, but I was strangely conscious of the fact that he was simply acting as an audible interpreter of the invisible Chairman. . . . I worshipped him from afar. I wept much under the spell of his eloquence." Wishard also remembered Anthony Comstock, author of the infamous censorship laws: "Anthony Comstock gripped me powerfully and in later years intimacy developed between us, the meaning of which is a prized possession." Weidensall, who, according to Wishard, "early attracted my attention," made a particularly strong impression when "he received me with all the greater cordiality because I was a college delegate. . . . I simply knew that he was one of the heartiest men that I had ever met, that he actually did welcome the obscure freshman to the Convention."[66] It was Wishard's admiration for Weidensall which inspired him to enter YMCA service for the advancement of student work. David McConaughy in turn recalled that he was attracted to YMCA work in 1879–1880 by the "personal magnetism" of Wishard.[67]

Anthony Rotundo has documented the existence of romantic friendship among young men in the nineteenth century which could include erotic elements. These friendships, he argued, were especially common among young college men, or men who found themselves in between full dependence on their parents and the independence of their own careers and families. The first generation of YMCA men came of age in this culture of masculine comradeship. Rotundo described "pairings" off, special relationships between young men which were recognized as such by their peers. Correspondence of R. C. Morse suggests that YMCA leaders were familiar with this male youth culture. In one letter, Morse recalled a "special" relationship from his college years very similar to those described by Rotundo: "In our class at Andover [Hendrie] was our second scholar & was always associated in our minds with Jack Taylor, our valedictorian both at Andover and Yale."[68] During his 1867 youthful travels in Europe, Morse met up with a former classmate by the name of Coe, who became a close companion. They explored the World Exposition in Paris together. They met and breakfasted together at each other's apartments and shared intimate conversations about many topics. Morse was delighted with his companionship and even compared it positively to his relationship with Dick Vail, another former classmate who happened to be in Paris at the time. Vail tired quickly of the exposition and became cranky when Morse insisted on a thorough tour. Coe, on the other hand, accompanied him everywhere, chatting with him, going shopping with him, attending the theater with him, and sharing meals with him. It was common among young middle-class men and women to travel abroad in same-sex pairs; allusions to this were frequent in Morse's travel correspondence: "Henry Grant & a young man his travelling companion were on board the ship. . . . Henry Grant & friend are on the way to Harbin, hoping to get there on or before May 28th. They will blaze the path for me to follow, sending me back word of their experiences!" [69]

According to Rotundo, however, the expectations of marriage and entry into the competitive world of American business denied mature men the male-male romantic pleasures and outlets of youth.[70] But correspondence from the YMCA indicates that male romantic friendship could continue to exist in the form of "Christian brotherhood" throughout adulthood and even into old age. Other historians, like Henry Abelove, David Hilliard, and Donald Yacovone have demonstrated that intense same-sex bonds played a particularly important role in other men's religious movements.[71] The emphasis on intense, male-male love in the YMCA appears to confirm a general pattern in which agape, or Christian brotherly love, provided the model for men's relationships in religious fraternities.

Rotundo argued that in an era before common awareness of homosexuality, the warmth, intimacy, and physical touch that characterized these same-sex friendships were viewed as natural and innocent, and were not at all associated with the crime of sodomy. Yacovone, Hilliard, and Abelove also agree that this emphasis on "brotherly love" provided a context in which erotic intimacy could be expressed without the stigma that would later be attached to homosexuality. I would argue that some men in the nineteenth century found this kind of physical and emotional intimacy so satisfying that they built their lives around it, forgoing heterosexual marriage. This kind of emotional and physical intimacy would be impossible today without attracting the label "gay" or "homosexual."

THE TORTURED SURVIVAL OF "FRIENDSHIP" IN THE 1920s

By the 1920s there was evidence that sex education campaigns undertaken since 1900 were beginning to raise apprehension about the traditional concept of male friendship in the YMCA. Growing anxiety about male relationships that were too intense posed a threat to the very social fabric of the YMCA. Friendship, the fostering of close bonds between men, was too central to the ideological foundation of the YMCA to abandon completely. Throughout the 1920s and 1930s rhetoric celebrating the beauty and goodness of close male friendship continued unabated. But it was accompanied by a counterrefrain of cautions against getting too close, and nervous discussions of the appropriate boundaries of true friendship. It was also plagued by warnings against homosexuality and the expression of worries that too exclusive a focus on male friendship might detract from "normal" relationships with women.

A comparison of guidelines offered by the International Committee in 1892 with official guidelines offered by its successor body, the National Council, in 1925, 1927, and 1936 is very instructive. The 1892 *Hand-Book*, a definitive compilation of advice and guidelines assembled by the International Committee and the most influential YMCA secretaries in the United States and Canada, described the warm, intimate relationship a secretary should have with young men in unqualified terms. In fact, it viewed "an intense love for young men, and a readiness to devote one's life to their welfare" as "*the special qualification required* in this work, as distinguished from other forms of Christian activity." It specifically continued, "Nothing will better gauge a secretary's influence . . . than the disposition to approach him with . . . personal confidences."[72] In 1927, thirty-five years later, *The Operation and Management of the Local Young Men's Christian Association* similarly suggested that the ideal secretary "makes many friends, takes time to talk over men's problems with them, visits the sick, sacrifices his personal convenience to the needs of others, . . . shows a genuine interest in all classes of people." But while the 1892 admonition added no qualifications to its advice, the 1927 manual warned secretaries about the need for "good judgment" in their relationships with the young men. It advised them to be "friendly but not familiar" and to "[choose their] associates carefully." In fact, the 1927 advice could even be seen as encouraging a sort of superficiality, when it suggested that the ideal secretary "smiles and greets people who come into his office, smiles easily, mixes happily with people in all walks of life, goes out of his way to talk to people, speaks to everybody, tells a humorous story well."[73] The overall image was one of friendliness rather than real friendship. Yet, despite signs that fear about excessive closeness between men might be flattening friendships in the YMCA, there were continuing expressions in handbooks in the 1920s of the importance of warmth and passion between men: "It is not by the multiplication of many activities and their formal administration that young men are helped to grow in their personal lives, . . . to grow manly souls, . . . but by the personal influence of men who are willing to place their lives alongside of their younger brothers."[74]

An examination of YMCA sex education literature shows how new ideas of sexuality were influencing YMCA evaluations of intense relationships among men which had historically been so important to the organization. Luther Gulick's *The Dynamic of Manhood* interpreted male social development in terms of "hungers" or drives. Gulick, the genius behind the YMCA's physical work philosophy, divided his book into four sections that are intended to describe four basic types of love: "Hunger for a Friend," "Hunger for Woman," "Hunger for Children," and "Hunger for God." "Hunger for a Friend" was the section in which Gulick described relationships between men, to which, incidentally, he ascribed nothing less than the foundation of civilization. "Hunger for Woman," curiously, devoted surprisingly few of its pages to the discussion of marriage. It did describe at length Gulick's theories about the evolution and etiology of sex. A sizable portion of the chapter discussed concerns about masturbation.[75]

Gulick's book, however, was written on the threshold of an era in which assumptions about gender were breaking down, in which women were demanding a new public role. *The Dynamic of Manhood* offered dramatic evidence of the impact of changing gender roles on conceptions of friendship. Gulick suggested that although traditionally men and women had been assumed to have a relationship that was by its nature physical, under the pressure of changes created by industrialization and urbanization, women needed to have an expanded role in the public realm and men needed to play a more active parental role. Gulick essentially offered a scientific rationale for "companionate marriage," a relationship in which men and women were expected to be friends as well as lovers. While Gulick still believed that women were more naturally disposed to "mother love" than to "spiritual friendship," he believed that the race would benefit from spiritual equality between men and women. Of course, the acknowledgment that male-female relationships might not be so different from male-male relationships introduced, by logical extension, the disquieting notion that friendship between men could include physical passion.

One of the reasons sex educators in particular were growing queasy about same-sex friendship was because of their tendency to view sexuality or the sex drive as the basis for all human passion and community. In stressing the link between sexual passion and love, they believed they were laying the foundation for a more holistic relationship between a man and a woman in marriage. But this had disturbing implications for passionate love in circumstances where a sexual relationship was viewed as grossly inappropriate—namely, in same-sex relationships. In November 1925, for example, Dr. Max J. Exner, one of the leading sex educators and physical directors in the YMCA, wrote a piece about sex education in *Association Men*. Exner described sex as "a normal, creative, enriching and socially upbuilding force when rightly guided." "Sex attraction," he continued, "was the starting point for the development of the whole range of sympathetic responses up to the finest expression of human love found in the world today." Not only was sex "the basis of love," but "the sex motive runs through the warp and woof of human life" and was the basis for all human spiritual values. Exner explicitly noted that sexual passion was the basis for male "comradeship and fellowship" as well, but at this point immediately turned to the dangers of allowing direct expression of passion. Passion between men "must find expression . . . by the long circuited route through all the high ranges of esthetic, emotional and spiritual responses of which the human personality is capable. Passion must be spiritualized." [76]

While Exner approached same-sex love carefully and indirectly through a theoretical discussion of the relationship between sexual passion and spiritual love, YWCA and YMCA sex educators Grace Loucks Elliott and Harry Bone approached it more directly and pragmatically, in *The Sex Life of Youth*. Elliott and Bone had been commissioned by a joint task force of the YMCA and the YWCA to study "sex matters" and prepare material suitable for sex education work in colleges. Their work was a direct outcome of the growing uneasiness with gender-segregated programs and efforts to engage in more "mixed work" in which young men could interact with young women in supervised YMCA and YWCA settings. Bone and Elliott distinguished between "the legitimate amount of emotion that belongs to friendship" and "the emotion that would normally find its expression in connection with the opposite sex." Note that the line between appropriate and inappropriate relations was not drawn at erotic activity, but between the appropriate "amount" of emotion and too much emotion. This created an area of ambiguity. How much emotion was too much? What was too intense?

Bone and Elliott noted that this ambiguity could become a source of painful confusion. "Many foolish and disconcerting things," they cautioned, "have been said about friendships which are supposed to be homosexual but which are actually normal enriching fellowships of especial depth." Elliott and Bone saw what they called "intense friendships" as the natural result of situations in which relationships with the "opposite sex" were unduly "hindered . . . by home influences or other circumstances," implicitly suggesting that sex-segregated YMCA social activities were partly to blame. "Whenever any normal outlets of life are denied, abnormal ones are likely to be substituted." Like Exner, they saw "sex attraction" between "two persons of the same sex" as natural, though they attributed this to situations in which "a woman may have the masculine characteristics which a woman would look for in a man and a man may have the feminine characteristics a man would look for in a woman." They counseled YMCA leaders confronted with a situation of "intense friendship" not to panic, but to gently guide the troubled individuals into more wholesome situations. Only in unusual circumstances would it be necessary to refer problem individuals to "expert help." They were confident that "modern science" could do much to alleviate problems that ordinary YMCA or YWCA secretaries were ill equipped to handle.[77] The distinction made by Bone and Elliott between true homosexuality and friendship that was legitimate but intense did not, however, provide a very useful guide to Association leadership for dealing with actual relationships. The fear of homosexuality, if broadcast too loudly and too widely, threatened to strangle the bonds and social dynamics that had made the Association prosper since its founding.

A July 1920 article called "Friendship" published in *Association Men* took another approach to preserving intense friendship while acknowledging the dangers of homosexuality. Arthur Gordon, the author of the article, assumed that "attraction," "desire," and "lust" were expected elements in relationships between all men. "Friends know each other at sight. How deep the bond may be is determined at first glance by a mutual appraisal that opens the heart just so much and no more. . . . All is a matter of mutual attraction, pitiless in its acceptances and rejections." But while Gordon acknowledged that passion and physical desire were an integral part of male friendship, he called for their repression and careful circumscription. Men were called on to put careful limits on how they interacted with each other. "Friendship," the article warned, "like every other beautiful thing, has the power to destroy utterly. . . . Let this man burn with a fierce desire toward that man, but let him not evidence that desire except by the actions of his eyes, his hands, and his heart. Let the other man keep his distance in the same way. . . . The relation between these two men, each ready to sacrifice all for the other, each tormented by the fear of unrequition, is the essence of Friendship." The article contained a particular, overt warning against sexual desire between older men and younger men or adolescents:

> The friend of boys should be a lover of boys—should have suffered because of boys until he has purged himself without pity of the lustful desires that come storming, whether he will or no, to take possession of him. . . . He must sublimate his friendship so that it moves on grandly, unrequited, like the friendship of a god. He is not worthy of the trust until he has been seared by suffering, scarred by battle, made sublime by the very passions that, but for his battle, might have been the victor instead of the vanquished.[78]

Gordon's article was illustrated with a photo of a statue called "Friendship" by Haig Patigian. The photo, which portrays two male nudes standing back to back and reaching toward each other or holding hands, evokes the central themes of the article: male-male eroticism, intimacy, repression, and denial (see fig. 5).

This unusual strategy for preserving male friendship was remarkably similar to views propounded by certain "literary" homosexuals around the

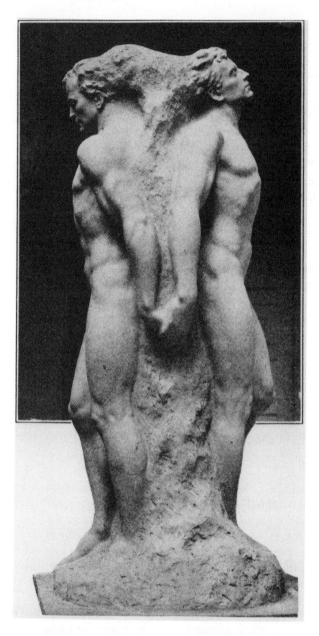

5. "Friendship," a statue by Haig Patigian. This illustration
accompanied an article of the same title published in *Association
Men* (July 1928): 498. The original caption read: "The compelling
statue . . . expressing friendship between men." Courtesy of the
YMCA of the USA Archives, St. Paul, Minnesota.

turn of the century, both in England and America. Individuals like Xavier
Mayne and John Addington Symonds were aware of medical and psychiatric descriptions of "sexual inversion," and acknowledged that they belonged to that category. Some romanticized male love, and saw it as one of
humanity's highest attainments. In this, they were in harmony with many
contemporary thinkers, like the YMCA's own Luther Gulick, who in *The
Dynamic of Manhood* argued that civilization itself had its foundations in
"the love of comrades." But despite the fact that literary homosexuals idealized male love, few granted that it could be allowed as a rationale for
physical love. Giving in to physical passion was a form of selfishness and
could only debase what otherwise would remain a true and pure relationship based on high motives. In this also, their views of sexuality were no
different from those of their nonhomosexual contemporaries. The understanding of sexual gratification as a form of selfishness governed Victorian
relationships between men and women as well as relationships between
men and men. The attempt to "save" traditional friendship by emphasizing
self-restraint was not bound to succeed, however, in the face of a growing
medical consensus that homosexuality was the characteristic of a mentally
ill minority. Increasingly, the strategy of choice was to deny that normal
men could experience this kind of passion.

Nevertheless, laments that the modern age was killing love between men
continued throughout the 1920s.[79] After describing the vast advances of science, technology, transportation, and communication over the course of the
last century, Victor Murdock asked, "Has friendship thriven in the same
degree as physical achievement has thriven?" He concluded that for many,
it had not, and called for a renewal of a spirit of friendship among men. His
Association Men editorial "The Need of Nearness" was accompanied by a
sketch of two bare-chested men in classical garb symbolizing a scholar and
a working man, reaching toward each other and holding hands across a great
chasm.[80] Despite nostalgic efforts to win back an unhampered, pure male
love, the increasing nervousness about homosexuality, accompanied by the
promotion of heterosexuality and a more heavy-handed emphasis on family
values, would by the 1930s transform the organization. The circumscription
and diminution of friendship as a central value in the YMCA would have
profound implications for the structure and mission of the organization, the
marital profiles and interpersonal relations of its leaders, its program emphasis, its membership criteria, and its self-image, for the rest of the twentieth century.

chapter 3

SINGLENESS AND THE
CONSECRATED SECRETARY

*Without father or mother, brother or sister, wife or child . . . he also unself-
ishly denied himself to social and all other calls, keeping himself only unto
"this work for Christ among young men."*—anonymous biographical sketch of
Robert R. McBurney

The ethos of intense friendship that characterized the YMCA
had a very concrete demographic manifestation in the nineteenth century. Despite a certain ambivalence among YMCA
men about bachelorhood, a disproportionate percentage of
secretaries were lifelong bachelors, and those who did marry
married much later than men in the general population. In
effect, significant numbers of men chose fellowship with one
another over marriage. For most, YMCA service was important enough to postpone marriage many years. For many, the
YMCA became the only family they had in any significant
sense of that word. Bachelor secretaries were instrumental in
creating the secretaryship and had a disproportionate influence on the early development of the organization, largely because their singleness permitted them to devote more of their
lives to service in the Association. But as the Association institutionalized sex education in its physical program, growing

attention was paid to male sexuality and marriage. Around 1900, the YMCA began to cater to the needs of married secretaries. As the twentieth century progressed, the phenomenon of the bachelor secretary declined, and by the 1930s YMCA secretaries were almost universally married.[1]

YMCA secretaries remained single in the nineteenth century despite a strong emphasis on the importance of marriage and the lack of positive images of male singleness in evangelical Protestant culture. Secular culture in the postbellum era also viewed the failure to find a lover and life mate as a serious inadequacy. As Ellen Rothman has put it, "everyone wanted to fall in love, and men especially seemed to feel a sense of obligation, even of desperation about it."[2] Lifelong singleness might possibly be viewed as a noble sacrifice made for the purpose of devoting one's life to other pursuits; more likely, it would be viewed as a lack, a failure; and for the most part it was not spoken of. The main form of discourse I have found in YMCA records regarding the failure to marry has been joking or teasing, sometimes good-natured, sometimes less so.[3]

Luther D. Wishard suggested in his memoirs that one obstacle to the enforcement of the YMCA's men-only membership requirement was the belief that such a basis for membership was unnatural, a belief expressed in the form of mockery:

> There was considerable jesting in the West about the number of bachelor members and secretaries of the Committee in New York, and there were in fact several such sinners, but some of them could not help it and never did help it, whereas others did escape from the estate wherein they were created at the first convenient season. It was because of this that a good deal of good natured raillery was engaged in whenever the Association membership test was discussed.[4]

The sole example of the jesting mentioned by Wishard which I have been able to find officially recorded in YMCA organizational records appears in an account of a reception held for R. C. Morse celebrating his twenty-fifth anniversary of service. Although the banquet was held in New York City, it is perhaps no coincidence that the raillery was engaged in by Thomas Cochran, a "westerner" from Minnesota:

> Now we are here to celebrate Mr. Morse's silver wedding with the Association. If Mr. Morse had done as he ought years ago we should have celebrated his silver wedding with Mrs. Morse some time ago; and as to that "hug," which our dear friend Dr. Cuyler wants given to Mr. Morse we are going to depute the ladies to do that! (laughter).[5]

Other examples of jesting were more likely to appear in private correspondences than in official records. A decade earlier, shortly after his marriage to Jennie Van Cott, Morse described an incident of casual teasing in a family letter:

> It has been quite an eventful month in our Association. One of the Secretaries of the N.Y. Assoc^n, James McConaughy was married April 16th & one of the International Committee's Secretaries, Mr. J[acob] T. Bowne on the 15th. Not a few of the brotherhood attribute these events to the influence of my example as one of the Senior Secretaries & I receive numerous inquiries as to the impending fate of other & more hardened cases! But I have nothing of a startling nature to reply to them or to mention to the [family].[6]

C. C. Hamilton's journal indicates that teasing about male-female relationships was common among YMCA workers, and not just on the International Committee, when he described a humorous incident that took place during his YMCA mission work in northern Wisconsin: "The cook told me that I spoke a little in my sleep about a person named 'Bertha;' of course they and Mr. T[erry] were joking about it this morning. I don't even know a person of that name unless it be E.G.B. T-r?!?"[7] Although in Hamilton's case the teasing was not strictly about singleness, it illustrates the kind of humor men engaged in when dealing with such subjects. Hamilton's incident was all the more significant when compared with the rest of the journal, since his relationship with Mr. Terry was usually characterized by the utmost seriousness; this is the only glimpse of their relationship in his journal which portrays any levity.

It is quite possible that John B. Brandt's 1886 letter to W. W. Vanarsdale commenting on the unmarried status of Robert Weidensall was intended in just such a jesting spirit (figs. 6 and 7):

> Weidensall is fifty is he? Just think of it. It seems but yesterday when we all thought we were boys. Isn't there some mistake? Why he is not even married yet. It is very unlike Robert to 'put himself forward' or in any manner claim what does not belong to him. Yet here he comes and says he is fifty and this important business of life is not yet attended to. It ought to have been done at least twenty five years ago. I am sure you will agree that we would not have thought this of one so conscientious and devoted to every known duty as this dear Brother of ours has always shown himself to be. But here is another sad example of the influence of Associates. If in the early days of our association work we could have kept Weidensall away from Morse & McBurney and altogether under good wholesome western influence all this might have been different. It is some encouragement that Morse has seen his error repented and is now trying to undo the mischief of nearly a life time. But McBurney seems to be obdurate as ever. Here he is right along side of Weidensall. Fifty years and no wife yet. I think some of you Chicago Brethren ought to lay aside all other matters for a year if necessary and teach these boys a thing or two. These young gentlemen should be shown up in their true light. They

6. Robert Weidensall (seated) with John B. Brandt, ca. 1890. Courtesy of the YMCA of the USA Archives, St. Paul, Minnesota.

1120 N 18 St

St Louis 4 - 14 - 1886

My dear Vanarsdale

Unfortunately for me our presbytery meets April 20ᵗʰ and owing to some special duties resting upon me, I cannot be absent. Of course when this time was fixed the Brethren were not thinking of Bro Weidensalls fiftieth birthday and that some of us would probably like to see him pass that important period. The fact is This is a startling announcement to most of us. — Weidensall is fifty is he? Just Think of it. It seems but yesterday when we all thought we were boys. Isn't there some mistake? Why he is not even married yet. It is very unlike Robert to "put himself forward" or in any manner claim what does not belong to him. Yet here he comes and says he is fifty and this important business of life is not yet attended to. It ought to have been done at least twenty five years ago I am sure you will agree that one would not have thought this of one so conscientious and devoted to every known duty as this dear Brother of ours has always shown himself to be. But here is another sad example of the

---

7. Letter, John B. Brandt to W. W. Vanarsdale, April 14, 1886. A passage in the letter chiding Weidensall and a number of other international secretaries for being unmarried is marked for omission. A typescript of the letter also appeared in the collection, with the offending passage removed. Courtesy of the YMCA of the USA Archives, St. Paul, Minnesota.

will be the ruin of the country if they are not stopped. You see already how Cree, Orr, Mather and many of our brightest and best are going in the same wretched way. Cannot something be done. . . .[8]

The letter contains several of the elements alluded to in Wishard's comment about jesting, and shares some elements with Cochran's teasing of Morse: it is a western secretary (Brandt was from Indiana) criticizing the singleness of easterners; it alludes to marriage as a "duty" that ought to have been "attended to" earlier; failure to marry is exaggerated into a "sin"; and Morse is goaded for having done his duty later than he ought to have. I originally doubted whether it was in fact a joke. There is evidence in the Weidensall papers of an attempt to have the comment suppressed. The papers also contain a letter from Brandt dated the day after the writing of the first letter attempting to verify that Cree, Orr, and Mather were indeed unmarried.[9] If the letter was intended as a joke, it is possible that it was not taken as a joke, or that it was censored for going beyond the bounds of good taste, for hitting too close to home in a sensitive area. (Weidensall does not appear to me to have been the type to take this kind of personal humor in stride.) But it is also possible that it was meant as a serious criticism.

An example of such more serious criticism appears in correspondence between David McConaughy and the International Committee regarding the scandalous resignation of Frank H. Wood, a YMCA secretary in India. Before Wood had even arrived in the mission field, McConaughy expressed doubts about having him come because he was single.[10] McConaughy later explained that single secretaries were acceptable only so long as they could be kept under the supervision of a senior, married secretary: "Whether he be married or single, it would not matter [in Calcutta] as it would at Madras, for should I come [to Calcutta], I should not have so much occasion to be absent on tour, but would devote a larger proportion of time to the local work, which really will demand the strength of two men."[11] Ironically, McConaughy was writing this letter to Robert R. McBurney, a lifelong confirmed bachelor, which suggests that the bias against singleness was so taken for granted that married men could self-righteously inveigh against it without fear of being challenged, even by single men who shared a strong commitment to the Association. Despite McConaughy's grudging acceptance of a single secretary, after Wood resigned McConaughy at least partially blamed the incident on Wood's singleness: "I wonder whether the Com^e realizes the mistake it made from the first to last, in relation to the sending of W. . . . In future send only such as have been tested by actual experience and if possible *married* men."[12] The underlying fear regarding unmarried men was that they were inherently less stable than married men. The case of Frank H. Wood seemed to bear this out disastrously. McConaughy's letter revealed the shame and harsh criticism that everyone knew could be due to men who failed to marry, and Brandt's letter, even if intended as good-natured jest, contained hints of this darker dissatisfaction with singleness.[13]

Ironically, it may have been the case that the demands of the general secretaryship decreased the possibility of marrying by curtailing a young secretary's social life. Writing of his impressions of one local YMCA's expectations of a potential secretary, L. W. Messer noted, "Mrs. Messer and I gained from friends at Selma the fact that a man who was too much in society would not command the respect and co-operation in Selma. . . . Knox I think would offend none, would be agreeable and dignified, but in no sense be a ladies' man or a leader in social life."[14] The YMCA general secretary moved in circles where his only contact was with young men. That fact would logically limit his ability to meet and enter into a relationship with a woman. Such expectations and requirements may also have attracted men who for whatever reason were uninterested in marriage but were motivated to devote their lives to social interactions with young men.

In at least one instance, a bachelor YMCA secretary offered a joke about his own failure to marry, though significantly it was not in a letter to other YMCA secretaries. Thomas Kirby Cree maintained a warm correspondence with his nieces during his travels in Europe. One letter, written in his later years from Paris, included this pun: "I saw at Pere la chaise [sic] the Cree-Mating establishment, feeling that the sere and yellow leaf was approaching, I visited it, only to find that it was for disposing of the dead and not for providing for the living. Such is life!"[15] This joke contained none of the elements mentioned by Wishard, or present in Cochran's speech or Brandt's letter. Rather than castigating himself for his failure to attend to a "duty," he seemed to be lamenting (tongue in cheek) the lack of facilities available for assisting him in his search for a spouse. He also noted in a tone of mock tragedy the passage of time that increasingly narrowed one's possibilities. Significantly, the letter was written by a bachelor uncle (now in his midfifties) to his unmarried nieces (probably in their thirties), and could be interpreted as a joke between singles. It made light of the social pressure brought to bear on them to do something that they refused to accept as a personal responsibility.

YMCA joking about secretarial singleness served two integrating functions. Men in the YMCA who never married were not conforming to the normal gender and sexual roles of their peers. This created tension, and the need to describe and account for this failure to fulfill marital expectations. Joking served first to remind men gently of what the expectation was, and perhaps even to prod those who had not fulfilled it to do so. Second, for those who apparently would never fulfill this "obligation," it normalized their status, and gave men the means to acknowledge their singleness in culturally appropriate ways. Wishard's statement is revealing along these lines, when he noted that "there were in fact several such sinners." "Some of them," he continued, "could not help it and never did help it, whereas others escaped from the estate wherein they were created at the first convenient season." Men joking about singleness reaffirmed the values of the community by portraying singleness as the natural state in which all men were born, and from which they found it desirable to escape as soon as possible. By joking in this way, they also simultaneously broke the tension caused by the acknowledgment that the YMCA had some "old sinners" in its midst. They were sinners not because of willfulness, but because they "could not help it." This claim of helplessness seems similar to Cree's tongue-in-cheek sorrow that there were not more facilities for matchmaking. If one was unmarried, it was not because one chose to be single, but because one had had bad luck in the search for a mate.

Anxiety about the degree of willfulness on the part of single secretaries, however, was also a major theme. The fact that they were referred to as "sinners"—Brandt's letter calls them "obdurate"—implies that there was more to blame than mere bad luck. To the extent that the statements were offered as jokes, they playfully accused singles of hardened willfulness even as they assumed that no real fault was implicated. But this manner of joking relied on the fact that there were only two types of discourse about men who did not marry: they were either unlucky in their search for a mate, or they were sinners severely remiss in a vital duty. There was no discourse that described lifelong bachelorhood as anything but a sort of failure, and no widespread discourse to suggest that it could be a positive choice.

An underlying assumption in the worldview of nineteenth-century white northern Protestants was that men needed women in order to be complete. Based on this assumption, the 1869 report of the president of the San Francisco YMCA painted a bleak picture of the fate of YMCAs should women be excluded from the fellowship: "I consider it a strange anomaly that woman is not in active membership in the Y.M.C.A. How thin and dry our regular meetings are. Month after month the hermits of the institution meet, look wise, eye each other in mute uncertainty or prattle a while and separate. No woman's voice livens the scene. Let us reform this altogether." [16] In fact, the San Francisco Association did reform it. They admitted women to full active membership for a brief period, starting in 1874. This quotation is striking for its highly unflattering portrayal of bachelorhood, referring to YMCA members as "hermits," and calling the absence of women an "anomaly." One phrase in particular—"eye each other in mute uncertainty"—was strongly evocative of homophobic anxiety. One could immediately understand why a man would take pleasure in and want to eye a woman. But to eye another man seemed fearfully inappropriate; the encounter produced "mute uncertainty." That the absence of women could suggest male-male sexual desire was not lost on YMCA men in the nineteenth century, as Cochran's joke about the infamous hug of Dr. Cuyler would suggest. Indeed, prison reformers of the 1830s had suggested that one of the ill effects of single-sex confinement was an incitement to the crime of sodomy. Such anxiety would not necessarily have been inconceivable in San Francisco of the 1860s.[17] Even if one ignores the homophobic undertones of the San Francisco report, the predominant image was that of withering. Without women men's lives are "thin" and "dry." The description was reminiscent of Cree's approaching "sere and yellow leaf."

THE BACHELOR YMCA SECRETARY

Given that men in the YMCA universally shared a belief in the necessity of marriage, and given the preference on the part of many YMCAs for married secretaries, it should come as something of a surprise to learn that the YMCA was overwhelmingly led by single men. Men who made a lifelong career out of the YMCA secretaryship married considerably later than men in the general population, and a significant percentage of them never married. Among those most committed to the organization, over one in five never married, compared to about one in eleven or one in twelve in the general population.[18] This generalization held even truer among the pioneers of the movement. Of the four men most credited with shaping the organization in its early years, Cephas Brainerd, Richard Cary Morse, Robert R. McBurney, and Robert Weidensall, two never married (Weidensall and McBurney) and one (Morse) married at the late age of forty-two. The list of distinguished bachelor YMCA secretaries is impressive in that it includes so many who played a formative role in the organization. I have already mentioned Thomas Kirby Cree, who like Weidensall was an early international secretary and pioneered YMCA fieldwork in the South. Will Cook shaped the YMCA's railroad work for three decades as the general secretary of the largest railroad branch in the country. Philip Augustus Wieting and Erskine Uhl were trusted workers in the International Committee, Uhl for almost four decades. Robert A. Orr was the man most credited with pioneering Bible study work in the YMCA. Sumner F. Dudley was regarded as the father of American camping and was a boys' work pioneer. Among YMCA secretaries in service in 1891 who had been in service more than a dozen years, almost one third never married.

The average age at marriage among YMCA secretaries in the nineteenth century was probably between thirty-one and thirty-three, compared to twenty-five and twenty-six among men in the general population. The majority of YMCA secretaries were young and unmarried. Two-thirds (66.5 percent) of all YMCA secretaries remained unmarried throughout the entire period of their YMCA service. Most served only for a few years and probably postponed marriage until after they had completed their YMCA service. But even those who stayed in service longer and eventually married while in YMCA service were postponing their marriages for years longer than men in the general population. After peaking in 1890, the average age at marriage in the United States steadily declined through the 1950s to about 22.5. Thus, in an era when men were postponing marriage longer than ever before or since, YMCA secretaries were on average postponing marriage about six years longer than their contemporaries. Approximately one fifth of those who stayed in service more than a decade were dispensing with marriage altogether. Correspondence, memoirs, autobiographies, and biographies of YMCA secretaries suggest that one reason YMCA men were postponing marriage or forgoing it altogether was because YMCA secretaries typically worked for a low salary, and, coming from middle-class backgrounds, may not have felt capable of supporting wives and families. Even if this is the case, these men were consciously choosing to work under conditions that would make it difficult for them to sustain typical middle-class family lives. They were choosing to give their lives in service to young men rather than to a family. The relatively high rates of bachelorhood among YMCA secretaries is even more impressive when compared with laymen who were not YMCA employees, but were board members and financial supporters of the YMCA. Among those on whom the YMCA Archives possess biographical data for the nineteenth century, none were unmarried.[19]

The question "Did they ever marry?" was most interesting and relevant for those who remained in service in the organization into their elder years. Qualitative biographical sources suggest that an intense, transcendent commitment on the part of these men to the organization was a strong factor in their decision not to marry. Secretaries who never married were much more likely to give longer terms of service than married men. Bachelor secretaries in the fifty-and-older age group gave on average 20.8 years of service to the YMCA, compared with an average of 15.7 years among married secretaries of comparable age. The pattern of increased likelihood of lifelong singleness extended beyond the pioneers like Weidensall and McBurney and was a factor in the organization as a whole throughout the nineteenth century. It is also worth noting that when broken down geographically this pattern of greater incidence of lifelong bachelorhood is strongest in the northeastern United States, confirming what, according to Wishard's memoirs, was common knowledge in the organization and a source of widespread joking and raillery in western associations. There were indeed many such "sinners." The degree to which they could or could not "help it" remains to be seen.

UNTIL THE EARLY 1880s, the institution of the YMCA secretaryship was still evolving. But after 1880, the first generation of YMCA leaders had established organizational principles and a model of leadership that formed the basis for future secretarial leadership. Between 1883 and 1891, there was dramatic growth in the number of employed secretaries. After 1891, the expansion in numbers of employed secretaries leveled off, though the secretarial workforce continued to grow at a moderate rate into the twentieth century. During this entire period of growth, the model for secretarial leadership was based on the principles established by key leaders like McBurney, Morse, and Weidensall in the decade between 1870 and 1880. But after 1915, the YMCA experienced major revisions in its mission, its structure, and in the complexion of its secretarial workforce as the result of its role as a major social service provider during World War I. Increasingly during and after the war, YMCA secretaries came to be viewed as professional service providers rather than the stewards of a religious movement.

As the institution of the YMCA general secretary came to be developed throughout the 1860s it was understood that the post required an extraordinary degree of commitment. This was probably not true to the same degree among the very first handful of antebellum employees of YMCAs, who were frequently librarians or corresponding secretaries, and whose job descriptions did not necessarily entail the same type of total oversight and management of the Association. YMCA historian C. Howard Hopkins commented on the level of commitment of these prewar employees as opposed to that of those who came after:

> With the exception of L. P. Rowland of Boston, none of those who served as paid Association executives prior to the [Civil] War remained in the work afterward or made the Y.M.C.A. a career. Thus, the secretaryship was created in the immediate post-War years by a few leaders, the outstanding figure among whom was McBurney.[20]

Besides McBurney and Rowland, this was the period when John B. Brandt, Thomas Kirby Cree, George A. Hall, Richard Cary Morse, Alfred Sandham, Lang Sheaff, Robert Weidensall, and Thomas J. Wilkie entered the service.

All these men helped shape the organization and ultimately committed many years to it. The list of men who entered the organization during the 1870s and early 1880s also included many distinguished names of men who were recognized as having pioneered or developed some major aspect of YMCA work. Robert J. Roberts (1875) was viewed as a father of the YMCA's physical program;[21] Jacob T. Bowne (1877) was cofounder of the Springfield YMCA Training School; Luther D. Wishard (1877) was the first international student work secretary and engineer of the YMCA's foreign service; David McConaughy (1880) was the first YMCA foreign secretary in India; L. Wilbur Messer (1881) was general secretary of the Chicago YMCA and a pioneer of the metropolitan system of association management.[22] After the early 1880s, once the secretaryship became more established and institutionalized, men who entered YMCA service did not necessarily have the same intensity of commitment. In fact, their longevity in the organization was no longer vital to its prosperity or survival. Once the organization had been built upon "established principles" (a term frequently used by the pioneer generation of secretaries) there was less opportunity for men entering the organization to imprint it with their own sense of mission; rather, they were carrying on a tradition whose broadest outlines had already been laid out.

As a group, secretaries entering service before 1882 were more mature. Their mean age on entering YMCA service was about 27.5 (median age was 26), compared to about 25.5 for all nineteenth-century secretaries (median age was 24). Because these secretaries entered service at an older age, and because they tended to stay in service longer, throughout the 1870s the average age of YMCA secretaries remained quite high—around 33 or 34. For this reason, it also appears likely that during the 1870s and 1880s, a higher percentage of YMCA secretaries were married than before or after.

Ironically, despite the likelihood that a higher percentage of secretaries were married during this period, the cohort of individuals contained the highest percentage of lifelong bachelor secretaries. Out of thirty-nine secretaries who entered service during this period and who left the service at the age of 55 or older, ten—or about one quarter—never married. Furthermore, as I have already noted above, these bachelor secretaries gave on average longer terms of service than their married counterparts. They had a disproportionate impact on the organization as a whole. Quite a few of these secretaries—among others Robert R. McBurney, Robert Weidensall, Erskine Uhl, and Thomas Cree—remained in service in the Association until extreme old age, when infirmity forced them to retire or they died in office.

After the early 1880s, the number of employed officers of YMCAs jumped. The workforce tripled between 1880 and 1885, and then tripled again by 1892. Throughout this period, the median age of YMCA secretaries steadily dropped, from 31 in 1880 to 27 in 1891. The percentage of YMCA secretaries who were married during this period for each year, as one might expect with the dropping average age, steadily declined from about half of all secretaries to about one quarter. In 1882 more than 100 men entered the secretarial workforce, more than in any previous year. From 1882 to 1891, a total of 2,490 men entered service. In 1891 there were 395 men entering the secretarial labor force. The vast majority of men entering were young—in their early twenties—and unmarried. It is interesting that one of the great fears among YMCA leaders in this period was that the "secretarialization" of the YMCA would place it in the hands of old men. It would cease to be an organization of and for young men. The problem, it was feared, with encouraging men to pursue the secretaryship as a life career was that secretaries would grow old, holding onto key positions of leadership beyond the age when they should have moved on , thereby disempowering the younger men for whom the organization supposedly existed. A glance at the demographics of the secretarial workforce shows that at least for this period these fears were unfounded. Secretaries on the International Committee, state secretaries, and general secretaries of the central branches of the larger metropolitan YMCAs did tend to be considerably older. But beneath this cream of leadership, the organization was overwhelmingly in the hands of young, single men, who held the vast majority of positions of leadership. In big cities like Boston, New York, Washington, Baltimore, Chicago, New Orleans, and San Francisco, the younger generation were general secretaries in the smaller metropolitan branches;[23] or in central departments they were assistant or specialized secretaries (financial, building, membership, or employment secretaries, or physical directors). And they were the vast majority of the workforce in town YMCAs and in the railroad and student branches.

In fact, the demographics of the organization suggest that the rhetoric about an exchange between old and young, of wisdom for youth and energy, was embodied in the leadership structure. The old guard were continually recruiting the more talented younger lights in the organization and constantly training them into leadership through service as assistant secretaries in the central branches or on state committees or in the International Committee. In 1877, for example, when Luther D. Wishard was recruited into the International Committee, he was still a quite young twenty-three years of age, while his mentors, Weidensall, Morse, and Uhl, were in their mid-thirties and early forties. In 1888, Wishard, then in his mid-thirties, recruited John R. Mott, a young man of twenty-three, onto the international workforce. When that happened, Weidensall, Morse, and Uhl were now in their late forties and early fifties. As older secretaries remained in the organization, they became a reserve of experience and know-how to all secretaries throughout the organization, intervening in times of difficulty or crisis, and advising in times of uncertainty. Their example and leadership made it possible for younger, less experienced men to take the risks of leadership. YMCA secretaries were very conscious of this passing of the torch. In the preface to his biography of Luther D. Wishard, for instance, C. K. Ober saw himself as the "hyphen" connecting the two great leaders of the student movement, Luther D. Wishard and John R. Mott. The demographic structure of the organization, in other words, served to promote strength, flexibility, and continuity in the organization and made possible a pattern of mentoring that promoted bonds of love and admiration within the YMCA's leadership.

Younger secretaries who offered more ephemeral terms of service gave the Association something it vitally needed as well: they were the foot soldiers in the secretarial army. Morse and other leaders often bemoaned how few secretaries there were who made life careers in the organization. T. S. McPheeters, an old-guard secretary from Missouri, once complained to a crop of young secretaries: "You're a fine bunch of fellows! My only criticism . . . is that you don't stay long enough in one place to accomplish much. Most of you stay long enough to make a nest; some of you stay long enough to lay some eggs; but mighty few stay long enough to hatch anything!"[24] But the YMCA probably could not recruit enough "egg hatchers" to staff all of the rapidly multiplying positions throughout North America. The plaintive cry of the International Committee throughout these years was "More men!" In repeated correspondence, Morse, Weidensall, Brainerd, and others found themselves short of men to respond to the growing number of calls from associations in city, town, and country for permanent secretaries. They devoted a major part of their labors to finding just the right men to fill these positions. While not all men were able to meet the need according to YMCA standards, and while the majority did not make life careers out of the YMCA, by the International Committee's own standards of success and failure, 90 percent of them served respectably and filled crucial positions in a rapidly expanding organization. (Only 10 percent were listed as leaving their positions owing to "failure.") Throughout this period, when the secretarial workforce expanded fivefold, approximately one-third of the paid positions in YMCAs were filled by men who gave less than five years of service.

The influx of new secretaries in this period laid the groundwork for a productive relationship between older secretaries who had pioneered the organization and a new generation of young, unmarried secretaries who found themselves attracted in ever-growing numbers to its mission. The result was a growing sense of community among these men as they worked to alleviate the growing pains of the Association. The primary problem was how to sustain the YMCA's impressive growth into the twentieth century as it brought Christ to the young men of America. By nurturing relationships between older and younger men, Association leaders succeeded in keeping the organization relevant. Far from declining in the hands of an aging leadership, the organization flourished. Its rank and file was overwhelmingly young and unmarried.

Between 1892 and 1894, the secretarial workforce declined for the first time, largely owing to financial cutbacks forced by the nationwide depression. By 1895, the secretarial workforce had recovered, and now entered a new period of growth that, if not as astonishing as that which had taken place throughout the previous decade, was stable and still impressive. During the period from 1892 to 1895, the workforce as a whole became older and more likely to be married. This could be expected, since the number of new secretaries hired dropped precipitously to pre-1886 levels while accelerating numbers of secretaries continued to leave the organization. Those who would be most likely to stay with the organization in such difficult times were those who were viewed as the most experienced and committed, and thus those who were naturally older. But the closing years of the nineteenth century saw a slow revival of the previous pattern of growth.

Despite an inability to talk about singleness in positive terms in the YMCA—it was typically joked about, laughed at, cloaked in silence, or viewed as a negative state from which it behooved young Christian men to escape at their earliest convenience—the organization was, throughout the nineteenth century, led by young single men. Furthermore, young men in the organization appear to have been postponing marriage in order to serve the organization, at a time when the average age at marriage was already higher than at any other period in American history. For a significant minority the Association fostered a type of commitment that found its expression in lifelong bachelorhood. Among those who committed their lives to the organization, a disproportionate number were lifelong bachelors, more than twice what could be expected in the general population for this time period.

This phenomenon parallels what took place among contemporary female reformers. Women in the gilded age who sought to play active roles in public service often postponed marriage until significantly later, and a much higher percentage of them never married than in the general population. But whereas women were almost required to free themselves from marriage in order to play a public role in nineteenth-century America, marriage was expected of men who played public roles. This was especially true of the YMCA's traditional constituency. While a higher than average proportion of YMCA secretaries were lifelong bachelors, almost all major lay businessmen who supported the organization as financial donors, as presidents, or as members of its boards of trustees were married. That this was the general expectation is underlined by the discourse that existed in the Association about singleness. Of course, nineteenth-century "spinsters" were also ridiculed and disparaged for failing to play their expected roles as housewives and mothers. But the difference was that acceptance of marital roles did not preclude for men, as it did for women, lives of public service. These men could have chosen to marry and could have kept their YMCA careers, but did not so choose in startling numbers. These men chose instead to give their lives to the organization and to develop productive relationships with a younger generation of secretaries, carrying the organization into the twentieth century.

The YMCA was not the only male single-sex institution around the turn of the century in which leaders tended to marry late or not at all. At least one other historian has noted a similar phenomenon among the Boy Scouts. Robert S. Baden-Powell, the founder of scouting, for instance, married at age fifty-five. E. M. Robinson and Dan Beard, early Boy Scout leaders in America, were lifelong bachelors.[25] Other historians have commented on the centrality of the YMCA's role as a "surrogate family" in an urban setting.[26] The possibility of avoiding marriage in order to pursue and develop alternative forms of family and community in a single-sex setting probably reflects assumptions that were broadly shared in the nineteenth century, and not just a quirk of the YMCA. Despite the tendency to assume that marriage was a normative state for men as well as women, the existence of bachelor secretaries reflects a worldview in which men and women were considered too different from each other to work together effectively. It also reflects the assumption that sexual self-restraint was considered a mark of virtue rather than as unhealthy. As the twentieth century progressed and new ideas about marriage, the body, and health entered peoples' consciousness, the single-sex emphasis and ethos of the YMCA would become suspect.

In the early twentieth century, man's need for woman came to be expressed not only as a social expectation but as a physical requirement. One particularly ironic statement of this came from Robert Weidensall, himself a lifelong bachelor, in his book *Man's Needs and Their Supplies*. According to Weidensall, "Man's" needs were perfectly matched in every detail by the supplies created by God to meet those needs. It was in this context that "male and female were created, [to insure] a continuance of Man on the earth." Woman was created from the bone and flesh of "Man" in order to meet "Man's" needs. Weidensall believed that scientific truth was simply one aspect of spiritual truth, and that violation of the divine laws regarding marriage brought not only a spiritual penalty but physical illness: "The misuse of these [unspeakable pleasures] of the Creator or the use of adulterations or substitutes for them, would not only be unsatisfying, but would render the needs, or need cells, themselves, abnormal and beget disease, pain, and suffering."[27] Although Weidensall did not suggest that abstinence from marital relationships would cause disease, he saw marriage as a relationship in which men's divinely created needs for sexual pleasure and procreation were supplied by a female life mate. When Weidensall penned these words, he was near the end of his life, long past the age when marriage would have been considered beneficial. It is interesting to consider how, in the light of his publicly stated beliefs about the necessity for marriage, he judged his own lifelong failure to marry, and whether his beliefs caused him any anxiety.

Robert Weidensall's statement on marriage in 1919 reflected some blending of what he considered to be divine law and scientific knowledge about physical health. His views were perhaps a remarkable testimonial of the impact of the YMCA's mind-body-spirit philosophy on an old-style evangelical who had publicly and privately professed Pauline asceticism as his personal creed. But if these ideas about the physical necessity of marriage represented Weidensall's beliefs, he did not live them. It is quite possible that Weidensall at some level accepted that marriage was a physical as well as a divine requirement. Yet he did not integrate these beliefs into an older and more fundamental conviction that God would reward physical self-sacrifice. All that mattered to him in the eternal scheme of things was true belief in the atonement of Christ.

The same was not true of Luther H. Gulick, one of the most important architects of the YMCA's mind-body-spirit philosophy. Gulick fearlessly applied his eugenic beliefs to his personal life. He actually broke off a romance at Oberlin College because both he and his fiancée "suffered with migraine headaches and had highly organized nervous systems."[28] Gulick himself claimed to apply his beliefs about eugenics, social hygiene, and scientific morality to the upbringing of his own family, even when to do so required some inconvenience. Gulick, in his book *The Dynamic of Manhood,* expressed the belief that the "love of woman" had a biological basis in the "need to reproduce." While Weidensall had sought to build character through self-renunciation and a celibate lifestyle, Gulick believed that "the road to fine, strong, loving character is best found for most through romantic love, marriage, and parenthood." Gulick saw "sex hunger" (which he, of course, assumed to have woman as its object) as an innate component of manhood: "It is manhood in its broadest totality, finding its complement in an equally extensive woman nature." Gulick believed that young boys should be encouraged with positive heterosexual role models through "romantic stories," usually in which men played the role of gallant heroes. "Historically," he wrote, "sex restores vitality, perpetuates the race, aids in the distribution of variations, and hence is basic in evolution. . . . Those who do not love do not reproduce, and hence are eliminated from the stream of life." After an extensive discussion of the social and psychological havoc wrought by masturbation and promiscuity, Gulick closed "the discussion of this complex subject by a most practical suggestion, which is, marry early." He suggested that parents and communities had a vital self-interest in supporting young couples financially so that they would not use lack of financial independence as an excuse for postponing marriage. Gulick's belief that sex between a man and a woman was vitally linked to good character, masculinity, and health represented a new view of marriage that would become increasingly widespread in the twentieth century, and which would make the single-sex ethos of the YMCA harder and harder to sustain.[29]

THE DEMISE OF THE BACHELOR SECRETARY

An examination of YMCA records between 1900 and 1940 suggests that by the 1920s and 1930s, the bachelor secretary was present only in the ghostly memories of "the Great General Secretary" McBurney and, until 1922, in Weidensall, the living relic of the pioneer years. Furthermore, comparisons of YMCA handbooks suggest that, while nineteenth-century writers of advice to local YMCAs went under the assumption that secretaries were unmarried, by the 1920s handbooks all assumed that secretaries were married—or if they were not that they should be. In 1900 the first efforts were made to acknowledge the existence of "YMCA wives"—many of whom were put to work around that time as trustees or secretaries of YWCAs. By 1940, the YMCA wife was an institution; there was even an official newsletter for YMCA wives called *Open Door*.[30]

Ironically, personnel records for the twentieth century are less complete than for the nineteenth century.[31] No complete survey of YMCA secretarial marital statistics for the period from 1900 to 1940 is available. What statistics I have been able to gather suggest that the YMCA secretaryship went from being a haven for unmarried men in the nineteenth century to a club for married men in the twentieth. While a majority of YMCA secretaries in the nineteenth century were unmarried and between 20 and 30 percent were lifelong bachelors, in the twentieth century less than 5 percent were unmarried. While in the nineteenth century YMCA secretaries were two or three times as likely as men in the general population to be lifelong bachelors, in the twentieth century YMCA secretaries were much less likely to be lifelong bachelors than men in the general population.

Foreign work records are one of the two most important sources on secretarial marital statistics between 1900 and 1940. They contain family information on most American secretaries in the YMCA's foreign service from

1889 to 1956. There is also a reconnaissance study of YMCA-YWCA relations conducted in 1930, which included a survey that was sent to a representative sample of YMCA general secretaries asking questions about their marital status. Of secretaries for whom marital statistics were available in the foreign service sample (76 percent of all the cases), only 3.9 percent of those who entered service between 1900 and 1956 were unmarried.[32] The reconnaissance study sample was considerably smaller than the foreign service records, consisting of only eighty-six cases. Of these, only two (or 2.3 percent) reported that they had never married, and both indicated that they "expect[ed] to marry within 2 years." It is unclear whether the response "expect to marry within 2 years" meant that they were engaged and had specific plans to be married, or whether it indicated only a commitment in principle to marry soon. If the former, it suggests that bachelorhood was rare indeed in the secretarial ranks by 1930; if the latter, it suggests that the minuscule minority of secretaries who were not yet married felt some pressure to get married soon. Although this sample was relatively small, the survey was conducted by a professional sociologist familiar with statistical method. It drew from a random sample representative of the geographic and urban/rural distribution of associations in 1930.[33]

Both data sets are biased in favor of YMCA men who were most likely to have made a major commitment—perhaps a lifetime commitment—to YMCA service. Young secretaries with shorter terms of service or lesser commitments would not have appeared in the reconnaissance study at all, since those surveys were addressed exclusively to "General Secretaries," the chief paid officers of an association. Younger secretaries would have risen to such a position in the smaller associations that did not have more than one or two paid officers; but in most of the larger associations, younger, less experienced secretaries would have served in specialized positions (education secretary, physical director) or as assistant secretaries. Young secretaries could and did enter the foreign service, though attempts were made to screen out those who did not have a serious commitment to the calling. These foreign secretaries and general secretaries were fortunately the two groups most comparable to the group of secretaries I examined to determine rates of lifelong bachelorhood in the nineteenth century—secretaries who were still in service beyond the age of forty-five. The dramatic drop in the percentage of unmarried secretaries in these groups, from 20–30 percent in the nineteenth century forty-five-or-older sample, to 2–4 percent or less in the twentieth century, seems especially significant since the twentieth-century samples included younger men who might account for some of the unmarried secretaries. It seems safe to assume that by 1930, YMCA leadership was solidly married, much more likely to be married even than their peers in the general population.[34]

An examination of YMCA manuals between 1890 and 1930 confirms that YMCA leaders were conscious of the shift from a predominantly single leadership to an exclusively married leadership. The 1892 *Hand-Book of the History, Organization, and Methods of Work of Young Men's Christian Associations* does not explicitly discuss the marital status of secretaries, but it is clear that the authors of the handbook had single secretaries in mind when they wrote the guidelines for secretarial qualifications and behavior. A lack of feminine influence and daily association "almost entirely with men" was feared to encourage "carelessness in dress and deportment." The remedy suggested was for the secretary to reside in "a boarding house where careful attention to polite details is a necessity." Secretaries were required to be "good housekeepers," a skill assumed "not often" to be "a masculine gift." The proposed solution: "The ladies must be called in as instructors, and after a series of object lessons the secretary should at least be able to imitate." The perceived problems in secretaries' personal lives, along with the suggested remedies, clearly assumed secretaries to be unmarried. But the most direct evidence of an assumption of singleness was in the *Hand-Book*'s guidelines regarding the secretary's social life: "A secretary must be guarded as to his relations to the other sex. If he be a young man of pleasing address and fond of ladies' society, this will be especially necessary. He had better make a recluse of himself than have attached to his name the unenviable reputation of a flirt."[35] Not only did this advice clearly assume that a secretary was not under the restraining influence of marriage, but it seemed calculated to complicate a secretary's relations with women and prevent social contacts that could lead to marriage. The expectation that a secretary display "a readiness to devote one's life" to the welfare of young men, that he associate "in his daily work almost entirely with men" was not likely to offer social contacts that would make marriage easy.

A comparison of the 1892 handbook with manuals published in the 1920s and 1930s offers a shocking contrast. Whereas allowances and guidelines were created in 1892 to compensate for and guard the presumed singleness of secretaries, in the 1920s advice was dominated by the assumption that secretaries were married and had families. This admonition reminding that the wife and children of a YMCA secretary might expect less time from their husband and father is typical:

> Perhaps in no realm of religious service are the requirements so exacting [as in the YMCA secretaryship]. The efficient secretary must do much of his work during the leisure hours of other men because these are the only hours when his committee forces can be assembled. This means absences from the home and the sacrifice of his family. . . . The secretary's family is left to shift for itself more largely than is true of other religious workers, a cost and a handicap which must be added to the usual sacrifices of the professional religious worker.[36]

Concern about the unique demands of the secretaryship upon the secretary's family and especially his wife led YMCA leaders to propose special remedies. "Y Wives Clubs" were recommended on the assumption that women could be induced to make greater sacrifices if they acquired "a better understanding of Association work" through exposure to other secretaries and their families. But the wives' clubs were also calculated to nurture relationships between secretaries "by strengthening friendships between the staff families." Handbooks also proposed "parties at the homes of staff members, the frequent coming together socially of the staff families." [37] If YMCAs were using wives' clubs and family-oriented events to strengthen secretarial ties and networks in the 1920s and 1930s, this would have focused attention on the marital status of single secretaries to a much larger extent. Before 1900, wives were never mentioned and mostly excluded from YMCA work and events. Social ties and networks promoted through wives' clubs would, by definition, have excluded single secretaries, adding to a sense of difference and isolation among them. This isolation was likely an additional pressure on them to conform and get married. The first year that the YMCA formally attempted to organize YMCA wives at a national conference was 1900. Though the conference was attended by only about sixty wives and was not repeated, it was a sign that the turn of the century was also a turning point in the YMCA's attitudes toward secretarial marital status.

chapter 4

MARRIAGE AND THE
SACRIFICIAL "Y WIFE"

If friendship was the highest type of relationship a man could have with another man, marriage was the highest type of relationship a man could have with a woman. In the nineteenth century marriage was rarely discussed in YMCA circles. Wives were virtually invisible in YMCA discourse. This was certainly due in part to the fact that the majority of YMCA members were young and unmarried. A majority of YMCA secretaries were also unmarried, and a solid core of YMCA leadership throughout the century were lifelong bachelors. But in the twentieth century the YMCA developed marriage preparation curricula, sponsored married couples groups, organized mixed gender social/dating groups, and shifted from a predominantly unmarried leadership to an almost universally married leadership. It is clear that the YMCA took a much more active interest in marriage in the twentieth century and began to promote normative ideas about marriage among its constituency. It is evident that much of the new emphasis on marriage was a result of the growing importance of sex education in the YMCA, and concern about the unhealthiness of singleness. The YMCA did not, however, abandon its historic emphasis on male bonding, friendship, and devotion. Leaders of the YMCA, who by the 1920s were almost all married, continued to devote the same amount of energy to the fraternity as previous generations of unmarried leaders, and as a result put unique pressures on their wives and their marriages. The universality of marriage among twentieth-century YMCA leaders, however, permitted them to preserve the Association's traditional ethos of male intimacy and intense friendship. It seems likely that such an ethos would have come under critical scrutiny in the twentieth century had the same percentages of secretaries remained single as in the nineteenth century.

As the YMCA wife became more visible, she played an important symbolic role. A discourse of the "sacrificial Y wife" developed in the twentieth century. This discourse rationalized the organization's demands upon the family and encouraged YMCA wives to acquiesce in their husbands' unusual degree of unavailability to them and their children. This discourse also made the wife an important ingredient in the success of a YMCA secretary. Richard C. Morse, general secretary of the YMCA from 1872 to 1915 and a representative of the older generation of Association leaders, had postponed marriage until the late age of forty-two. He forwent the possibility of having children in favor of a lifetime commitment to the YMCA. But by the twentieth century the assumption that marriage was a necessity for YMCA secretaries made celibacy or late marriage—logical alternatives—unthinkable. Increasingly evident in the careers of Mott and his successors was a knowledge of and major emphasis on sex education, accompanied by heightened concern about marriage. Secretaries like Mott and his successors were marrying early. They were then left rationalizing or apologizing for their inability to give the same devotion to their wives and children as "normal" men.

The comparison of three marriages can illustrate the growing normative emphasis on marriage in the twentieth century, which complicated the male homosociality that had been a foundation of the YMCA in the nineteenth century. This chapter will compare the marriage of Richard C. Morse, a prominent YMCA leader of the nineteenth century, with the marriages of two prominent twentieth-century YMCA leaders, John R. Mott and Eugene E. Barnett. Morse was born in 1841 and came of age in the 1860s at a critical time in the YMCA's early growth and development. Mott was born in 1865 and came of age in the mid-1880s, when the YMCA was beginning the era of its most prodigious growth. Barnett was born in 1888 and came of age in the early 1910s, when the YMCA and American churches generally were undergoing profound transformations as they sought to resolve the conflict between ascendant liberalism/modernism and militant fundamentalism. Mott was Morse's successor in 1915 as general secretary of the YMCA in North America and remained in that position until resigning in 1928. In 1936, Barnett returned to the United States from YMCA service in China and occupied a key leadership role in the national organization. In 1941, he became the general secretary of the National Council, and retired in 1954. Morse, Mott, and Barnett thus represent three generations of YMCA leadership spanning the years from 1870 to 1940 and beyond.

RICHARD AND JENNIE MORSE

The marriage of Richard Cary Morse to Jennie Van Cott is of particular interest. Morse was the general secretary of the YMCAs of the USA and Canada from 1872 to 1915, a period of momentous change for the YMCA. During a significant portion of his service, however, Morse, like most leaders of the YMCA, was a bachelor. All of his successors in the twentieth century, by contrast, were safely married before they ever assumed the reins of leadership. Morse presided over the organization mostly during an era when the YMCA emphasized men's relationships with one another. But during the last half of his tenure, the YMCA began to assume a family orientation. The wives of YMCA general secretaries came to play an important ceremonial role. Representations of YMCA wives became an important part of how the organization portrayed itself.

Private correspondence of the Morses showed how their marriage was influenced by late-nineteenth-century ideals of companionate marriage, stressing mutuality and partnership. Furthermore, the Morses' marriage did not fit the stereotypical expectations of a marriage: they were both quite old, they never had children, and Mrs. Morse was a public figure in her own right with a prominent position in the Presbyterian Church's mission work. But public representations of their relationship excluded Mrs. Morse from all but a few circumscribed ceremonial or symbolic roles, roles similar to those that were stressed in public representations of other YMCA wives in the twentieth century.[1]

Although the wedding represented the joining of two prominent New York families, the occasion took place quietly and unobserved. Colleagues and friends of Morse from the YMCA were generally excluded. In a letter to Edwin Shipton, a prominent British YMCA secretary, Morse described the lack of general notice: "We were married very quietly. I sent no cards of invitation except to the members of our family & our immediate home circles."[2] Morse's family correspondence confirmed that the marriage happened relatively quickly. Engaged in mid-March 1883, he was married by the end of June. Furthermore, Morse's discussion of the marriage in his correspondence with his family was terse. The first mention of Jennie Van Cott did not appear until the actual announcement of engagement. There was no evidence in the family letters of any sort of courtship. Morse claimed in his autobiography that there had been a long relationship between the Morse and Van Cott families. This was confirmed by a mention in his 1867 travel diary of a Van Cott for whom he had ordered some china while at the World Exposition in Paris. He also took note in his travel diary of the marriage of his friend Henry Stebbins to a Van Cott daughter that same year. But if there was a long courtship (and it is quite possible that there was not), it was Morse's personal secret until he was ready to announce an impending marriage.[3]

Though the privacy of his courtship was not unheard of in an age when marriages were assumed to be individual rather than family affairs, it was unusual for two people of Richard's and Jennie's social class. Furthermore, the small and quiet wedding is worth noting. Although American weddings in the antebellum era had been small family affairs held in private homes, not unlike Morse's marriage,[4] by the gilded age American weddings had evolved into large and festive affairs, with much publicity.[5] That is perhaps why Morse found it necessary to explain himself in his letter to Shipton. A quiet wedding would not have been unheard of, but the relatively advanced age of both marriage partners may have been an incentive to avoid attracting undue attention to the event. Given the social pressures on young men to marry, Morse may have considered it embarrassing to draw attention to the fact that only now had he finally taken a mate. In his autobiographical summary of their marriage, Morse noted that "children have been denied us, to our great sorrow."[6] But given Mrs. Morse's advanced age, it was likely that she was entirely incapable of bearing children by the time they married. This fact leaves one wondering whether his lament was not somewhat disingenuous. In the minds of some Christians, entering into a marriage where it was clearly impossible to have children would have defeated the purpose of marriage. It is possible that the Morses preferred to avoid this type of censure: the two partners did not move in together until almost a year after their marriage. But the silence about Mrs. Morse was consistent with a pattern of restricting the visibility of YMCA wives to certain roles.

Morse's public discussions of his marriage were sparse.[7] In this, he was not different from other nineteenth-century YMCA secretaries. Only in the twentieth century would increasing attention be drawn to the home and family life of YMCA secretaries. In his autobiography, *My Life with Young Men*, Morse discussed his relationship with his wife in reserved terms and allotted her only a few pages. The only really extended passage he devoted to her was toward the end of his memoirs, where he described her role as an entertainer and hostess. Morse was not the only YMCA leader to devote little or no space in his official memoirs to his wife. Although Luther D. Wishard's memoirs, "The Beginning of the Students' Era in Christian History," discuss his childhood, upbringing, and personal life in great detail, there is no account or even mention of his marriage. His wife was mentioned once in passing; otherwise a reader would have no idea that she even existed.[8] By contrast, both he and Morse offered lengthy and intimate accounts of their relationships with men. Other memoirs do not mention wives at all.[9]

This relative silence did not mean that Morse had no feelings of attachment to his wife. Surviving correspondence with his wife during separations he experienced from her in 1894, 1907, and 1910 demonstrate the depth of emotion he felt for her.[10] On the other hand, his unwillingness to publicly share intense emotions that he felt for his wife cannot necessarily be taken to mean that Morse saw the sharing of any kind of emotion in a public setting as inappropriate. As I have already documented in previous chapters, Morse expressed powerful emotions in his discussions of relationships with other men in his memoirs, in speeches, and other writings in public (that is, YMCA) settings. At least in the YMCA, intense emotions and expressions of love were not necessarily viewed as private. YMCA secretaries clearly shared an emotional/affective life together that was expressed publicly. Furthermore, the distinction between public and private was blurred in the case of men like McBurney, Weidensall, and Cree, who never married and whose lives virtually belonged to the YMCA. But the distinction also appears blurred for all lifelong YMCA leaders. The YMCA movement claimed these men's personal lives as much as their families did. Morse himself recognized that, both in the writing of his autobiography and in his decision to leave family and spousal correspondence to the YMCA rather than to other relatives. Morse's general silence about his feelings for and life with his wife could not really be viewed as a defense of privacy. Rather, it likely reflected the attitude that men's relationships with women were viewed as belonging to a completely separate sphere from their relationships with men.[11]

Morse did come close to sharing with the public an intimate event in the relationship between himself and his wife: her death. A note that appeared in his family league correspondence indicated that he had originally intended to publish a very long—and sentimental—account of his wife's death. The following text appears there with a small note:

> Written for but not printed on page 52 of "My Life with Young Men." During these last months (1917) of our joint work upon this volume the sorest bereavement of my life has come to me in the home-going of Mrs. Morse after thirty-four years of loving growing fellowship. With the sorrow has come, also from our Lord unspeakable consolation.[12]

The text that he had originally intended to publish was taken verbatim from the description he offered in his family league letters of his wife's death and his own bereavement. Morse may eventually have decided to exclude the account of his wife's death because it was so intimate, though his decision not to publish it was consistent with a pattern of circumscribing her visibility in YMCA settings.

If Morse considered discussing his wife's death in public at all, it may have been because it included a testimony to his faith in the afterlife. "Another smile passed over her face as she said to me: 'I shall not live to see the book.' . . . 'Oh yes, Jennie,' I said, 'you *may* read it when it comes out. Who knows.' 'Yes!' she replied, 'that *is* so.'" But the account also stressed Morse's relationships with other YMCA leaders. On her deathbed, Jennie asked Richard to give her farewells to friends and family for her. She even went to the trouble of enumerating by name who should receive them. After she had gone through the list of people Richard should greet for her, she apparently had still not included any YMCA secretaries and needed some prompting from Richard: "Then she asked: 'Have I forgotten anybody?' . . . Then I said: 'There are our Secretaries at the Building & elsewhere.' 'Yes,' she said, 'say farewell for me to them and to their wives. How good they have been to us.'"[13] Morse did in fact convey these sentimental farewells to YMCA secretaries, as in this letter to P. A. Wieting: "Among her last messages to the Secretaries '—all of whom had been'—she said—'so good to me.' I promised to convey her farewell and you are certainly of the number."[14] While this ritual of conveying farewells was undoubtedly a way for Richard to work through his grief, it also symbolically reaffirmed the bonds that connected him to other YMCA secretaries, and underlined his wife's ceremonial role as an ambassador of good will.

Although Morse had functioned as the general secretary of the YMCA for so many years as a bachelor, and although the absence of children in the Morse household freed Jennie for service outside the home, it was clear after his marriage that Jennie would become an important symbol of Christian domesticity. In a family letter, Richard described Jennie Morse's "exceptional opportunities of intercourse with women . . . of her class in society & Christian & church work [throughout the world]. She belongs also to a class of women who address audiences & engage in the deliberative & executive activities of the women of this modern time."[15] But in his memoirs, although he briefly mentioned the fact that her "ministry to others" extended "beyond the family circle," he confined concrete description of her activities to her role as a homemaker and hostess.[16] This role was alluded to in an anecdote that Morse recounted in his memoirs, describing a meeting of the International Committee at which his father-in-law made an address.

At the close of the evening, when the speaker was lamenting to a group of the staff of the smallness of the contribution he was able to make to a work in which he was so deeply interested, he encountered a chorus of protest with an emphatic assertion that in the person of his daughter he was making a contribution of value altogether incalculable in the terms of finance and inestimable in the coinage of character and cooperation.[17]

Jennie Van Cott Morse was a "contribution of value" to the Association not in a literal or direct sense. Rather, she provided valuable emotional support and domestic service for one of its prominent leaders.

Among other things, his acquisition of a wife enabled Morse to open his home to "Association friends and fellow workers from this and other lands." They could now be "frequent and welcome guests," which had been impossible when he was a bachelor.[18] Jennie's ceremonial importance as a hostess was highlighted in Morse's correspondence with his family describing a visit of his friend Henry Stebbins shortly after his marriage:

At home we have greatly enjoyed a week's visit from my friend Mr. Stebbins & his wife. It is the first time in our friendship of 28 years that he has been a guest under my roof & at my table. During his visit our entire household joined him & Mrs. Stebbins in an evening call at Seven Oaks in memory of the many good times we had enjoyed together in that home of hospitality, merry-making & the best of cheer.[19]

A man was not capable of entertaining friends "under [his] roof and at [his] table" unless he was married. It was not that Morse the bachelor had been incapable of entertaining. During his stay in Paris, Morse was frequently entertained and fed at the apartment of his single friend Coe. Perhaps it was assumed that in the relationship between a bachelor and a married man, the married man would always entertain, since he had a wife to play hostess. Or perhaps it would be considered an imposition for a man and his wife to expect hospitality from a single man (despite the fact that the single man probably had more expendable income). What is clear is that the difference in marital status created a clear inequality in social standing and expectation; less was expected of a man who was unmarried. This expectation of less carried over into other realms: the bachelor was considered less stable, less reliable, less successful. The acquisition of a wife represented an important step, a crucial milestone in the development to full masculine maturity. Morse's apparent pride that he was finally—after twenty-eight years—able to entertain his friend Henry Stebbins clearly manifested this social reality. After his marriage, Morse entertained the Stebbins family at his home at least once a year for an extended visit: "This week will be known as Farrar-Stebbins week with us, for my old friend Henry Stebbins &

his wife have been our guests & we have attended all the Farrar lectures, enjoying them very much." [20]

Another important ceremonial role played by Jennie Van Cott Morse was to accompany her husband on some of his travels to major YMCA conventions. He commented regularly in his official memoirs on this role. This fulfilled an expectation that, as Samuel M. Sayford once commented in a letter to Charles K. Ober, "No married man ought to take such a [long] trip as this without his wife." [21] In this capacity, she also met and socialized with YMCA and YWCA leaders, government officials, and businessmen and their wives. In 1900, as I will discuss in greater depth below, her role at a conference of YMCA secretaries' wives was to calm some of the discontent and criticism that was expressed there and channel it into support for the Association. Her presence and good will was apparently considered a necessary part of YMCA diplomacy. Sending greetings between wives was a common way to close letters: "Mrs. Morse joins me in affectionate regards to Mrs. Wishard & yourself." [22]

Although Jennie Morse seemed for the most part to have been delegated the role of hostess and YMCA diplomat, there were some examples in Morse's correspondence of attempts at a more cooperative partnership. In one letter to his family, Morse described an interesting incident in which he gave a lecture while his wife operated the "stereopticon." According to Richard, Jennie "announced to Mr. & Mrs. Allen that this had opened to her the prospect of a joint career for us. We could not act in the singing role of some of our married friends, for *I* cannot sing & *she* cannot play, but here at last was her opportunity. I could lecture & she could manage the lantern & slides!!" [23] Richard also apparently shared confidential details about YMCA work with her. For example, in a letter dated May 31, 1907, Richard discussed with Jennie the "confidential" dilemma over whether to devote secretaries to the promotion of YMCA work in the Chinese capital, where little work had been done and there was less of a foothold, or in Tientsin, where much work had been done, but where a successful YMCA had less potential to gain national attention and influence. Undoubtedly in her role as both assistant and confidant, she fulfilled her wifely duties as a helpmeet but was also acknowledged as a companion in her husband's labors.

Yet, as the stereopticon incident demonstrated, wives of YMCA secretaries who wished to share in their husbands' work came up against a fundamental dilemma. YMCA work was by definition a work "by men for men." While Jennie's role in the YMCA always had to remain circumscribed as a ceremonial and diplomatic role, Morse could openly celebrate the participation of male members of the family in the YMCA. He showed considerable enthusiasm for drawing male nephews into the fellowship of YMCA leadership. Morse's brother Oliver was an important leader on the International Committee and at the YMCA Training School in Springfield. Some of Morse's nephews became YMCA secretaries and lay leaders.

> I began to feel that, as a YMCA prophet I was beginning to get honor & opportunity not only in my own country but among my own kith & kin. Gilbert's visit resulted in Mr. McBurney's and my attending a few days after (Oct. 8) in Orange a meeting of young men by whom an Association was organized. . . . Gilbert has been chosen President!![24]

The exclusion of wives from YMCA circles had an emotional element. Morse's official conveyances of greetings almost always included a reference to his wife. But greetings of special warmth, which were intended to underline the emotional bond between him and another man, rarely did. One dramatic illustration of this came at the end of a letter to P. A. Wieting, where Morse closed with this warm acknowledgment: "These and only a few hurried words of affectionate greeting from two old friends one of whom is more than ever Faithfully yours Richard D. Morse." The word "one" was circled in a different pen, and scrawled in the margins was the reminder "No! Two!! J. V. C. M." The note was a reminder of the ambiguity of Jennie's relationship to the YMCA. The nature of Richard's relationship to the rest of the brotherhood was clear: he nurtured numerous working relationships in the context of warm—sometimes romantic—friendship. Jennie maintained social relationships with many of the brotherhood. She had the opportunity to do so to the extent that she accompanied Richard in his YMCA work and travels and to the extent that he entertained YMCA friends and colleagues at home. Richard's greeting duly mentioned Jennie in an official way, but in the special expression of warmth he included only himself. It may not have occurred to him that Jennie could have special feelings of warmth, since she was officially excluded from the brotherhood. Jennie may, on the other hand, have experienced some annoyance at Richard's assumption that he was a part of an emotional community that by nature excluded her.

The exclusion of women from the YMCA was manifested in physical separation as well. Although Jennie accompanied Richard on some of his larger YMCA trips, more often than not Jennie was excluded, and they were frequently separated. Many of these were separations of fairly short duration when Richard traveled to YMCA state and local conventions. In 1910, Morse was needed in Europe and was forced to leave his wife for a longer period. In this case, Mrs. Morse apparently wanted to accompany her husband but was forced to remain in the United States. Richard attempted to reason with Jennie and console her in the aftermath of some hard feelings about her inability to accompany him:

It was hard to go, but alas harder much harder for you to stay, and sorry am I to think of this. But your reward is sure—even though it be as yet in the future—that blessed future when we shall surely see that "All things *did* work together for our good," because the love of God to us does evermost so work *not* for those who deserve it but for "those who love Him" though undeserving—[25]

It was painful to leave you in the mood we were both in the night of the 10th & the morning of the eleventh. I hope better days were ahead of you.[26]

Future generations of YMCA wives would find forced absences of their husbands a major hardship. Many of them had to contend with realities that Jennie Morse did not. She had no children yearning for an unavailable father. Throughout their marriage, she was involved in the Presbyterian Church's foreign missions board and had opportunities for leadership that afforded her sources of fulfillment and identity outside the home. That Richard and Jennie married as mature adults in their forties with established separate social networks, and that they remained childless, made their marriage a special case. Their circumstances created less occasion for conflict between the demands of their relationship and Richard's role as general secretary of the YMCA. The same would not be true for the increasing numbers of women who were becoming Y wives as the Association entered the twentieth century.

THE SACRIFICIAL Y WIFE

The gender-exclusive nature of the organization was dramatically demonstrated by the fact that the pioneer secretaries—Morse, McBurney, and Weidensall—had all been bachelors in the formative years of the organization. In those years they created a model of leadership for those who would follow, and they established principles and procedures that could be relied upon to make the organization flourish. McBurney in particular had been hailed as "the Great General Secretary," the man who, more than any other, had created the institution of the secretaryship. If there was one trait in particular of the pioneer secretaries which was seen as definitive, it was sacrificial consecration to the work, a willingness to give oneself entirely and unreservedly to the welfare of young men. For the pioneer secretaries, this total giving of oneself flowed naturally out of the passion that drew them to the YMCA in the first place. It was an unstated but central part of the reason these men never married or chose to marry so late in life. This model of leadership was in harmony with the private lifestyles they had chosen for themselves. Indeed, it was sometimes hard to distinguish between these men's private lives and their commitment to the Y. McBurney, for instance, lived in the Tower Room of the Bowery Branch YMCA and was on call virtually every hour of the day. This merging of private passion with public service was idealized by YMCA leaders and was held up as a model. The total commitment of the pioneer secretaries did not conflict with their private lives as bachelors.

Indeed, their bachelorhood enhanced their ability to play the public, professional roles and life callings they had chosen. The same was not true of married secretaries, for whom the YMCA secretaryship competed with wives and families for time and attention. Because YMCA men took for granted the primacy of religious callings in general, the YMCA secretaryship had a tendency to invade their private lives and require the sacrifice of their wives and families. In order to accommodate marriage to the secretaryship, YMCA leaders developed a discourse of sacrificial YMCA wifehood. Regardless of whatever other callings they may have had in life, the wives of YMCA secretaries also had a calling of service to the YMCA. This calling was fulfilled primarily through a willingness to relinquish their husbands to the YMCA. It involved additional burdens of household management and child-rearing to make up for the increased absence of the YMCA secretary from the home. It also included other forms of service, such as a willingness to host, at a moment's notice, guests from the YMCA, participation in YMCA fund-raisers, and leadership in the YMCA women's auxiliary. Because YMCA work was a work of men for men, however, whatever direct service YMCA wives performed for the organization had to be unobtrusive and behind the scenes. Wives could not, for instance, accompany their husbands in committee meetings. In other words, the ideal YMCA wife was to provide increased domestic service so as to facilitate the YMCA secretary's work and relationships with other men.

In 1900 an early attempt was made to reconcile YMCA wives to the neglect they suffered as a result of their husbands' intense commitments to young men. The wives of married secretaries, who as of 1900 were still a minority, were invited to accompany their husbands to one of the many leadership conferences that took YMCA secretaries away from their families. This was done so that they could attend a parallel "Wives' Conference." The conference was presided over by none other than Jennie Morse and was attended by a total of sixty-four wives. The purpose of the conference was to provide wives of YMCA secretaries with emotional and social support. The proceedings of the conference were to be published and distributed to all those who were unable to attend. Organizers also hoped that future similar conferences would be held, and could grow into a regular form of support. It was assumed that the wives' conferences would change YMCA leadership trainings from one more occasion where a YMCA secretary was separated from his wife to an opportunity for spouses to travel together at least once a year. Unfortunately, there is no record of any additional wives' conferences. In fact, in standard histories of the YMCA there is no mention even of the wives' conference of 1900. At the end of the conference, the organizers themselves expressed uncertainty as to whether another one would be organized. After expressing the belief in the "great helpfulness to the wives of secretaries" of such conferences, they submissively noted that "this expression is made with the understanding that it is not intended to convey any opinion as to the wisdom of holding a second conference."[27] Secretaries' wives apparently were never again given such an opportunity to organize independently. By the 1920s, local associations were organizing wives' clubs, which were not separate women's organizations, but consisted of socials for secretaries and their wives.

If the YMCA did not see any "wisdom" in continuing the conferences, it is possibly because of the clear anger, discontent, and frustration expressed by so many of the conference's participants, among them wives of very prominent secretaries. Jennie Morse and other conference leaders attempted to channel that discontent into constructive support for the YMCA, but in the course of the conference YMCA secretaries endured harsh criticism for the neglect of their wives and children. In speech after speech, wives lamented having to play the role of "both mother and father," raising their children almost as if they were widows. They had to spend week after lonely week at home by themselves as their secretary husbands were absent in an endless round of meetings, activities, and social events, sometimes abandoning their wives for weeks at a time at conferences. The wives reminded each other that their sacrifice of loneliness was their contribution to the work of the Lord, though some were less sanguine. "I always advise a young secretary (if I'm asked) not to marry," said Mrs. C. B. Willis, wife of a prominent secretary, "unless he is very sure he knows how to treat a wife." She continued: "I have seen some desperately homesick young wives and have not much wondered at their disgust with married life and association people generally. . . . Our husbands have the importance of their work so impressed upon them that they are ready to sacrifice themselves and all who belong to them."[28] YMCA secretaries had developed a culture in which such direct, open, and harsh criticism was almost unheard of. Willis's use of phrases like "disgust with married life" and "sacrifice . . . all who belong to them" was tantamount to open rebellion. There was even criticism of the unmarried secretaries in a speech of Mrs. William M. Danner, wife of another prominent secretary, who scolded "some few secretaries, bachelor and otherwise" who "believe that the 'sharp treble of a woman's voice should never cut the air of a Young Men's Christian Association building.'"[29]

Mrs. E. C. Brownell went so far as to indirectly criticize the personal choices that led so many secretaries to a life of celibacy: "It is a fact that we all know, and the *unmarried secretary hardly realizes*, the great supplementary power that comes from the relationship of a wife with the association friends."[30] Willis, Danner, and Brownell all resented the fact that women were not allowed to play a more active role in the life of the Association and that they were excluded from the male-only fellowship, resulting in the loss of their husbands to Y work. Some blamed their husbands, others blamed the influential circle of bachelor secretaries, and some blamed both.

But if the conference allowed wives to vent criticism of the YMCA, it also established a code of sacrificial YMCA wifehood as the proper relationship of secretaries' spouses to the work. Organizers of the conference employed a discourse that became common by the 1920s and 1930s, and began socializing YMCA wives to accept the organization's demands on their families. Jennie Morse rallied the women in the composition of a letter to wives of secretaries laboring abroad. This letter included a classic statement of what the organization came unofficially to expect of YMCA wives. It stressed "sacrifice" and obedience to "His will," "patience and long-suffering with joyfulness, giving thanks unto the Father." It enumerated the duties of YMCA wives: procuring the support of "influential Christian women" for the Association; assisting the work of YMCA women's auxiliaries; "developing the associations' social life" (meaning holding banquets, decorating the rooms, and hosting friends of the secretary); and nurturing good relations with the YWCA (or sometimes actually playing a leadership role in the YWCA). Although the letter acknowledged some of the stress and pain expressed at the conference regarding "unsettled family problems," it emphasized the importance of learning "how to relieve the secretary of all domestic duties," and "reconciling ourselves to the bringing up of . . . children" without much input from the father. Wives were to focus on the physical maintenance of the associations and of their secretaries, rather than on spiritual or intellectual pursuits. "We may perhaps reach higher attainments in studying the 'browning' of beans [preparing food] for Bible classes, than studying the Browning of literature." These burdens were interpreted not as an unfair imposition but as evidence of wives' importance in promoting God's work. The conference was compared to "a training school for secretaries' wives."[31]

A survey of the wives of YMCA foreign secretaries in 1920 confirmed that by the second decade of the twentieth century, they had been more or less successfully socialized into their roles as sacrificial wives. That the survey was directed at foreign secretaries' wives living in China, India, and Japan is all the more significant, since there is clear evidence that these women were self-consciously modeling "true womanhood" and appropriate family roles for the peoples they were there to proselytize. The survey was conducted by a member of the International Committee, W. B. Smith. He intended to use material from the survey in the writing of a pamphlet for secretaries' wives, that is, to assist in the continuing socialization of secretarial spouses. The survey was also significant in that by the 1920s married secretaries had become the majority in the Association. The survey represented an open acknowledgment that secretaries had families and that the success of the YMCA's work depended on the cooperation of secretaries' wives. Smith asked them to discuss the "influence of the home" on YMCA work. The degree of uniformity in the women's responses is striking, suggesting that YMCA wives had already been socialized through informal channels, by their husbands and by other secretaries and their wives.

The common themes that emerged included uncomplaining maintenance of the household and raising of the children, buoying up their husbands emotionally through a positive disposition, entertaining YMCA guests, and doing supplementary work as fund-raisers, preparers of food, or Sunday school teachers. "I personally think," wrote Cornelia S. Mills from China, "that there is nothing a Secretary's wife can do as important as the use she makes of her home. . . . I feel that whatever of good I may have been able to accomplish was not through teaching and other outside work that I did, but through what I was able to do in the home." She stressed maintaining an orderly home and entertaining guests.[32] Edith L. Brown saw her first duty as keeping her husband "happy," followed by entertaining guests, teaching Sunday schools, and working in women's clubs.[33] Julia H. Trueman listed holding bazaars as fund-raising events for the YMCA, entertaining guests, doing the housework, and "keep[ing] up the men's spirits."[34] Foreign secretaries' wives also performed duties not expected of wives in the United States: teaching English to children and teaching non-Western women Western cooking and household etiquette. Again, there was evidence in the letters that these roles empowered YMCA wives at least somewhat by allowing them to share in the sense of mission of their husbands. Especially as wives of missionaries, they had opportunities for leadership and service which they might not have found otherwise: "I have been on the field long enough now (almost ten years) to wonder how people can be contented to stay at home when such tremendous opportunities and privileges are offered over here."[35]

It seems unlikely that in the 1920 survey wives would openly express the discontent that was aired at the 1900 conference, since they were being polled one-on-one by a male YMCA secretary on the International Committee. But in the 1940s, wives of secretaries started an independent newsletter that once again gave women a forum to complain to each other about their lot as secretaries' wives. The newsletter was called *Open Door*, which symbolized the hostess role that wives of secretaries supposedly played more often than most wives. One woman, of the same generation as the women who raised their laments at the 1900 conference, wrote "looking back over forty years as a Y-wife," and found the central defining experience one of "waiting" for her husband to come home, hearing his constant refrain, "I'm sorry dear." [36] Another Y wife warned prospective secretarial spouses that they would spend much of their lives waiting for their husbands and raising their children alone.[37] Some managed to find some wry humor in the situation. Mary Dickson, wife of the man who was general secretary of the Dayton, Ohio, Association for twenty-one years, was reported to have said after the death of her husband, "Henry's funeral procession must never pass the YMCA. If it should I just know he would raise [*sic*] up and say, 'Hold on boys, I have to run in the "Y" a minute.'" [38] Esther McCaslin of Detroit, Michigan, recounted a joke about a Y secretary and his wife who awoke one night in the middle of a tornado and found their house "de-roofed" and themselves "soaring through the sky" on their bed. After landing, the wife began to cry, and her husband "[congratulating] himself on being at home instead of at the Y in this time of crisis" said, "Don't be afraid, honey. I'm here and I'll take care of you." "Oh, I'm not crying because I'm afraid," she replied, "I'm crying because I'm so happy. This is the first time in ten years that we've been out together." [39]

The *Open Door*, like the 1900 wives' conference, however, largely sought to help wives manage their frustration rather than alleviate its source. Most of the laments usually ended with the refrain "But in spite of it all, 'Y' Wives are happy wives." [40] The joy of sharing the man's sense of mission was always affirmed to outweigh his increased absence. The *Open Door* also occasionally became a forum for YMCA secretaries to instruct their wives on how to be appropriately supportive. Thomas P. Pearman held up as a model a Y wife who "never did complain much" and who made "the best of this present situation because she has learned that a husband doesn't discharge all of his home responsibilities by the number of hours he spends at home." He also promoted the notion that the spiritual benefits of being a secretaries' wife outweighed the prospect of virtual single-parenting: "While a 'Y' secretary has less time to spend with his family than husbands in some other professions, I like to think that perhaps he brings more into the home than do others who spend more hours there." He even quoted a widely cited quotation of Leila Mott, wife of John R.: "I would rather have Dr. Mott three months in the year than any other man for all the months of the year." Y wives who had "a real sense of partnership" with their husbands would gladly accept the burdens.[41]

It is clear from almost fifty years of discourse about the Y wife that these women shared with most other women the expectation that their husbands be present in the home in a significant way, as the rearer of children but also to meet their emotional needs. The wife's desire for continuing romance with her husband was assumed to be valid, and any reasonable woman could expect it in marriage. There was also some expectation that husbands and wives have shared interests and that in some very real sense wives be partners in accomplishing the husband's life work. Morse's attempts to involve his wife—even in very limited ways—in YMCA work were evidence of such expectations in the 1890s. But YMCA wives were not visible or vocal until the turn of the century because until then they represented only a minority of the YMCA's secretarial workforce. Only as married secretaries became a majority were the needs and concerns of their wives given YMCA forums for expression. Despite the expectation on the part of their wives that men marry and devote significant time and energy to their families, however, YMCA secretaries maintained the primacy of homosocial relationships and culture well into the twentieth century. Wives were offered, as compensation, the knowledge that their domestic labor constituted a form of partnership with their husbands in the work of bringing young men to Jesus Christ. Nineteenth- and twentieth-century YMCA secretaries were alike in their commitment to homosocial service. What separated nineteenth-century YMCA secretaries from their twentieth-century successors was their greater willingness to translate homosocial passion into a celibate calling. After 1900, such an interpretation of the mandate to "devote one's entire life to the service of young men" was no longer possible.

JOHN AND LEILA MOTT

Like Richard C. Morse, John R. Mott was drawn into the YMCA by love and friendship in the context of an all-male fellowship. John R. Mott was strongly influenced in his early Christian life by the active personal interest shown in him by a Methodist circuit rider:

> This rarely equipped pastor [Horace E. Warner] identified himself with me. Again and again he visited me while I was at work in the lumber yard. He interested himself in my reading. He generated in me the desire and purpose to get a college education and convinced my parents so that they made this possible.[42]

At the time Mott was fourteen years old and Warner only twenty-four. But the man Mott actually credited with his conversion to Christ was J. W. Dean, YMCA state secretary of Iowa, who also took an interest in him during an evangelistic program in Iowa in 1879. When Mott went to college at Upper

Iowa University in 1883, the love for the YMCA inculcated in him by Dean manifested itself when he helped organize and became a charter member of that university's first YMCA. After transferring to Cornell, he immediately joined the student chapter of the YMCA, known as Cornell University Christian Association (CUCA). Mott quickly rose to prominence in the CUCA and was elected to be its delegate to the state college YMCA convention. Later the Association elected him vice president of its executive committee. The greatest advantage to being involved in the CUCA, according to Mott, was that it brought him in contact with "the best young men of the school."

Mott experienced his call to Christian ministry in much the same way as Richard C. Morse—through an intense friendship with a roommate. His sense of call to the ministry caused him some agony because of his fear of "weakness and imperfection." Like Morse, Mott found himself able to resolve his doubts about the ministry with a soul mate and friend. Mott met Arthur H. Grant through the YMCA. Grant was president of CUCA. He found himself "in a comparable inner struggle" to Mott, and experienced a sense of dilemma about his call to the ministry. Mott and Grant became roommates and regularly discussed their internal spiritual struggles with each other. They finally resolved the issue together, on Tuesday afternoon, January 12, 1886. Putting their books away, they discussed the matter in depth, "closely examining" one another, according to a letter Mott wrote his parents the following Sunday. Then they kneeled down together and prayed until they had both received from God a confirmation that they were called to work "in his vineyard." In the letter to his parents, Mott described himself as "wholly consecrated." As a sign of his sense of consecration, Mott turned down a prestigious graduate fellowship at Cornell in order to pursue his calling as a YMCA secretary.[43]

Mott's career in the YMCA, like Morse's, was characterized by a series of intense relationships with men as mentors, coworkers, and friends. J. E. K. Studd, former sports hero turned evangelist, played a role in Mott's emotionally intense "second conversion." L. D. Wishard and C. K. Ober, who recruited him into the student work, also established warm personal relationships with him (19–20, 38, 59, 80). Mott expressed open admiration for Robert R. McBurney, to whom he turned as a role model in his YMCA work (82). Mott in turn played a role in drawing other men into the fellowship as well, establishing intense friendships with men like Fletcher S. Brockman, Nathan Söderblom, and Wilfred Monod (79). His decades of close friendship with J. H. Oldham were a major impetus in Mott's career as an ecumenist (339–340). During his YMCA career, Mott adopted models of leadership training very similar to Weidensall's "discipleship" plan and Ober's "fellowship" plan, which sought to foster personal loyalty between men in an intimate setting (217). Mott developed an electric appeal to younger men which fed the dynamic of homosocial passion and intensity. One admirer wrote:

> I have never forgotten that evening when I saw John Mott for the first time, and I never shall. He was just forty-five years of age; his height, the beauty of his face, his straight, intelligent look, the energy which radiated from his whole personality, the unusual authority which emanated from his words and gestures, all combined to impress the students with a sense of moral nobility, absolute conviction and spiritual power. . . . I went away deeply moved, overwhelmed by what I had just heard, and still more by the certainty that I had just met *a man* in the fullest sense.[44]

In summary, the pattern of male homosocial bonding that characterized the YMCA throughout the nineteenth century was no less prominent in Mott's YMCA career than it had been in Morse's or that of any other secretary who had come before him.

But Mott, unlike Morse, married at the age of twenty-six, approximately the average age of marriage for men of his race and class in the 1890s, and only one year after the "ideal" age, according to Indiana secretary John R. Brandt, that a young man should marry. Although it would be impossible to prove that concern about avoiding censure as a single man was a motivation in Mott's decision to marry when he did, it is worth noting that Mott was an outspoken promoter of sex hygiene and sex education throughout his career as a YMCA secretary. As a leader of Cornell's student YMCA in 1883, he was an active promoter of the White Cross Army from its inception.[45] Grover Cleveland, the only bachelor ever to have been elected president of the United States, and father of an illegitimate child, was despised by Mott, who called him "that great national disgrace." When Benjamin Harrison was elected in 1889, two years before Mott's own marriage, Mott praised him using a family-values trope that would grow commonplace among YMCA secretaries after the 1910s: "It seems good, don't it, to know that we are to have a man and a family at the head of this nation which will have family prayer in the White House" (58). In 1893, he declared to the World's Parliament of Religions at the World's Columbian Exposition in Chicago that guarding students "against the many bodily temptations" was a primary goal of YMCA college work. Throughout 1894 he made sexual morality a topic of primary concern in his public speaking. Mott was especially concerned about the sexual morality of foreigners, and against the advice of friends, pushed himself to exhaustion delivering "the old talk on personal purity" during his tours of China and India where, he believed, "it was needed on every street corner" (152, 179).

Mott's emphasis on purity continued after 1900 in speeches like "Temptations of Students in All Lands," "Universal Sins in Student Life," "Be Sure Your Sins Will Find You Out," and "Temptations of Young Men." Like other purity preachers, Mott often followed his speeches by private interviews with penitent students in search of sexual purity advice (221, 248, 255–256, 262). Mott continued to stress sexual morality throughout the 1910s and after his ascension to the position of general secretary of the YMCA in 1915 (416). It is clear that years before his marriage to Leila, and throughout his subsequent YMCA career, Mott was attentive to issues of sexuality and stressed marriage and family as an indispensable feature of Christian manhood. It is also reasonable to argue that this concern shaped Mott's early personal decisions about marriage, without inferring that his affection for his wife was anything less than genuine. This is especially true in light of a career that gave him precious little time for wife and family. It was a career where a decision to give up family life might have seemed more logical in an earlier decade.

By the 1910s, the concern about the need for marriage that Mott had held early on came to dominate the organization of which he became a leader. It would influence the way the organization presented itself to the public. Mott himself, sometimes called the "embodiment" of the YMCA, and his family life became an important part of that presentation. After Mott became general secretary, the fact of his marriage and his four children made it convenient for the YMCA to promote a family-oriented image of Mott in its publicity and propaganda. YMCA propaganda in the war years and after stressed that the YMCA was a "home away from home" to young men. That image was buttressed by media stories like that featured in *American Magazine*, which "presented Mott as . . . a family man—with an informal photo of all six Motts at the Lac [des Isles, the Mott family's private resort in Canada]" (531–534).[46]

John R. met Leila White through a male associate, who introduced him to his three sisters. They married within a year after Mott was appointed to the post of senior student secretary on the International Committee. He had already committed his life to the YMCA and had accepted a more onerous set of responsibilities in the Association than he had ever shouldered before. Mott spent most of their honeymoon in California organizing student YMCAs with colleague Harry Hilliard—leaving Leila and Mrs. Hilliard to keep each other company in their absence. As Mott biographer C. Howard Hopkins put it, Leila "would accept and adapt to his total preoccupation with 'my work.'"[47] As Mott's career progressed, not only was he inordinately busy with YMCA work, leaving little time for his wife and family, but he was increasing absent on extensive travels. After 1905 Mott typically spent more time each year on the road than he did at home. During the war years, he would find himself at home with his family for only a total of three weeks. The fact of Leila Mott's "YMCA widowhood" was widely talked about in the Association and even held up as a positive role model. Ethan Colton, a friend of Mott, praised the example she set in raising her children alone for most of the year. He also praised her for responding, when asked, that "she would rather have John for one week than anyone else she had ever known for the rest of the year." She "set an example and was a great encouragement to the wives of the staff around the world," and was a model of "sacrificial service." [48]

There is no doubt that John's affection for Leila was genuine or that the romance between them was strong. "You have been in my thoughts and heart every waking moment since those holy moments together last night," he wrote, after a particularly painful parting in 1906.[49] But he also experienced moments of self-doubt, as when he learned by mail of her pregnancy in March 1907: "I feel guilty not to be near you and yet we have seemed to be on the path of duty. Certainly God has been using me along the line on matters calling urgently for my help. . . . Everywhere secretarial problems must be dealt with in person." [50] He was clearly seeking to convince not only Leila, but himself, that his calling as a YMCA secretary justified his absence during her pregnancy. Even as Mott was increasingly portrayed as a family man in YMCA propaganda, he was spending less and less time with his family. Mott was, of course, an extreme case. Few YMCA secretaries were expected to have the kinds of work and travel schedules that he did as senior student secretary, and later as general secretary. But the fact that he—and his marriage—were held up as models was proof that by the mid-1910s, YMCA leaders took it for granted that absentee marriage was better than no marriage at all.

EUGENE AND BERTHA BARNETT

Eugene E. Barnett was a less extreme case than John R. Mott and was probably much more representative of the average YMCA secretary. But an examination of his life, YMCA career, and marriage show that similar themes, concerns, and attitudes prevailed and affected his relationship with his wife and family. Like Mott and Morse, Barnett was drawn to the YMCA by its burning sense of mission and the warmth of its male fellowship. Like Mott, and unlike Morse, Barnett was also exposed to YMCA sex education early in his Association career and gave concrete expression to his concerns about sexuality in his first YMCA work. Barnett married even earlier than Mott, in 1910, at the age of twenty-two. Like Mott, his YMCA career kept him separated from his wife and family for long stretches of time and ensured that he had less time than most men to commit to them. Barnett also recorded regrets and perhaps some guilt that he was less present as a husband and father. They were accompanied by the plea that it was justified by the demands of Christ's work. Like Morse, Barnett in his later years decided on the necessity of writing an autobiography, to preserve in writing his memories, life experiences, and achievements. But Barnett's memoirs clearly indicated a much stronger sense of the indispensability of marriage and family in the life of a Christian man than Morse's. While Morse self-consciously addressed his autobiography to the "young men" he had labored with and given his life to, Barnett was writing primarily to "my children, and perhaps their children." "If any others," he continued, "chance to look over the family's shoulder, I shall not object."[51] Barnett's wife received a much more visible place in his memoirs than Morse's had in his own. Barnett was born in 1888, a generation younger than Mott and two generations younger than Morse, and wrote his memoirs in 1963, from the perspective of an entirely different era. He was seventy-five years old when he wrote his memoirs, one year younger than Morse was when he wrote his in 1917.

Barnett's first encounter with the YMCA took place at Emory University, where he "promptly joined . . . and took part in its various activities." He and the other young men involved in Emory's student Y met, as so many YMCA men before him had, in the intimate setting of its president's bedroom. Barnett began to attend regional and national student YMCA conferences representing his university. Barnett, even in old age, recalled with fondness the sense of fraternity that prevailed in the Emory YMCA: "We were young, full of spirits, an extraordinarily congenial company, and gaiety came easily upon us." Like the young Wishard at his first YMCA convention in 1872, Barnett at the Nashville Student Volunteer Movement Convention in 1906 was completely awed by the charismatic young men who organized and led the convention—John R. Mott, Robert E. Speer, and James M. Thoburn. He was so taken by the sense of mission and the powerful rhetoric of that convention that he immediately formed his own SVM band at Emory. Barnett was also impressed by other YMCA leaders he met: Richard C. Morse (by that time, sixty-nine years old), Robert Weidensall (age seventy-five), C. K. Ober, George J. Fisher, F. S. Goodman, and George B. Hodge. "These men gave us intensive courses in YMCA history and principles," he recalled, "and the fact that they were themselves makers of that still-short history and formulators of the principles they propounded made them both interpreters and evangelists." He was eventually recruited to the secretaryship by W. D. Weatherford (43–63).

While men of the pioneer generation that Barnett looked up to, such as Morse and Weidensall, had expressed hesitation and doubt about the role of sex purity or sex hygiene work in the program of the YMCA, Barnett, like Mott, saw it as central. Barnett's ideas about YMCA work were shaped in an age when Christ-centered Bible study and evangelism were combined matter-of-factly with social settlement work in Nashville, race-relations studies, and antiprostitution campaigns. One of Barnett's proudest achievements as leader of the Emory YMCA was the role he played organizing a crackdown on prostitutes who had set up camp near the university. The "strumpets" and "loose women," as he called them, were meeting young men in a field not far from campus. Barnett led a posse of YMCA men to the scene and, in what he jocularly referred to as "the Battle of Cemetary [sic] Ridge," the women were rounded up and taken to the county seat where they were jailed (56–61). Later in his YMCA career as a missionary in China, Barnett would rally the YMCA in another antiprostitution campaign. This time he sought to nip in the bud an initiative to allow licensed prostitution in Hangchow. The campaign was accompanied by a sex education program at the Hangchow YMCA. These classes and literature had been commonplace in North American YMCAs for a decade, but were a novelty to the Chinese (119).

When Barnett married, there was some indication that he saw marriage as a prerequisite for the type of YMCA service he was about to enter, namely, the foreign work. His engagement and marriage occurred very quickly. His fiancé had grown up in his hometown, but when they married he had seen her only once in the last eight years, during a YMCA-sponsored tour of Jasper, Florida. After their day-and-a-half reunion, they corresponded until their decision to wed. Their marriage occurred literally on the eve of their departure for his missionary work in China (62–66). Perhaps he assumed that this would be his last chance to marry before entering a foreign mission field, where his marriage prospects would be much more difficult, or where marriage to an eligible American woman would necessitate a return to the United States. But his description in his memoirs of his wife's role also indicated that he saw a wife as a necessary partner for a successful YMCA missionary. A clue to Barnett's sense of the importance of marriage in the life of a Christian man was revealed in one of the activities he organized under YMCA auspices in China: a Tuesday evening married couples club. According to Barnett this was an innovation and "broke new ground." At the time married couples clubs were an innovation not just in China, but in

North American YMCAs as well. But in China their introduction seemed especially novel since, according to Barnett, Chinese culture saw public mixing of husbands and wives as inappropriate (114).

"Going to China," he wrote of his wife, "meant for her no real change in life purpose or in her basic manner of living, only a change of locale." He described her as pious. Her life was geared toward service and offering food and flowers to "the lonely, the ill, and the poor." He stressed the "quiet" influence for good she exerted on others. This penchant toward silent labor and passive but pious "influence" were seen, in combination with her experience as a Sunday school and normal school teacher, as suiting her perfectly for the role of missionary's wife. When discussing his wife, he usually praised her in vague terms for being a "partner" in his work: "I was fortunate in following a vocation which was also an avocation, one, moreover, into which my wife could enter so fully" (157). Yet, while Barnett frequently described intense friendships with men in the China field, men such as S. L. Fung, Chi Min-lan, Sin Fung, Hsia Ting-Lou, and H. L. Zia, his wife appears infrequently in his recital of the work achieved in Hangchow. She was occasionally mentioned as a travel companion. In a postscript on their work in Hangchow, Barnett summarized in a single paragraph his wife's work teaching Sunday schools, organizing children's church services, conducting cooking classes for Chinese women, holding women's Bible study and prayer groups, directing a choir, and of course playing hostess at Y functions held in his home.

Barnett's description of his wife's role was remarkably similar to the "sacrificial Y wife" discourse that had been evolving in the YMCA since 1900. And like the proverbial sacrificial Y wife, Bertha often found herself tending and raising the children alone. Even during his furloughs, Barnett was usually on the road while his wife and children "visited around" (124). For the four months of his second furlough, he "saw almost nothing of my family but much of America" (188). At numerous other points, he documented continuing long-term separations from his wife and children (e.g., 266). At a certain point in his memoirs, Barnett felt it necessary to dwell at length on the problem of his frequent absences and unavailability to his family. He attempted an apology: "There were times when my family must have felt that the YMCA absorbed too much of me" (157). Barnett also apologized for the lack of narrative about his family in personal memoirs which were, after all, specifically written to his children and grandchildren. He could only excuse it with the words: "After all the YMCA was my reason for being in Hangchow." On the other hand, he saw as one of the major assets of his wife that she complained so little, even through serious health crises, allowing him to devote more energy to the work (173). "I have seen not a few men's careers wrecked by their wives," he continued, in volume 2 of his memoirs; "My difficulties would have been compounded beyond endurance had Bertha chosen to whimper or complain. Instead she stepped into her new tasks and relationships as if they were the most delightful and challenging opportunities a body could wish. In cramped quarters and in uncongenial surroundings she made home a pleasant and attractive place for her family—and many others."[52] After moving to White Plains, New York, Barnett served in the national YMCA in New York City. His work kept him commuting daily by train, which meant that "White Plains never became for me much more than a bedroom of New York City," while for his wife "it became indeed our 'home town.'"[53] It was only a heart attack and retirement from the YMCA that finally allowed Eugene to live a "normal" life with Bertha in their old age.[54]

Bertha Barnett was one of the many wives who responded to W. B. Smith's 1920 survey of foreign secretaries' wives. She described her role as the wife of a YMCA secretary in terms very similar to those of her husband and to the wives of other secretaries. This should not be surprising, since Mrs. Barnett listed as one of the duties of a YMCA wife taking the wives of recently arrived secretaries under her wing and teaching them how to assist their husbands in their work. In frequent staff get-togethers, according to her letter, wives would talk, and would listen to their husbands talk about their work. In this way wives could be socialized. They knew what was expected of them as Y wives. Like most of the Y wives' responses, most of her letter focused on the value of her work as a homemaker and entertainer of guests. Other duties included church service, assistance with YMCA fund-raising, and conveying Western marital and family values to Chinese women. Although Y wives were partners with their husbands in the sense that they provided invaluable auxiliary labor, it was not true in the sense of spending a lot of time together or having equal say in and control over the work. Bertha's advice to incoming secretaries' wives stressed the rewards of obedience and waiting: "Whenever the wife joyfully and expectantly accompanies her husband she will find unlimited chances for service and abiding joy in her work."[55]

IN THE TWENTIETH CENTURY, YMCA leaders came to expect marriage and family of each other. One dramatic illustration of this assumption occurred at the death of Richard C. Morse in 1927. The British National Council of YMCAs passed a condolatory resolution which read:

> The Members of the National Council of the Young Men's Christian Associations of England, Wales and Ireland, *desire to express their sympathy with the National*

Council of the United States, also with Mrs. Morse and Members of her family in the irreparable loss they have sustained through the death of Mr. R. C. Morse.[56]

The lapse is surprising, given that Jennie Morse had been dead for a decade, and especially since Morse had traveled to the British Isles since her death. With as many acquaintances as he undoubtedly had there, it is startling that no one on the National Council noticed the mistake. It leads one to wonder whether the reference to "members of her family" was not an equally presumptuous reference to children which the Morses never had. It seems quite possible that members of the National Council simply assumed that a YMCA leader of Morse's stature had to be married with children.

The model of the sacrificial Y wife was consciously promoted by YMCA secretaries and by their wives. It reflected the Victorian dual spheres ideology, conceptualizing women's roles in the public and private spheres in terms of their motherhood. But it also demanded a degree of separation between men's and women's work which most twentieth-century wives found trying, and which a few rebelled against. The occasional references to Y wives who had ruined their husbands' careers by complaining or refusing to cooperate suggest that not everyone was as attentive, silent, and obedient as Jennie Van Cott Morse, Leila White Mott, or Bertha Barnett. Discourse of the sacrificial Y wife or the YMCA widow rationalized the intense demands that Y work made on secretaries. It promoted an inflated view of the "influence" Y wives could exert for "good." It required of them auxiliary labor and additional domestic duties to make up for the greater absence of their husbands, without giving them any real power in the organization or control over their husbands' schedules. It essentially justified the absence of the father in the name of Christian service, encouraging him to channel his energies and affections into an all-male fellowship while his wife tended the home front.

The sacrificial Y wife was not inevitable. It was the creation of a series of organizational and personal choices and cultural pressures. It was, if anything, the result of an organizational ethos that romanticized male bonding in the context of an all-consuming, sacrificial mission combined with a new emphasis on the need for marriage at an age no later than one's late twenties. Twentieth-century YMCA leaders saw marriage as a duty and were—unlike their nineteenth-century predecessors—almost universally entering it. But they did not want to relinquish the sense of shared masculine adventure that had always made the YMCA so dynamic. Women also could share in the sense of mission of their husbands, although their enjoyment of that mission was often vicarious, as they were by definition excluded from most of the YMCA's central activities.

chapter 5

WOMEN AND THE YOUNG MEN'S
CHRISTIAN ASSOCIATION

*Our experience is adverse to the admission of ladies as members; perhaps
as a compromise it would be well where there is a demand to make them associate members. I would exclude them where I could without making any
hard feelings, and in other cases give them as little as possible. Of course, we
need their sympathy and aid; this we cannot afford to do without.*
—Cephas Brainerd to Robert Weidensall, 1868

*Certain it is that the easy, friendly intermingling of men and women in our
parlors, cafeteria, and occasional program features gives a "hominess" to the
building which is difficult of accomplishment when the two basic features of
home (man and woman) are separated.*—C. A. Schell, c. 1930

Despite its name, the Young Men's Christian Association
struggled over the question of whether women should be included in the organization during the first three decades of its
existence in North America. By the 1880s, the question had
largely been resolved in favor of excluding women. The official policy of the International Committee of the YMCA was
to refer women seeking YMCA-type programs to the YWCA.
But the issue flared up again with new vigor in the 1920s, and
this time was not resolved until the YMCA amended its national constitution in 1933 to allow women full membership
privileges on an equal basis with men.

In the nineteenth century only a minority of YMCA members and leaders argued that women should be full members. Some complained that it was more normal for men and women to be together. Some argued that women deserved access to resources that were unavailable to them in the YWCA, which was generally smaller and more poorly funded than the YMCA. The majority remained convinced that it was most normal for men and women to be in separate organizations because men and women were fundamentally different. In the nineteenth century the presence of women in the YMCA was largely viewed as disruptive. Women were allowed to play a role in the organization only in capacities that were motherly and nurturing, as members of YMCA women's auxiliaries.

But in the 1910s, a drive began to organize programs where women could participate side by side with men. By the 1920s, a majority of YMCA leaders and members were convinced that gender-segregated organizations were unnatural and were undermining "the family as a unit." Those who believed that the YMCA would lose its clarity of mission if women were allowed to join dwindled to an embattled minority. Just as women's auxiliaries in the nineteenth century were rationalized on the grounds that they could help create a more homelike atmosphere for the men, the drive to include women as members and to develop programming for them in the twentieth century was also justified as a measure that would strengthen the family. What was new in the twentieth century, however, and what gave the creation of mixed-gender programming an air of special urgency was the growing belief that the lack of women in the organization was causing homosexuality. For the first time in its history, YMCA leaders in the 1920s and 1930s expressed the belief that the promotion of "healthy heterosexuality" was essential to the overall mission of the YMCA to develop young men "mentally, physically, and spiritually."

IN ORDER TO understand the context in which the YMCA abandoned an eighty-year policy of excluding women from membership in 1933, it is necessary to examine what claims nineteenth-century women advanced in favor of inclusion, and how those claims were rejected. The strongest argument in favor of allowing women access to YMCA programs and facilities on the same basis as men was that women could benefit from what the YMCA had to offer, and that women had contributed vital community resources to the YMCA. These arguments, while practical, were rejected by the organization as a whole for the sake of preserving the Association's mission: to reach and save young men. The presence of women would complicate or disrupt the pursuit of that mission. Women and men were deemed to be different enough that their needs could not be fully met in the same organization. Furthermore, men were believed to be at greater risk of falling

into temptation. Society depended to a greater extent on male uprightness, increasing the urgency that the Association focus exclusively on men's
needs. Women were welcome to play helping roles behind the scenes. Indeed, as guardians of household piety who needed God-fearing husbands,
it was in women's interest to further the mission of the YMCA. But in actual
proselytizing, only a man knew how to reach the heart of another man. The
task of saving young men could most effectively be accomplished in an organization that excluded women. In the 1920s, such arguments collapsed in
the face of institutional homophobia, and the old practical arguments in
favor of including women were revived.

Nineteenth-century YMCA leaders acknowledged that women offered
the Association critical resources and support that often made the difference between success and failure. Women's support offered the Association
a mantel of public respectability, and oiled the gears of cooperation between
the YMCA and churches. Women offered the Association considerable financial gifts, likely greater than those of men in proportion to their financial
means. Women also provided valuable services to YMCAs by organizing
fund-raisers and social events, preparing food, and cleaning and decorating
YMCA buildings, most of which they did free of charge through women's
auxiliaries. Furthermore, the wives of YMCA secretaries who served both
in the United States and abroad often performed considerable unacknowl-
edged labor for the YMCA.

Women's financial contributions were critical to the survival of many
YMCAs in the nineteenth century. Concerted efforts of a women's aid association saved the Cincinnati YMCA from collapsing into debt in 1855.[1] In
the late 1850s and again in the 1870s, the efforts of women fund-raisers re-
lieved the Boston YMCA, one of the nation's leading associations, of its
debts.[2] Not only did women's auxiliaries organize valuable fund-raisers, but
individual women of means donated huge sums of money. In the 1880s,
Mrs. D. P. Stone was the first to donate money for a new Association building in Boston—a grand sum of $25,000—which encouraged other wealthy
donors to contribute. Mrs. William E. Dodge was known for her generous
giving to the YMCA, which included a $25,000 gift to the San Francisco
YMCA. Her daughter Grace H. Dodge contributed $2,500 to the same fund,
while half a dozen other women contributed over $60,000.[3] Mrs. Freder-
ick L. Billings was probably the single greatest contributor to the YMCA
Training School, giving $30,000 within the space of two years (1901–1903).
She also donated considerable sums to the San Francisco YMCA. The salary
of Professor Ralph L. Cheney at the Springfield school was paid for some
years by Mrs. Billings, and another $6,000 came from a woman acquain-
tance of Cheney in Hartford.[4]

R. C. Morse credited two women of means for enabling the International Committee to acquire its building in New York.[5] Luther D. Wishard acknowledged that "the financial pathway of the work has been literally lined by generous women." Wishard's foreign work fund-raising was greatly aided by women, as when Mrs. J. Livingston Taylor paid for a YMCA building in Tientsin, China.[6] Other women well known for their generous contributions to the YMCA were Miss Helen Gould and Mrs. Russell Sage. Wealthy women often also left sizeable bequests to the YMCA, like Anna H. Wilstach and Mary Lewis Smith, who each left the Philadelphia YMCA $10,000.[7] Miss Frances S. Moody, another major contributor, left $10,000 of her estate to the training school and provided for the purchase of an island for boys' camping. Mrs. Eleanor S. Woods, a friend of the training school, donated $18,000 during her lifetime for the erection of a new dining and social hall, and left $5,000 to the school from her estate when she died.[8]

YMCA leaders were aware of the inequitable flow of time, energy, and resources from women to men in the organization. But as one YMCA convention delegate declared: "Auxiliary members [women] should not ask privileges of the Association. 'They come to minister, not to be ministered unto.'"[9] YMCA leaders developed a rationale for this flow of energy, suggesting that men were "more susceptible to temptation" than women,[10] that urban young men were more vulnerable and yet more critical to the functioning of American government and society. An 1883 YMCA bulletin pontificated that "some consider our meetings too exclusive, they being confined to young men only, but it must be remembered that the Y.M.C.A. has a specialty, and that specialty is *young men.* Our limited room also is a sufficient reason in itself for not having mixed meetings. Our lady friends, however, have a standing invitation to visit our rooms."[11]

Women who worked for the YMCA occasionally pioneered activities under the aegis of the Association which benefited working-class girls and women, although these activities were the first to be curtailed in the late 1860s and 1870s. YMCA women held "ragged schools," teaching basic cooking and sewing skills to working-class girls.[12] They also held mission Sunday schools that taught working-class children how to read. In 1915, reviewing the history of YMCA work, Robert Weidensall derisively complained about this type of service: "Some of these Associations would be engaged in anything but work for young men, and call it a Y.M.C.A. In DesMoines they had in the Y.M.C.A. work a class to teach poor little girls to sew, then gave them the garments they made, etc., etc."[13] Male YMCA leaders did not necessarily see such work as lacking merit, but they refused to see it as a legitimate work of their organization. "The Association," wrote Weidensall, "as such cannot consistently take any prominent part in moral reforms, however good in themselves, that do not involve in their efforts the leading of young men to Jesus Christ as their personal saviour." [14] Throughout the nineteenth century the International Committee persistently rooted out all activity that did not relate directly to this end.

Many women, especially wealthy middle- and upper-class women, accepted and promoted the policy excluding women. They believed in the rationale that YMCA outreach would strengthen the home by preparing men to be good Christian husbands and fathers. Numerous nineteenth-century women's historians, including Mary Ryan, Ann Douglas, and Barbara Welter have argued that women used religious voluntary societies to promote domestic values. Pamela J. Walker's study of the Salvation Army suggests that at least in some religious circles women were able not only to domesticate men through religion, but to win them over to a more egalitarian view of the sexes. [15] Nineteenth-century men, on the other hand, were abandoning the church in droves because they perceived it to be a female-dominated (or at least effeminate) institution. Women outnumbered men in churches by about two to one. Some women may have perceived the YMCA as a taming and civilizing force among young men. At least some data support this interpretation of women's involvement in the YMCA. [16]

An article in a YMCA newsletter of 1883 suggested that middle-class women supported the Association because they saw "in this institution the means raised up to answer their prayers for sons and brothers, that they may be kept from the sins of this wicked world. Save the sons and brothers and you have the husbands and fathers for Truth." [17] A speaker at a YMCA women's auxiliary convention in 1889 saw the role of the auxiliaries as reminding young men of "the teachings of [their] dear Mother and her desire that he should become a follower of Christ." [18] Elizabeth Spence (fig. 8), widely credited as the person who inspired the first YMCA college work, wrote a poem, "All hail to the new formed Christian Alliance!" which rhapsodized about the need for men to "strengthen [their] virtuous resolve." The poem exhorted young men that

> If you, like your Master, be scorned and derided,
>> Then welcome reproach for the name which you bear . . .
>
> True greatness stoops down to the lowliest labor,
>> And looks at the cross when an insult is given;
> Seeks only to show what is duty, then does it;
>> The humblest heart is the nearest to Heaven. [19]

It appears likely that the YMCA prescriptive literature encouraging passive, pious virtues in men appealed to women.

8. Elizabeth K. Spence, mother of the man credited with founding the YMCA's first college association and purported in YMCA lore to be its inspiration. Courtesy of the YMCA of the USA Archives, St. Paul, Minnesota.

Men generally accepted this feminization of piety, which went hand in hand with the sentimentalization of motherhood and the dual spheres. In Samuel M. Sayford's account of his conversion, the salesman-evangelist who brought him to Christ was unable to break through the emotional barriers Sayford had erected against him until he invoked Sayford's deceased mother: " '[Your mother] must have been a godly woman. Only yesterday [your father] was telling me about her death, and the great triumph of her faith.' He had touched the tenderest spot in my heart. Any reference to my mother wakened the most affectionate memories."[20] The saving of young men from temptation in the city was usually associated with helping men stay true to the teachings and desires of their mothers. In Sayford's account of his conversion, the man who brought him to Christ convinced him to pray by reminding him that his mother had been a "praying woman." In a speech regarding YMCA work at Cornell University, F. W. Kelly expressed confidence in the efficacity of "the prayers of mothers and sisters . . . constantly offered on behalf of loved ones away from the influence of home."[21]

It is, of course, important not to overdraw the feminization of the church. Despite the fact that women participated in larger numbers than men and found opportunities for public service there which they might not find elsewhere, the church still maintained an exclusively male leadership, used exclusively male images of God, and preached a theology that dichotomized women as the source of temptation and original sin or as the model of sainted and silent purity. Nor is it clear that the YMCA actually succeeded in "domesticating" young men.[22] It is equally possible that the YMCA represented a male flight from a church that men perceived to be feminized. YMCA rhetoric about "manly Christianity" and "muscular Christianity" could be seen as an expression of nineteenth-century male paranoia that women were taking over the church, and reassured men that they were indeed America's rightful spiritual leaders. But to the extent that women accepted the dual spheres ideology, it is understandable that some women would perceive the YMCA's gender-exclusive approach to be natural and to their advantage.

Women made considerable contributions to the YMCA, but almost all of these contributions emphasized women's domesticity. From the end of the Civil War through the 1920s women's auxiliaries were the most popular form of organized women's service in YMCAs. By the late 1890s, such auxiliaries numbered five or six hundred.[23] A women's auxiliary was to a men's organization what a wife was to a man. A Rochester YMCA ladies auxiliary report compared the auxiliary to a "faithful spouse" and the Association to a "husband."[24] YMCA literature also referred to its auxiliaries as "help-meet" organizations.[25] In 1881, the San Francisco YMCA dropped its constitutional clause allowing women to be members of the YMCA, and instead organized its women friends into the Ladies Central Committee. In addition to fund-raising, the L.C.C. sponsored Thanksgiving and Christmas dinners for young men who were away from home. In 1901 the Ladies Central Committee reorganized as the San Francisco YMCA Women's Auxiliary, whose mission was "to increase the membership of the YMCAs, to keep the rooms tidy, to attend the social gatherings, arrange floral decorations, to make the place attractive, to visit sick young men and to 'administer to their wants and comfort in divine and temporal things,'"[26] in other words, to mother them.[27] A speech made at a convention of YMCA women's auxiliaries emphasized the role of auxiliaries as surrogate mothers to the "boys": "Keep the rooms supplied with flowers. A flower is a little thing, but the Holy Spirit can use it to draw a young man's thoughts away from a cheerless, hardworking life, back to his Mother's garden."[28]

Although women could not be hired as YMCA secretaries, they were occasionally hired as help staff. Even this could occasion controversy. The proposal to hire a female stenographer at the San Francisco YMCA in 1886 elicited complaints until it was pointed out that she could be hired at "much less expense" than a man.[29] It is significant that the first formal work that women did for the YMCA was in the area of boys' work, an area where a motherly presence was seen as an advantage. In fact, it was the mothers of the boys themselves who took an active part in promoting this work.[30] Ellen Brown pioneered boys' work in 1881 in Buffalo, New York, working for five years as a volunteer. She was hired as the boys' work superintendant in 1886. Though for all intents and purposes she was a YMCA secretary, Laurence L. Doggett noted a reluctance on the part of "most of the writers on [the subject of boys' work] . . . to name Miss Brown as the pioneer secretary," because of their evident discomfort with the fact that "the first secretary was a woman."[31] Other women's work for the YMCA, like women's war relief efforts under the auspices of the YMCA's United States Christian Commission during the Civil War, and overseas war work in France during World War I, were similarly tolerable only to the extent that they emphasized women's roles as nurturers. Writing of women's work in the United States Christian Commission, Bishop Simpson declared:

> This has elevated woman in the eyes of the world. She has taught us that man will be more manly and brave, as well as purer and more refined, wherever Christian woman goes. What part she is to have in the future of humanity I know not, but I fancy that her aid in some form will be essential in correcting these forms of vice which now degrade humanity.[32]

BUT IF MANY nineteenth-century women accepted the exclusively male outreach of the YMCA and were content to participate in it simply as helpmeets and auxiliaries, significant numbers of urban women, working women, and college women began to demand access to YMCA facilities and programs. Women who joined the YMCA clearly sought to benefit from the resources it offered. As early as 1853, women began to join the Boston YMCA in order to take advantage of its library.[33] YMCAs also offered a variety of self-help classes and kept employment bureaus and boarding registers, all of which could assist single working women in the city. Furthermore, young urban women claimed to be vulnerable to the same temptations and evils as young men. They saw the YMCA as a moral and spiritual resource that was every bit as important to them as it was to young men. Women sought out YMCA Bible studies, prayer groups, and urban revivals as well as its more secular programs. In colleges, YMCAs were evolving into a major center of campus social life. College women, who were usually a minority on male-dominated campuses, wanted access to the resources and social life available there.

In the earliest years of the YMCA in North America, there were no national policies governing membership, and some associations had women members. Between 1851 and 1854, the Springfield, Brooklyn, and Worcester associations granted women full, active membership on the same basis as men. The first convention of the YMCAs of the U.S.A. and British Provinces in 1854 made provision for the autonomy of local associations in setting their own membership qualifications. Thus, although most associations excluded women from full membership, it was possible for associations to include women if they wished. After the Civil War, however, North American YMCA conventions set standards by which new associations could be admitted to the convention. At the convention of 1867 in Montreal, a handful of women delegates were refused seats, and the convention voted that in the future representation at YMCA conventions (which was proportionate to the number of members in each association) could be based only on the male membership. An attempt to overturn this resolution a year later at the 1868 convention was defeated, and the policy remained in place until 1933.[34]

The tradition of local autonomy that had shaped the YMCA since the first international convention in 1851 determined the official response of the International Committee to women members. This made for some ambiguity. Local associations could still allow women members, while the International Committee encouraged local associations to focus on work "for young men only." C. K. Ober recalled that "Association leaders in the period from 1870 to 1885, were not entirely agreed as to what constituted a true Young Men's Christian Association."[35] After the 1880s, however, the International Committee more aggressively promoted an exclusively male membership policy. Although they never claimed to have any power over the internal workings of local associations, it was not uncommon for the International Committee to make financial and other aid contingent on conformity to what they called "established principles." Thus, for example, international field secretary Thomas K. Cree refused to organize a fund-raising canvas that the San Francisco YMCA desperately needed until they agreed to revise their constitution to exclude women from the membership.[36] A common tactic for excluding women from YMCA membership was to couple exclusionary clauses with the formation of a women's auxiliary, as was done in San Francisco in 1881 and in Chicago in 1888.[37]

The status of women in the YMCA had high symbolic importance to YMCA leaders. Few YMCAs ever granted women full, active, voting membership, but even the granting of associate member status could cause controversy. Although the second constitution of the Chicago YMCA, drafted in 1863, clearly stated that it sought the "spiritual, intellectual and social improvement of all within its reach, irrespective of age, sex, or condition," female Chicagoans were restricted to auxiliary membership that granted them—in exchange for a five-dollar fee and a commitment to serve the Association through its women's auxiliary—the material benefits of YMCA programs. Auxiliary members were not allowed to vote or hold office.[38] But even this second-class membership status rankled the International Committee in New York, which was not satisfied until the Chicago YMCA revised its constitution to read "[improving the] spiritual, mental, social, and physical condition of young men."

Such wrangling about words was typical of the way in which the YMCA settled the status of women in the organization. The San Francisco YMCA allowed women to attend Association meetings after September 1854 without having to apply for formal membership, provided they recognize that the mission was one of "benefitting the young men of this city." Women were also allowed access to the library for the payment of a three-dollar yearly fee, provided they received a recommendation from a (male) member of the YMCA. This compromise was crafted after defeating a proposal that would have granted women associate member status. Even when the San Francisco YMCA constitution was revised to allow women to be members in 1873, they were granted only auxiliary membership, which was dropped again in 1881 under pressure from the International Committee.[39] In 1894, when the Association allowed women to use YMCA gymnasium facilities, they could do so only on condition that "the ladies would in no sense be considered members."[40] Although women's access to YMCA resources and their level of participation in YMCA leadership did not significantly change in all this time, the labels used to describe or justify women's presence caused considerable tussling.

The most dramatic example of International Committee arm-twisting was in the concerted effort to segregate the many western and midwestern college associations into Young Men's and Young Women's Christian Associations. Luther Wishard explained sheepishly in his memoirs that he had organized some sixty to seventy-five "mixed" associations in the Midwest

by 1882 because of prevailing local attitudes that sex-segregated associations were not normal. When the International Committee learned what he
had done, they summoned him to New York.

> We all recognized that we were up against a proposition as difficult as one con-
> cerning which John Pierpont Morgan once remarked, "It is difficult to unscramble
> eggs." We saw at a glance that we could do nothing hastily and could do nothing
> at all for the mere sake of conforming to a technical requirement in the member-
> ship basis; we must discover some solution which would in no wise sacrifice the
> interests of the young women, so we separated and literally began a campaign of
> watchful waiting.[41]

C. K. Ober described Wishard's subsequent three-year campaign to separate
women from the Association (1883–1886) as "delicate, difficult, and pro-
longed."[42] Obviously the seriousness with which the International Committee considered Wishard's error and the energy and care they invested in its
undoing demonstrated that they considered the policy more than a mere
technical requirement. The most significant victory of the "unscrambling"
campaign came in 1888, when the Chicago YMCA revised its constitution
to bar women from membership.[43]

Hall and Sweet, the authors of a 1940s history of women in the YMCA,
explained the nineteenth-century exclusion of women "more by a determination to keep this a men's movement than by a determination to discriminate against women." This was, in fact, the explanation most commonly
offered by YMCA men at the time, although it begged the question of why
they were determined to keep the YMCA a men's organization. Nor did such
an explanation consider that the systematic exclusion of women from a
large public service organization drawing on a disproportionate share of
community resources might itself be discriminatory regardless of the moti-
vations. Hall and Sweet suggested that there were other, more psychological
motives: "There was evidence that . . . some fear of the influence of women
lurked in the minds of Association leaders."[44]

If contemporaries and later observers all insisted that the exclusionary
policy was not a matter of discrimination, it is likely because the controversy hinged not on whether women should be treated as equals (most assumed that they should not), but rather on what constituted true masculinity. Men who argued for the inclusion of women generally believed that
the YMCA should promote heterosexual familial models of masculinity,
where the proving ground of masculinity was men's ability to sire families,
and where it was assumed that normal, healthy men would desire the presence of women. Those who argued for the exclusion of women focused on
business and political leadership as the proving ground of masculinity,

and assumed that men could learn best from other men about how to perform in the world as men. In this vision, women's presence would be seen
as a distraction. Robert Weidensall made a classic statement of this vision
in an open letter to the YWCA. According to Weidensall, separation of men
and women was natural, since men were called to a more public, business-
oriented lifework, while women were called to a more quiet, behind-the-
scenes work in the home:

> The Young Men's Christian Association may, and perhaps will, be more before the
> public, for it has to do with persons in public life, but the work of your Association
> will have a more constant force, will work more steadily, will have less friction . . .
> will not be opposed by the complications of business, etc., will work through the
> home, the first divinely appointed organization.[45]

Men who opposed the exclusion of women did so because they felt that
the intermingling of the sexes was more conducive to the promotion of heterosexual marriage. The association president who succeeded temporarily
in integrating the San Francisco YMCA, complained that the absence of
women in YMCAs led to an abnormal social situation: "We want social re-
unions, where the young of both sexes can meet and find social companionship. . . . The feet of the young run naturally toward gladsome pleasures,
and religion cannot prosper if it makes war upon all the instincts which the
God of nature has implanted in the heart of youth."[46] Other statements in
favor of admitting women as active members suggested that women would
make the meetings more "interesting." Luther Wishard observed that members of western associations found the idea of segregating associations ri-
diculous, making it the subject of "raillery," and concluded that "it was better to have mixed Associations in the colleges than none at all."[47] Similar
pleas against the abnormality of gender segregation came from women, including this speech at a YMCA annual meeting: "In spite of all its masculine
exclusiveness even the YMCA has discovered the fact that 'it is not good for
Man to be alone.'"[48] These nineteenth-century complaints about the abnormality of sex segregation did not, however, move most YMCA leaders or
the International Committee. Though there were a few local exceptions, and
though there was more support for gender-integrated associations in the
West and Midwest, the vast majority of conventiongoers and the largest and
most prestigious associations rejected full membership status for women.
Women's auxiliaries and YWCAs were seen by the majority as an acceptable
compromise that honored women's and men's distinct natures.

If two different visions of masculinity were at the root of the conflict, then
Wishard's observation that attitudes toward the male membership requirement were different in the West than in the East makes more sense. The

largest, most influential associations in the country—New York, Brooklyn, Boston, Philadelphia, Washington, Baltimore, and Toronto—were eastern, urban associations that were dominated by upwardly mobile, middle-class businessmen. These men would have considered success in the men-only world of business as the primary determinant of masculinity; they would have looked to the Association as a place for networking, and a place to come to terms with the anxiety of the competitive world they worked in. Most western associations, while including clerks and small merchants, would have had a much larger mix of men from rural backgrounds for whom marriage was a prerequisite to establishing independence and beginning one's own farmstead. In western, rural culture, youth groups would have been seen as marriage markets as much as anything else. The thought of excluding women from membership or organizing segregated groups would have seemed queer indeed. In Chicago and San Francisco, which in the 1850s and 1860s were essentially booming frontier towns, early YMCAs admitted women as members at a time when their communities had extreme male-to-female sex ratios. After the 1880s, as these cities stabilized demographically and developed strong mercantile middle classes to serve as the backbone of association leadership, these YMCAs stepped into line with the eastern associations and adopted exclusionary policies. The fact that associations that included women had no commitment to women's equality was freely admitted. As Wishard put it, in such associations "the young women occupied a very subordinate place in offices and on committees and in promoting intercollegiate relations."[49] Women in these associations were relegated to the subservient, service-oriented roles it was assumed they would play in marriage.

The motives for segregating associations by sex went beyond meeting the social needs of urban men, however. Had that been the case, rural YMCAs might have been left alone to determine their own membership policies. For the eastern leadership, the symbolic importance of a male-only organization and a male-only leadership was too great. Especially with the rise of a visible, national women's rights movement in the 1880s and 1890s, there was too much at stake in the construction of masculinity to allow exceptions in the YMCA's organizational fabric to threaten it. Even for those who did not feel personally invested in the male-only vision (like Luther Wishard, for instance), solidarity with the eastern leadership was so important that they eventually came into line. Wishard, despite his initial doubts, became a true convert: "I shall ever believe that the disconnection of the men and women in the college Associations has resulted in vastly increasing the efficiency of organized Christian work in the colleges and cities for which these two kindred movements [YMCA and YWCA] stand."[50] In its campaign to segregate the western associations by sex—to "unscramble the eggs"—the YMCA employed the good services of YWCA spokesperson Fanny Beale, whose watchword was "Only a girl can reach the heart of a girl." According to Wishard, wherever she uttered this statement, she "convulsed the house" with applause. The usefulness of such a device was not lost on the male leadership of the YMCA, as Wishard noted: "Dear old McBurney never got over quoting that remark. . . . We returned [from hearing her speak] crying 'Eureka,' and we had." Wishard recognized that adherence to the motto implied commitment to a society in which core identity was determined by gender. "The mixed Association," he maintained, "really ignored the identity of young women." Separate associations merely recognized that men and women were fundamentally different and that a mission of spiritual, social, intellectual, and physical improvement could best be carried out separately.[51] This explanation for maintaining a gender-segregated movement remained compelling to the vast majority of YMCA leaders until the 1910s.

Though this argument was convincing to a male leadership committed to the cultivation of masculinity in a male-only environment, it was rejected by a significant number of women in the YMCA. College women challenged the separation on the grounds that they would not have the same opportunities for intercollegiate relations in a separate organization. Nineteenth-century women's enrollment in mainstream academic institutions was considerably below that of men's enrollment, so this should have been a special consideration in the college associations. At the national level there were too few women's collegiate organizations to make a separate structure numerically viable.[52] Furthermore, women did not have access to the same financial resources that the YMCA typically attracted in the business community. Not only that, but YMCAs drew significant financial support from women of means, who might otherwise have contributed to YWCAs. This argument was a difficult one for the eastern leadership to overcome, which is why they quietly agreed to attempt segregation of the associations where possible, but not to push the point where they encountered entrenched resistance. One letter from Richard C. Morse to C. K. Ober cynically acknowledged this fact, with the caution that it would be best not to do anything to draw attention to the disparity of resources between YMCAs and YWCAs: "You may find that your work by giving impulse to the work of the college *boys* only may make yet more unfavorable the contrast between them & the girls' organization."[53] Morse admitted that the most reasonable response to this disparity of resources—short of allowing women to participate freely in the YMCA—was to assist in the building up of YWCAs. But rather than do that, he suggested that Ober keep his visit short to avoid drawing attention to the greater resources of the "boys'" Association. That arguments for integration based on women's lack of resources were largely pushed aside in the nineteenth century is significant, since this became one of the most popular rationales for integrating YMCAs in the 1920s.

THE HETEROSEXUALIZATION OF THE YMCA

Opposition to the integration of YMCAs began to break down in the 1910s, came under open attack after World War I, and was abandoned by the YMCA's national council in 1933. In the mid 1910s, YMCAs across the United States and Canada sponsored increasing numbers of mixed-sex activities. Some YMCA secretaries became quite aggressive in creating programs for women and girls. This represented a significant shift away from the YMCA's historical focus on single urban men. Before 1920, even when YMCAs were offering services to men who were presumably married, they never considered that allowance should be made for the participation of men's wives in the program.

Although women had been allowed access to some local YMCA activities or resources throughout the nineteenth century, never had the leaders of these YMCAs attempted to formulate a consistent philosophy to justify such inclusion. Often they were under pressure from the national leadership to discontinue such services and refer women to the YWCA as the appropriate vehicle of service to women. But after 1915, those favoring exclusion were on the defensive, and new philosophies of sex-integrated activities circulated among YMCAs engaging in "women's and girls' work." Usually these philosophies appealed to "changing relations between the sexes," the need to "treat the family as a unit," or "nature" and "normalcy." Debates about women's and girls' programming in the 1920s clearly reflected a familiarity with and concern about the implications of popularized Freudian theory.

The growing emphasis on gender-integrated YMCA programs reflected three concerns. YMCA leaders were concerned about the rise of dating and the increase in unsupervised leisure activities where young men and young women interacted with each other.[54] There was also anxiety about the women's movement, women's growing independence, and women's pursuit of careers outside the home. Finally, YMCA leaders were increasingly anxious about homosexuality, and fearful that a half century of gender-segregated activities might be turning out "abnormal" individuals whose "normal" sex impulses had been frustrated by a lack of appropriate outlets.

Hedley S. Dimock, a YMCA secretary who was an outspoken proponent of integration, implied that Victorian prudishness alone had been responsible for the policy of exclusion. He further argued that "there have been coeducational activities, for example, since boy first met girl, yet many of our youth-serving agencies today are built essentially on the principle of segregating the sexes."[55] By 1935, William H. Morgan, in his *Student Religion during Fifty Years*, could declare that "it is increasingly assumed that the development of wholesome personalities in the one sex requires comradeship with the other in more and more areas of experience."[56] The YMCA was not so much being integrated as it was being heterosexualized.[57]

Since the YWCA had been created and promoted under the rationale that the sexes needed separate organizations to meet their unique needs, the abandonment of that rationale by YMCA secretaries in the 1910s and 1920s provoked a crisis in the relationship between the YM and the YW. YMCA-YWCA relations in these years were revealing of the momentous cultural changes taking place. The growing emphasis on gender-integrated activities met resistance within the YMCA from men who embraced a more traditional understanding of the YMCA movement and more traditional views of gender and sexuality. It also met resistance from the YWCA, which saw the growth of mixed programming as an encroachment on their constituency, an attempt to undermine their autonomy, and a calculated move to subvert their role in the woman movement. On the other side, YMCA leaders began to express suspicion of the YWCA, characterizing it as an organization subversive of the family and accusing it of harboring lesbians.

Although some YMCA leaders claimed that the increase in mixed activities under YMCA auspices promoted women's equality, YWCA leaders saw it promoting the opposite. While a majority of YMCA leaders in the 1920s clearly favored mixed programming, an even greater majority of YWCA leaders were vehemently opposed to it. YWCA protests throughout the 1920s against unilateral moves on the part of YMCA leaders to integrate women into the YM resulted in a series of consultations, conferences, summits, and studies, all to no avail.[58] Despite impassioned pleas from YWCA leaders, in 1933 the YMCA changed its constitution to grant full membership rights to women, laying the basis for a full-scale entry into the field of women's and girls' work. In 1931, as the YMCA was still contemplating these constitutional changes, Emma Bailey Speer, president of the YWCA's National Board wrote an open letter to Francis Harmon, president of the YMCA's National Council:

> Our committee voted that I should write to you expressing our surprise and deep concern that a responsible group of your members should contemplate an action

that would tend toward the establishment of an organization competitive to our own. We particularly regret this at a time when so much advance has been made toward a more truly cooperative relationship between the two organizations in their joint field of work with young people.[59]

YWCA efforts at cooperation with the YMCA had been undertaken partly to forestall such a constitutional change.

Not only were YWCA leaders concerned about competition with the YM, but experience had taught them that women and girls were treated as second-class citizens in the YMCA. They were ambivalent about cooperation because of sexist attitudes on the part of YMCA leaders. A statement typical of many made by YWCA leaders throughout the decade of the 1920s was presented in a report, "Relationships with the Young Men's Christian Association," published in the 1928 Biennial Report of the National Board of the YWCA. The report complained about refusal on the part of YMCAs to acknowledge the needs of women and girls to be as important as the needs of men and boys. It cited instances in which YWCA work had been hampered because the YMCA had successfully monopolized community resources in its fund-drives. It expressed concerns about a racially segregated YMCA trying to impose its policies on the YWCA in cooperative endeavors that involved black women and girls. Finally, it underlined that "a Young Women's Christian Association is *not a program for women*. It is an *organization of women*." No YMCA efforts on behalf of women, no matter how well intended, could offer women the same opportunities for leadership, or the same ability to advance the woman movement as the YWCA. The YWCA noted the existence among YMCA secretaries of an attitude that "the Young Women's Christian Association is objectionably feministic, subversive of the best interest of women and of the family." They also cited accusations of lesbianism.[60] One YWCA secretary wrote, "There is an undercurrent of real antagonism to women's organizations, to women's independent action, and a distrust of their dependability and permanence in united action."[61]

Between about 1925 and 1930, the YMCA and YWCA conducted a number of studies and surveys to determine to what extent these and similar accusations were true.[62] One such study, conducted by a committee jointly appointed by the YMCA and the YWCA, documented forty-six case studies of YMCA-YWCA relationships. Although there were a few exceptional cases of exemplary cooperation, most of the cases involved friction, suspicions, and conflicts, most often provoked by the YMCA. The Monmouth, New Jersey, YMCA not only accused the YWCA of being irreligious because it allowed dancing, cards, and movies, but also refused to cooperate with a YWCA liaison who had been sent to work with them. The Philadelphia

YMCA began women's and girls' work over the opposition of the YWCA on "the theory of treating the family as a unit." The Philadelphia case was particularly revealing, since its mixed work had been held up as a model in the pages of *Association Men* since 1923, and Walter Wood fancied himself a progressive in the area of women's rights.[63] The general secretary of the Athens, Georgia, YMCA expelled YWCA girls from the YMCA campgrounds when YWCA leaders complained that they were not being allowed equal access to the facilities. He then refused all attempts at communication from the YW, "contend[ing that the] community [was] unwilling to support two organizations" and "that men's and women's work should be done together today." "Open warfare" was reported between the YMCA state secretary in Kentucky and his YWCA counterpart. The Hartford County, Connecticut, YMCA held the "theory that men's and women's work should be done together today," but it was "mostly [a] men's program; women prepared food." Although the YWCA complained that women received inadequate programming, the YM was "satisfied." Not only did YWCAs not provoke conflicts with the YMCAs, but there were even documented cases of YWCAs deferring to YMCAs when there was a clear conflict of jurisdiction. The Springfield, Tecumseh District, Ohio, YWCA was poised to enter boys' work, but refused to, "because there is a city Y.M.C.A." As of the writing of the case study, they were still "waiting for the Springfield Y.M.C.A. . . . to take some action." Another more comprehensive study conducted in 1930 to determine whether YMCA attitudes toward YWCA secretaries posed a problem, found "the existence of opinions on the part of General Secretaries of the Associations, which may militate against successful cooperative activity." It found "no guarantee of willingness to work with women on a genuinely cooperative basis."[64]

From within the YMCA, an ever more beleaguered minority of secretaries resisted integration on the grounds that it would undermine the essential, historic mission of the YMCA. One of the more outspoken opponents of women's and girls' work, Paul Super, argued that young men were "the most important element for good or evil in a community," and thus needed special attention. They were "more exposed to evil influences than any other class," but were less successfully reached by the church than young women. Finally, he was firmly convinced that young men could most successfully be reached only by their peers. The presence of women in the organization would make it more difficult to win their trust.[65] Many of Super's argument's against mixed work were echoed by a minority of YMCA secretaries in various surveys. Many YMCA secretaries simply believed that young men and young women were different; they had different needs, experiences, and social roles, and they needed different programs.[66] Super's defense of gender-segregated work, made two years after the Philadelphia YMCA had embarked on a major experiment with mixed work, essentially recapitulated the same arguments that had been offered in defense of segregated work throughout the nineteenth century. Super's assertion that men simply wouldn't be attracted to an organization that had women was out of step with the times. Many of his peers were beginning to assert that young men couldn't—or shouldn't—be attracted to an organization *without* women.

Jay A. Urice, another opponent of women's and girls' work, was less chauvinistic than Super and more sensitive to the concerns of the YWCA. As the conflict between the YMCA and the YWCA came to a boil, Urice regularly stayed in touch with YWCA leaders, and was a channel for many of their concerns in YMCA circles.[67] "Y.M.C.A. men speak with considerable confidence," he wrote a YMCA colleague, "about policies the merits of which are flatly denied by the Y.W.C.A. and other persons. . . . Any one who speaks dogmatically regarding 'joint work,' 'work by Y.M.C.A. for women and girls,' 'what communities demand,' etc. is on most uncertain ground." Urice also expressed anguish that action of the YMCA "seriously threatens the very existence of the Y.W.C.A." Urice accused YMCA men of pursuing "the welfare of women and girls" in a way that would destroy women's autonomy, without regard "for the welfare of the organization which has developed among women and girls themselves." But Urice had his own reasons for resisting integration. "Most of the present experiments," Urice confided to a colleague in 1928, "imply an abandonment of the 'movement' characteristic of our organization. Few local boards have looked at the matter squarely when they have commenced to sell privileges to women." He feared that doing work for women, rather than doing work of and for men, was continuing the process, accelerated during the YMCA's World War I service, of turning the YMCA into a dispenser of social services rather than a Christian men's movement. Despite Urice's honestly expressed profeminist sentiments, like Super he also worried about "a distinct 'feminization' of the Association profession."[68] What was at stake for the defenders of the old order was the loss of an ethos of male solidarity, a "movement" in the early YMCA sense. The importance of preserving the Association as a movement was crumbling under the pressure to heterosocialize, to turn Y social events into a dating service, to shuffle men into marriage rather than to "build character."

But opposition from within and without the YMCA could not overcome the determination of a growing majority of YMCA secretaries who saw mixed work and YMCA work for women and girls as inevitable. One secretary wrote Jay Urice comparing separatists to a couple of tandem motorcycles about to be run over by the "Mack truck" of heterosocialization on the highway of progress.[69] One way to appease the integrationists was through the promotion of joint endeavors of the YMCA and the YWCA, which would supposedly give young men and young women the opportunity to interact socially and yet allow the YWCA to maintain its organizational integrity. But these attempts were undercut by the tendency of YMCA secretaries to simply commence their own mixed work without consulting the YWCA. The 1930 reconnaissance study of YMCA-YWCA relations conducted by Herbert Shenton, an outside researcher from Princeton University, surveyed 1,035 YMCAs and 543 YWCAs across the United States, and found that about 60 percent of YMCAs had already—without the authorization of the YMCA's National Council, and against the stated wishes of the YWCA—begun doing work for women and girls. This was occurring in spite of the fact that 70 percent of YWCAs were already attempting to cooperate with YMCAs in joint endeavors.[70]

The most commonly cited YMCA argument in favor of integration suggested that it was necessary from the viewpoint of economic efficiency. YWCAs were generally smaller, had fewer financial resources, enjoyed less community support, and were not organized in as many locales as the YMCA. Some YM secretaries conceded that the theoretical ideal would be for YWCAs to provide women's and girls' programming. But in situations where they were unable, couldn't YMCAs, with their ample resources, more efficiently provide those services until the YWCA could get organized? Actually, this was one of the few circumstances in which YWCA secretaries generally acquiesced in YMCA work for women and girls. But in practice, once YMCA women's and girls' work had been organized, it became more difficult for the YWCA to break into the field. What was really needed in order for YWCAs to get organized was a base of community financial support, and the eagerness with which YMCAs entered the field of women's and girls' work preempted YWCA efforts to establish that base. What the YWCA actually preferred, if YMCAs were so eager to promote women's and girls' work, was assistance in setting up an independent base of community support. But many YMCA secretaries were engaging in mixed work on the theory that most communities were unwilling to support more than one young people's Christian association, and had no intention of sharing the field with the YWCA then or ever. Attempts at resource-sharing (in which, for instance, a YWCA used YMCA gymnasium equipment) frequently caused more problems than it solved, with conflicts breaking out over access, and the usual YMCA assertion that boys and men should have priority. The reconnaissance study, according to Shenton, "disclosed no serious significant advantages achieved by those [YM] associations which were operating with and for women." He saw no evidence that community resources were being used more efficiently through efforts at mixed work or YMCA work for women and girls. On the other hand, it was resulting in the "preemption or diversion of financial resources otherwise available for the Y.W.C.A."[71]

In evaluating the claims of YMCA secretaries that economic efficiency was the primary reason for integrating women, it is very instructive to compare the integration of African Americans into the YMCA with the integration of women. On paper, the YMCA integrated racially in 1946, but the decision to integrate was essentially made from the top down. It took decades to bring local associations into compliance with the national mandate. The integration of women, on the other hand, was a bottom-up movement; a majority of local associations were already including women by the time the National Council officially ratified it in 1933. While claims of economic efficiency featured prominently as an excuse to integrate women into YMCA programming over the protests of the YWCA, similar concerns did not move YMCA leaders with regard to issues of race, even after black leaders began demanding inclusion in the 1940s. Indeed, in the 1930s while YMCAs were expanding women's and girls' programming for whites, already underfunded and ill-equipped African American programming was in danger of being cut owing to funding considerations resulting from the depression. No white YMCA leaders were suggesting that blacks' needs would be better met by using buildings and equipment of white associations.[72] The 1930 reconnaissance study, as well as widely documented YWCA experiences, suggested that YMCA secretaries' claims about more efficient use of resources were either disingenuous or ill founded. And even if arguments about efficiency were honestly advanced, why did they seem compelling now, in the 1920s, when they had been largely rejected throughout the nineteenth century, an era when the disparity of resources between YM and YW had been even greater? When pressed, most YMCA secretaries agreed that arguments about efficiency were not enough. There had to be compelling spiritual, moral, scientific, or sociological justifications to permit such a momentous transformation of YMCA programming.

By the mid-1910s YMCA secretaries were producing such justifications. Much of the "scientific" basis for the new rationale was coming from the YMCA's physical department, and the spiritual and moral basis from its purity and sex education work. This new philosophy had the enormous advantage (from a YMCA point of view) of appealing to very traditional YMCA concerns and using YMCA rhetoric that had become widely accepted since the 1880s: "ministering to the 'whole' man," "meeting young men's needs in mind, body, and spirit." But it also called into being a new rhetoric, a rhetoric that sounds eerily familiar today in the wake of the Moral Majority of the 1970s and the Christian Coalitions of the 1980s and 1990s, namely, "family values." In the 1920s family values rhetoric was more self-confident, less shrill than in the 1990s. The YMCA's family values agenda had three major components: (1) expanding supervision of youth social interactions and developing guidelines for dating; (2) promoting marriage; and (3) combating homosexuality.[73]

Homosexuality was a particularly sensitive issue. Many YMCA secretaries were becoming uneasy about the Association's gender-segregated basis, believing that past organizational practice had actually been guilty of promoting homosexuality. Concern about homosexuality came up in position statements regarding the need for mixed work as well as in surveys of YMCA secretaries who were asked to discuss their feelings about including women and girls in the organization. A YWCA report noted that not only were YMCA secretaries accusing the YWCA of attracting lesbians, they were also convinced that the YMCA was attracting "abnormal types."[74] A 1930 YMCA report, "Activities That Unite Young Men and Young Women," warned that "one of the natural drives in the young man 18 to 24 is his relationship to the opposite sex. . . . *Too much activity within his own group is quite abnormal and may lead to homo-sexual tendencies.*" The report expressed the desire to provide young men with a more "normal experience."[75] In surveys of YMCA secretaries' opinions about the need for mixed work, satisfying "the natural impulse of young men," promoting "social normalcy," and concern about the "unwholesomeness" of keeping young men and young women "completely separate" featured prominently. In 1931 one YMCA secretary demanded that the YMCA "should provide opportunities" to develop "a wholesome hetero-sexuality" through "happy relationships with the opposite sex."[76] The terms "natural" or "normal" appear to have been code words warning against homosexuality, and they were invoked repeatedly in the justification of gender-integrated work.[77] Although such widespread and open criticism of the YMCA by its own secretaries on the grounds that gender-segregation was promoting homosexuality did not come to the surface until the early 1930s, YMCA secretaries had been exposed to sex education ideas since at least 1905 which reinforced that view. Concern about homosexuality was not a new idea in the YMCA of the late twenties and early thirties. It had been circulating for almost two decades, and was likely responsible—at least in part—for the groundswell of unauthorized mixed work that secretaries had been embarking on for years.

Much of the imagery used by YMCA secretaries to justify the inclusion of women reflected exposure to popularized Freudian psychology. The movement to integrate YMCA programming was usually compared to an unstoppable force, or a raging flood, which could not be dammed but could be harnessed to "run our machinery." One secretary wondered "if they [the

YWCA] wouldn't get further if they would stop trying to dam the Y.M.C.A."
Instead, they should find a way to absorb "this great store of energy."[78] One
secretary wrote, "Burlesque shows, cheap movies, and the like exist because
they answer a fundamental need in certain folks' natures. We engage in a lot
of waste[d] energy when we attempt to reform the show."[79]

Historians have noted the rising emphasis in American society after
World War I on women's role as housewife and mother and on the heterosexual relationship. The "sexual revolution" of the 1920s had the effect of
putting greater pressure on women and men to interact socially as well as
sexually, and put more emphasis on heterosexual marriage as the means
to lifelong happiness.[80] The YMCA played a role in promoting a marriage-
oriented vision of American society, and in popularizing Freudian views
of sexuality and concern about homosexuality. The obsession of YMCA
secretaries in the 1920s with marriage was most evident when the actual
content of YMCA mixed work was observed. One YMCA report conceded
with a certain amount of embarrassment that "We only get young men and
young women together when we want to talk about their personal relationships."[81] Virtually all YMCA mixed work could be accounted for in
two categories: social events whose sole purpose was to allow supervised
mingling, a sort of group dating service; and sex education or marriage
preparation classes. The noble sentiments expressed by a few secretaries
that mixed work should prepare young men and young women to cooperate
in a world where women were playing a larger public role[82] went by the
wayside in favor of socializing and preparation for family life.

After World War I, economic prosperity and the mass production of the
automobile were creating social circumstances in which young people could
interact with each other free of parental supervision, and were paving the
way for a sexual revolution. Clearly, a major motivation for mixed work was
analogous to the nineteenth-century YMCA's decision to acquire gymnasiums and billiard rooms. It was better to provide young men with a supervised outlet for natural desires, than to lose all control over them when they
went elsewhere in search of pleasure.

But it was no doubt also a relief to YMCA leaders to consider that mixed
programming would no longer leave the Association vulnerable to accusations that it was producing abnormal individuals. The drive to bring
women into the organization was a logical concomitant to the decline of the
nineteenth-century culture of Christian manhood and intense friendship.
Sex education had increased anxieties about same-sex relations and made
homophobia a force in the organization. The intensity that had once characterized male relationships was now suspect, and leaders began to raise
warnings about men's relationships with each other. But in order to alleviate

fears about the health of the organization, it was necessary to address male-female relations as well. Since sex education programming was a major component of YMCA mixed work, and since most YMCA sex education included warnings against the dangers of "abnormal" friendships between members of the same sex, the fact that young men and young women were being herded together in mixed groups to receive such warnings suggests that the YMCA was interested in more than just "providing an appropriate channel" for presumably preexistent heterosexual desire. They were actively promoting heterosexuality.[83] In 1932, Percy Williams of the Toledo, Ohio, YMCA could proudly and unselfconsciously report that their mixed programming "has been very effective in . . . bringing about happy relationships."[84]

chapter 6

GETTING PHYSICAL

With a Y.M.C.A. building the young men of Jonesboro will be protected from many temptations, and many a boy who would otherwise go astray may grow into a useful citizen.
—*Jonesboro (Arkansas) Evening Sun*, April 9, 1906

In the 1880s and 1890s, the YMCA committed itself to a building/gymnasium-centered program. YMCAs that owned their own buildings before the 1880s were a rarity. Given that the Bible study, prayer, and self-help that were the staple of early YMCA programming required only the simplest of accommodations, and given the limited membership and financial means of early YMCAs, it shouldn't be surprising that buildings were considered something of a luxury through the 1870s. But after the 1880s, with the shift in emphasis to physical work, the YMCA building, specially designed to promote the YMCA's fourfold work and the moral uplift of young men, came to be considered essential. The new buildings provided public space where men related to one another primarily on a physical level, and could even relate to each other sexually. Public, urban spaces where men could meet provided the opportunity for male-male sexual relationships, but the new stress on physicality, masculine strength, and male beauty that evolved in the YMCA's physical culture actually encouraged the sexualization of men's relationships.

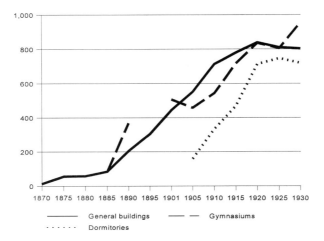

9. YMCA buildings, 1870–1930, United States and Canada. General building statistics are unavailable before 1870 and after 1930. Statistics on gymnasiums are available only from 1885 (except for 1895) and were no longer recorded after 1930. Dormitory statistics were available only between 1905 and 1930. After 1930, YMCA yearbooks summarized physical plant holdings in dollar value of property only, not in numbers of buildings.

The YMCA entry into physical work and building-centered programming set the stage for the lively homosexual cruising scene that evolved there and is associated with the YMCA to this day. Even as sex education and sex hygiene were increasing anxiety about homosexuality in the YMCA, the emphasis on physical work ironically set the stage for the flourishing of a sexual underworld on YMCA premises.

A SOCIAL HISTORY OF THE YMCA BUILDING

In the twentieth century, the YMCA had come to be associated with a particular kind of building. This had not always been true. The building-centered view of the YMCA was actively promoted through YMCA building campaigns of the 1870s and 1880s. It was only after 1885 that YMCA building construction really took off (see fig. 9). C. Howard Hopkins has described the rise of a "building-oriented" YMCA, as contrasted with a "program-oriented" or "community-oriented" YMCA. The shift to a building-oriented program between 1870 and 1890 had numerous implications for the YMCA as a whole. It required a solid commitment to the fourfold conception of YMCA work. It made vast fund-raising efforts a permanent feature of YMCA work, in order to pay for the buildings and raise the salaries for permanent building staff. The existence of permanent overhead put pressure on YMCAs to "sell" membership privileges to a broader constituency. But last, and most significant for the purposes of this study, the fact that YMCA buildings were physically oriented, male-only spaces, easily accessible, largely free of supervision, and safe from police surveillance made them an ideal setting for same-sex sexual activity.

YMCA leaders first argued that buildings were essential to their mission of Christian character-building in the 1860s. They believed that young men in the city were naturally attracted to certain pleasures and amusements in settings that exposed them to morally deleterious influences. The proposed solution was to offer the same pleasures and amusements in a properly supervised, morally uplifting environment. Men might initially be attracted to the pleasure, but gradually could be drawn to higher purposes and converted to evangelical Christianity. In order to do this, the YMCA needed to create urban meeting spaces that were controlled exclusively by the YMCA and were specifically designed to promote moral uplift. At least one historian has referred to the YMCA's building philosophy as "environmental evangelism," the belief that physical surroundings literally shaped morality and character for better or for worse.[1] In *The Association Building*, Louis E. Jallade, one of the proponents of a "YMCA architecture," called the YMCA building "an intricate instrument for the improvement of young men."[2] YMCA buildings would shape young men's character in two ways. The buildings were to be new, clean, well-lit, spacious, and comfortable, and would thus help inculcate a spirit of cleanliness, responsibility, honesty, and well-being in the men who inhabited them.[3] Second, the buildings would be designed to facilitate supervision from centralized locations, to insure that men's behavior was beyond reproach at least during the time they spent on YMCA premises.

Supervision was the primary concern of YMCA leaders from the beginning. The earliest definitive instructions regarding YMCA architecture were published in 1888 and again in 1891. The International Committee advised local associations to commission buildings with a single reception room that was to "be the initial or focal apartment, by which all enter, from which the various rooms or departments are all reached, and through which every one must again pass in retiring." This would bring the building "under the supervision of the officer or committee in charge; a very important matter in connection with control." It was believed that centralized control of the entry would assist the chief officer in "recognition of strangers, and personal contact with members and others frequenting the rooms."[4] Similar advice was echoed in almost all subsequent YMCA architectural advice literature.[5] In later years, the concern about supervision was refined. In recognition of staffing problems, YMCAs were encouraged to organize "the units so as to secure the smallest number of points at which constant supervision is necessary." Concern that excessive supervision was detracting from the intimate environment that YMCAs sought to achieve was expressed in advice that "the attendants should not have the appearance of policemen who are there to maintain order. If supervision over the entrance lobby is exaggerated, it will kill the sociability spirit [sic] that should be maintained if the work of the Association is to be conducted efficiently."[6] In some sense, this concern about supervision expressed in 1919 was analogous to the dilemma over how much friendliness and intimacy were appropriate or needed in the relationship between the YMCA secretary and the young men. The spontaneous friendship and intimacy that were needed to achieve the mission of the organization might be killed by excessive supervision, yet there was fear of the consequences of such intimacy if left unsupervised.

There is evidence that an awareness of the existence of homosexual cruising was having an increasing impact on concern about supervision, especially after 1912. In 1912, a major homosexual scandal at the Portland, Oregon, YMCA implicating some fifty men and youth undoubtedly drew the attention of YMCA leaders across the country to the problem of supervision. Although I will discuss this scandal at length in the following chapter, for the moment it is enough to note that in its aftermath YMCA leaders were expressing special concern about supervision in parts of YMCA buildings where cruising was most common. In a 1913 report on YMCA dormitories, Dexter A. Rau noted that "every Association that has a dormitory" had to deal with the problem of "immorality." Specifically noting the outbreak of "sex perversion" that had been uncovered at Portland and "broadcast over the country," Rau concluded that "eternal vigilance is necessary."[7] While 1891 advice regarding YMCA buildings suggested that toilets "should be conveniently placed, but not in too public a position," 1913 advice completely reversed this injunction by suggesting that the "public toilet . . . must be in a direct line with some point of supervision" in the main lobby.[8] By 1923 a lecture on YMCA architecture raised concern about "lingering in the shower room" and the fact that "there can be no central supervision as it is not arranged in a proper manner." The lecture called for more supervision not only of showers but locker rooms as well.[9]

Despite the high level of concern about supervision, YMCAs largely failed to achieve the kind of control they envisioned in their advice manuals. They failed for a number of reasons. First was that YMCA dormitories and gymnasiums—the two main sites of cruising—were deliberately separated from the main buildings, defeating the purpose of centralized supervision. Secondly, it was assumed that supervision of the main entrance would be adequate, since it was believed that "troublemakers" could be screened out by visual inspection. Probably out of concern for modesty, YMCAs made specific provisions to protect young men's privacy in locker rooms, shower rooms, bathrooms, and dormitories. It was impossible to supervise *and* offer privacy, and YMCAs believed that sorting out the "bad" types at the entrance would provide sufficient control. As I will demonstrate at greater length in the following chapter, however, homosexual activity was engaged in by men who belonged to the YMCA's main constituency— respectable working- and middle-class men from Protestant backgrounds. The YMCA's main supervision strategy was thus inadequate to control cruising. Finally, throughout the most active years of the YMCA building movement—roughly from 1870 to 1920—YMCAs suffered from chronic staff shortages. These staff shortages would be exacerbated in the war years by a tremendous influx of soldiers and military support personnel seeking to use YMCA physical facilities. They were further exacerbated in the interwar years by the depression, since YMCAs generally sought to cut expenses by cutting staff.[10] Thus, even the minimal supervision that YMCAs proposed could not often be implemented for lack of personnel.

These staff shortages were most acute in areas where YMCA homosexual cruising was most common—in the gymnasiums and dormitories. By 1890, after YMCA gymnasium building and physical education had taken off, the ratio of physical directors to gymnasiums was less than one to three. In startling contrast, the ratio of YMCA employees to physical plant for all other programming was four to one. The ratio of physical directors to gyms had improved somewhat by the turn of the century, though from 1900 to 1930 it fluctuated between about 1:2 and 2:3. After 1915, the physical programs drew ever larger numbers of men until they had all but dwarfed the religious and educational programs. In 1915, YMCAs reported a total of 477,731 young men involved in YMCA physical work, and 194,402 men in YMCA dormitories, compared to 152,160 men enrolled in Bible classes and 81,920 men enrolled in other educational programs. Roughly three times as many men were involved in YMCA physical education as were involved in YMCA Bible study. By 1935 that ratio had risen to 10:1, and by 1940 to more than 20:1. The hiring of YMCA physical directors did not, however, keep pace with this expansion of physical program. Throughout the entire period under study, physical directors consisted of between 10 and 15 percent of the YMCA's personnel.[11] In summary, while most YMCA activities—religious, educational, and social—were highly structured and well supervised, the physical program, which was attracting the bulk of YMCA members by the 1910s, was highly unstructured and unsupervised—sometimes even chaotic—throughout the entire period.

The problem of supervision and control in the YMCA dormitory was even more acute and, in the minds of YMCA secretaries, posed a much

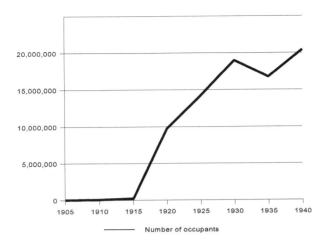

10. YMCA dorm residents, 1905–1940, United States and Canada.

greater problem. Even though YMCA dormitories had been in existence since 1886, as late as 1905 fewer than 9 percent of all associations in North America had acquired residences. But in the 1910s, YMCA dormitory services took off. Between 1915 and 1920, YMCA dorm residents grew in number from the tens of thousands to the millions (see fig. 10). By the mid-1920s, YMCA leaders generally agreed that in order to cope with the dormitory problem adequately, it would be necessary to employ building secretaries. But in actuality, dormitories were usually overseen by the general secretary, assisted by a handful of help staff—lobby clerks and janitors. The general secretary was usually too preoccupied with other aspects of YMCA administration and program to give the dorms more than the most superficial attention, and help staff were not always chosen for their understanding of or commitment to YMCA values. The situation faced by YMCA leaders in the dorms was similar to that faced in the gymnasiums: YMCA dorms had become the gathering place for large numbers of urban young men whose activities on YMCA premises were largely unstructured and unsupervised.[12]

YMCA leaders had a very specific idea of the place YMCA buildings should have in the urban landscape. In 1891, the International Committee advised that "in a large city a location is generally sought near some center of travel. Several associations, in determining the sites for their buildings, have ascertained by actual count the spot in the city passed by the largest number of young men in a given time, and have purchased lots at that point."[13] During the early years of the YMCA building movement, associations sought buildings in the downtown business districts. In later years, they sought to position themselves on the border between up- and downtown, so as to be conveniently located for men who were traveling between residences and their places of work.[14] In any event, ideally, YMCA buildings were placed in the locations of greatest access for young men. This was crucial in order to achieve the YMCA's evangelistic goals. But it also, ironically, made YMCAs ideal locations for homosexual cruising. Access along the routes of greatest circulation, combined with large facilities where physical contact between men was easy, and where relatively little supervision was provided, was the perfect formula. Added to this was the fact that unlike other public spaces where cruising occurred, YMCAs were virtually free of police harassment because of their Christian reputation.[15] YMCAs were one of the safest spaces for men to connect sexually.

MEN EXAMINING MEN

The YMCA's shift toward a building-oriented and physical-oriented program did more, however, than merely provide the physical setting for same-sex sexual liaisons. It created a culture that facilitated and shaped same-sex sexual desire. The YMCA's physical program elevated public discussions of the physical in general, and men's bodies in particular. Increasingly, a man's physical appearance was consciously factored into all of his relationships. Furthermore, through the integration of sex hygiene into the physical program, it intensified the association between the body and sexuality, and helped spread awareness of homosexuality as a possible expression of desire. Though homosexuality was stigmatized, physical culture generally gave men permission to focus their attention on other men's bodies. YMCA physical culture granted such permission in a Christian setting.

YMCA physical work provided a setting in which it was impossible for men not to notice each other's physiques. L. L. Doggett noted in his history of the Boston YMCA that in early physical work, the use of "flesh-colored tights" by YMCA physical instructors was common, though sometimes controversial because of the degree to which they simulated nudity.[16] Fitness talks frequently used live models. L. L. Doggett described YMCA bodybuilding exhibitions using live models that attracted hundreds of young men.[17] A typical description of such bodybuilding exhibitions described a dumbbell drill performed by "fifty men in dark full tights and sleeveless jerseys, [accompanied by] beautiful rhythmical music and the rapid vigorous drill [that was] fully appreciated by the audience."[18] YMCA leaders were proud of the physique art that they created and disseminated. Doggett, in his history of the training school, believed that the YMCA had made a unique contribution to the world of art in the "statuesque tableaux" produced by YMCA physique artist Leslie Judd "in connection with the 'gym' team exhibitions."[19] The contemplation of male anatomy—both in pictures and in living models—was promoted not only in YMCA gyms across the country but in the Springfield Training School, where physical directors were formed. The second Springfield Training School catalogue (1886–1887), which had the first physical program, noted that "Anatomy will be studied particularly in relation to the living model. . . . The students will have access to a fine library of works on physical culture," works that included abundant images of the male physique.[20]

YMCA physical directors were attracted to their work partly because of their own interest in the contemplation of male beauty. Robert J. Roberts, acknowledged by the YMCA as one of the founders of its physical work, declared that his physical work philosophy was built on three principles: "unity, symmetry, and beauty."[21] This philosophy legitimized male contemplation of masculine beauty directly, without even having to mediate it with the rationalization of the need to strive for physical health. According to an interview with his daughter, Luther Gulick was also drawn to physical work because "the love of the beautiful" was a "controlling factor" in his life. Gulick encouraged the contemplation of male physical beauty by stressing the importance of anatomy in physical education and advocating the use of photography to study body movement.[22]

The artistic display of the male physique was apparently an effective way of promoting YMCA physical work from the beginning. Robert J. Roberts publicly displayed his own body to promote YMCA physical work (fig. 3). A popular YMCA advertisement featured "Robert J. Roberts' back."[23] His article "The Home Dumb Bell Drill" was illustrated with images of a muscular Roberts stripped down to tight briefs demonstrating the various physical drills. In his biography of Robert J. Roberts, Luther Gulick even indirectly invited men to see if they "measured up" by offering Roberts's measurements: "Height, five feet five inches; weight, 145 pounds; chest, forty-three inches; waist, thirty-two inches; biceps, fifteen inches; thigh, twenty-three inches; calf, fourteen and one half inches. He was a favorite model with the artist of those days, especially so with the great artist Rimmer."[24] According to L. L. Doggett, not only did Roberts receive "good remuneration" for his work as an artistic model because of his "fine physique," but he actually developed his light exercise program in order to perfect his physique for his work as a model.

That men were noticing each other's bodies was evidenced in comments and comparisons that were appearing in YMCA literature (fig. 11). In an article on physical training in the YMCA, in a section subtitled "Why You Should Be Athletic," the author wrote,

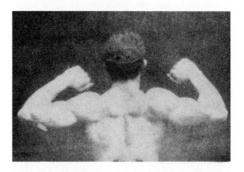

11. "Some Superbly Developed Association Men." Physique photos published in *Association Men* (March 1902): 236. The text accompanying these photos includes body measurements, and rhapsodizes about the "pleasant companionships" and "strong rivalries" occasioned by sport and physical exercise. It also warns against "the seamy side of athletics." Courtesy of the YMCA of the USA Archives, St. Paul, Minnesota.

All admire a deep chest, well developed arms, back, legs, or neck—if their owner is also erect of carriage. Slim arms, a small or flat chest, or a weak back, are *defects*—always seen and not pleasant to look at. . . . A man of well-developed body, neck and limbs, and of good carriage, always makes a favorable impression. If he adds to it a mind bred to steady, hard work in important matters, and has, as he is likely to have, an agreeable expression, he is still more attractive. If his character is also strong and high, and has stood the strain of many a fiery trial, he is apt to be of noble personal presence.[25]

The observation and contemplation of male beauty played a key role in Robert J. Roberts's formulation of a new philosophy of physical work, as his own widely published account indicates. Roberts described his impressions of physical work done in the most popular gymnasiums of Boston prior to the development of YMCA physical work: "I felt in my heart, even at the time, but did not care to express it, being so young, that Dr. Winship's [program] was too hard, for I noticed that all his most powerful members, while they had large, powerful muscles and fine-shaped bodies, had pale, white, sickly-looking faces, and I felt that the two should not go together."[26]

Young men were encouraged to focus new attention on the development of their muscles. In "The Home Dumb Bell Drill," Roberts gave young men practical advice about how to shape their muscles as well as their overall physical form:

If you wish to grow very strong and gain a showy muscular development, work hard, slow, and long, and put strong action into all parts of each exercise, as though you were using five-pound bells. . . . If your chest is *flat*, follow the hint that is given with the flip, and don't go beyond a vertical, and practice the front chest elevation an *extra* number of times. If your chest is narrow, pay much attention to the *faithful* practice of the side chest elevator and the vertical push. When the chest is flat and narrow, everything should be done to quickly increase the size of the chest, *practice deep breathing, indoors and out. . . . You have no excuse for not taking exercise when you know this drill. . . . If you have time to eat, you have time to exercise.*[27]

Association Men began to carry a regular column called "Muscle Questions," accompanied by a drawing of a classical nude statue. One issue reminded its readers that "a flabby muscle is not only a chasm between willing and doing but it may also be the defective link in an otherwise strong chain." The same article counseled against overdoing it, warning against the "haggard look frequently seen on the face of a professional strong man," but offered advice for ways to obtain the "healthiest and most enduring physique." The article reassured young men who were feeling inadequate about the size of their muscles that there was an optimal muscular development, one that was neither too flabby nor so overdeveloped that it limited dexterity.[28]

The presence of a physical program made it natural for YMCA leaders to focus on good physique as a qualification for leadership and as a dynamic of the organization's social life. L. W. Messer wrote to Fred S. Goodman regarding the qualifications of a potential secretarial candidate: "He has a good physique, an attractive face and manner, [and] is a fair gymnast."[29] R. C. Morse held up the German delegation at the Paris Conference of 1905 as an example of the beneficial effects of YMCA physical work in creating "virile . . . large, fine looking men."[30] Physical masculinity came to be seen as a foundation upon which men could relate fraternally. One secretary noted that fraternal intimacy "cannot be so well secured in any other manner" than through daily exercise.[31] John Brown, Jr., believed camping to be beneficial not only because it was physically invigorating, but also because it afforded "personal contact with virile men."[32] R. C. Cubbon wrote: "Beyond doubt THE attraction is the SOCIAL ATTRACTION. . . . All are seeking for helpful fellowships, and they can be found in great abundance *in the properly conducted physical department.*"[33] William Blaikie waxed lyrical about the possibilities that the YMCA's physical program offered young men to interact as friends: "What pleasant companionships they will effect, what strong rivalries, and how they will make the sky bluer, the grass greener and life sweeter and stronger from their very existence."[34]

By associating spiritual values with the building of the male physique, the YMCA adopted a stance that was not essentially different from the homosexual emancipation movement in Germany at roughly the same time period.[35] Early physical culture in America was actually imported from Germany, so the North American physical culture movement in fact had a demonstrably common influence.[36] The spiritualization of the male physique was compatible with a contemplation of its natural beauty. Through its philosophy of mind-body-spirit, the YMCA elevated bodybuilding to the level of a moral necessity. The YMCA made a moral duty out of gazing upon the athletic male figure, out of considering its goodness and necessity in God's scheme of things, and of desiring it for oneself. That the appropriation of an athletic body was promoted for all in a quasi-religious setting opened wide the gates. The YMCA was granting universal permission to young men to express more openly than ever before their homosexual desire.

The use of physical culture magazines as a form of male pornography consumed by men is beginning to be documented in the emerging discipline of sexuality studies. Modern gay pornography in fact evolved from early physique magazines, in some cases being produced by the same publishers.[37] One scholar has described how Bernarr McFadden, publisher of the magazine *Physical Culture,* faced obscenity trials in 1907 and after because of the sexually ambiguous nature of the photographs and stories carried in his magazine.[38] Yet a perusal of physique illustrations in *Physical*

Culture shows that they were no different from images commonly carried in *Association Men* and other YMCA publications. All of them featured photographs of nude or seminude men demonstrating various feats of physical skill or serving as models of an ideal male physique. In the *Physical Culture* obscenity trials, McFadden, himself briefly a YMCA physical work assistant at the 23rd Street YMCA in New York City,[39] defended himself by arguing that the photographs were necessary in order to show young men how to achieve good health and a balanced physique (fig. 12). This rationale for including photographs of virtually naked men was apparently acceptable to the editors of YMCA magazines as well. The YMCA was likely protected from similar harassment by its reputation as a Christian association, and by the assistance it occasionally offered police in the prosecution of obscenity laws. But the YMCA's Christian aims and reputation did not eliminate the erotic ambiguity posed by the use of male models and seminude photographs. Luther Gulick, for example, opposed the use of tights, which was common in YMCA gymnasiums and gymnastic exhibitions, because they were too revealing. He dismissed the argument that tights would less hinder certain kinds of physical activity by pointing out that nudity would hinder physical activity least of all.[40]

Another way in which male-male erotic interaction was intensified through YMCA physical work was through the spread of the examination room. Gulick saw the examination room interview between young man and physical director as central to the success of any physical program. Gulick advocated the use of the examination room to probe into men's "personal problems," particularly "sex problems."[41] The examination room could create an emotionally charged setting for the exchange of sexual knowledge. The physical director had privileged access to young men's erotic lives, and in turn offered them knowledge about sex to which they could have access in no other setting. The context in which sexual knowledge was exchanged had to intensify men's anxieties about their own bodies, and about the desire that drew them to the gymnasium. An image in the January 1922 issue of *Physical Training* illustrated the changes that had taken place in the first two decades of the twentieth century, heightening attention to the male body, submitting men's bodies to greater scrutiny by other men, and magnifying the authority of YMCA physical directors. The photo, from the Lincoln, Nebraska, YMCA showed sixteen men standing fully naked in a line, being examined individually by two fully clothed men (fig. 4). The caption held the Lincoln YMCA up as a model, and informed the reader that twenty to fifty men were examined in this manner every week.[42]

Despite—or rather, perhaps, because of—the growth of discourse about the masculine physique and the emergence of an economy of admiration and desire, there is evidence of a growing male discomfort with touch. My

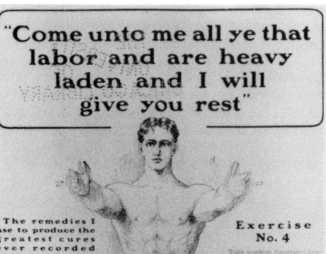

"Come unto me all ye that labor and are heavy laden and I will give you rest"

The remedies I use to produce the greatest cures ever recorded

The reader has doubtless noticed my advertisement from time to time and has wondered how I could produce the great results I claim. No doubt you believe I have some secret by which these remarkable cures are made. Perhaps you think that I have discovered some wonderful tonic or purgative. Perhaps you imagine that I hypnotize my patients, but, my dear reader, such is not the case. The cures that I perform are accomplished through the agency of **proper feeding, watering, ventilating, exercising and resting,** the most common sense method of cure on earth. I advise the patient so that he is able to add to his vitality and through this increased vitality purify and rebuild the body. In reality he makes his own cure, I simply acting as a director or trainer. The foods that I give consist of cereals, nuts, fruits, milk, eggs and the fresh vegetation which is pleasant to eat. My instructions regarding the ventilation of the body are original and have never been equaled. They teach the individual to ventilate his body as thoroughly as he would ventilate a room. My patients resort to me every week and I **give such instruction as their individual case requires,** reading and dictating all of my correspondence personally. The following exercise, which is one of the many I employ, will demonstrate the simplicity of the movements I teach, and yet these movements have even copied all over the world.

Copyright, 1903, by
JULIAN P. THOMAS, M.D.

SEE NEXT PAGE

Exercise No. 4

Take position illustrated herewith. Raise chest, breathe deeply and regularly, using the diaphragm. Extend arms forward even with shoulders, bend arms slightly at elbows, throwing in and out rapidly. (See Arrows.) Continue exercise ten seconds. Relax muscles thoroughly.

Results

The effect of this exercise is to concentrate the thought, strengthen the mind, free of all impurities from each cell, composing the muscles in the front upper chest and back of shoulders, thus making room for new food to develop them. It also tends to draw the spinal vertebræ in proper position, thus removing abnormal pressure from the spinal cord and nerves, soothing the nervous system, causing the person to become more erect and powerful. It materially strengthens the internal organs underlying the contracted muscles, drawing the organs into perfect position and causing their healthful action, thus making the outlines of the body perfect and the organization healthy. This exercise will have the foregoing results, PROVIDED THE INDIVIDUAL IS PROPERLY FED, WATERED, VENTILATED, EXERCISED AND RESTED.

12. Frontispiece of the July 1903 *Physical Culture.* Note the religious theme.

conclusions in this regard are only tentative and impressionistic, given the scarcity of evidence. While there is abundant evidence of the discomfort YMCA men felt about sex, there is almost no evidence about how they regarded physical touch. An intriguing comment of Robert Weidensall in his 1919 book *Men's Needs and Their Supply* gives a hint of growing discomfort with same-sex touch that did not exist in the days when George Williams shared a bed with Christopher Smith: "[Jesus Christ] indulged Peter in his forwardness of speech; *John in reclining upon his breast;* Thomas in his doubting expressions; and Judas Iscariot in his scrupulous regard for the treasury; but so tenderly and affectionately rebuked the flagrant abuse of the same, as to prevent repetitions of the offenses and gain for himself the esteem and love of the offenders."[43] Although there are scriptural accounts of Jesus rebuking Peter, Thomas, and Judas for the offenses named by Weidensall, nowhere does Jesus rebuke John for reclining on his breast.[44] The most plausible explanation for Weidensall's error is that in his mind it would be so difficult to imagine Jesus not rebuking same-sex physical intimacy that he subconsciously classed such behavior with other "sins" that Jesus did rebuke. Weidensall's false memory of Jesus's response to John, "the Disciple whom Jesus loved," is all the more interesting when compared to a biblical account in which Jesus rebuked a Pharisee for complaining about a prostitute who washed his feet with her tears and dried them with her hair.[45] The Gospels do not portray a Christ who was uncomfortable with intimate touch, although that is how Weidensall remembered it.

A study of about eighty-five YMCA physical work team photographs from 1900 through the 1950s offers a hint regarding men's attitudes toward touch. Although nowhere in the photos do men seem to allow themselves the same degree of physical intimacy that women could allow themselves, touch appears to have been more acceptable before 1920 than after. From a sample of about twenty-five team photographs taken before 1920, roughly half portrayed easy physical contact between members of the team. Men were portrayed with knees, shoulders, or elbows touching; leaning against or on top of each other; with a hand casually placed on another teammate's thigh; with a leg sprawled across another teammate's thigh or calf; and even with teammates holding hands. (See figs. 13 and 14.) In none of the sixty photos I examined from 1920 on was such easy physical contact between team members portrayed. Team members were lined up, with visible space separating them from each other, standing in an attentive, rigid pose (fig. 15). The exception to this rule was in photographs of boys' teams, which generally appeared to be less posed and more disorderly. (There were no boys' photos available before 1910.) In interesting contrast to these photographs of men's teams, the one photograph in the YMCA of the USA photo

13. Waterbury, Connecticut YMCA baseball team, 1900. Note the team mates in the center holding hands. Courtesy of the YMCA of the USA Archives, St. Paul, Minnesota.

14. YMCA International Training School, Springfield, Massachusetts, basketball team, 1906. Courtesy of the YMCA of the USA Archives, St. Paul, Minnesota.

15.Barton Heights Baptist Sunday School basketball team, 1926. Courtesy of the YMCA of the USA Archives, St. Paul, Minnesota.

archives portraying a women's basketball team (dated 1901) portrays two women leaning their heads on the shoulder of another, and two other women leaning their heads on the same woman's lap (fig. 16).

These photos do not reveal whether the unwillingness to show easy physical intimacy reflected the anxieties of the photographer, the YMCA physical director who arranged the photographing sessions, or the teammates themselves. At the very least, it is reasonable to assume that the photos were intended to represent the YMCA's physical program, to display in some sense the values embodied in that program. Earlier photos showing easy physical contact between teammates stressed the emotional bonds, the

16. Colorado Agricultural College (Fort Collins) women's basketball team, 1901–1902. Courtesy of the YMCA of the USA Archives, St. Paul, Minnesota.

friendship and interdependence that existed between teammates, while later photos portrayed individual physical prowess and independence. The change in team photographic representations certainly suggests a greater self-consciousness about how male bodies were being shown to the public. If the photos do indeed reflect a discomfort on the part of YMCA men to be shown physically touching other men, it is indirect evidence of the emergence of an economy of physical attraction and desire in YMCAs. It suggests that all physical touch between men—even that which occurred in a context of team spirit—was being sexualized to some extent. And if all physical touch was being sexualized, men's bodies in general were being sexualized, as was the gaze in which men looked at other men's bodies.

CONCLUSION

There is plenty of irony in the story of the YMCA's creation of a physical program. In order to shape men's physical and sexual development, the YMCA found it necessary to develop an enormous and costly physical plant, but also to create discourses and programs that focused on men's bodies. Both of these moves set the stage for the emergence of a flourishing same-sex sexual underground on YMCA premises. Men now had easy access to safe spaces where they could relate physically to one another, with minimal (if any) supervision. Furthermore, they were being shaped by programs that heightened attention to men's bodies, and even created opportunities for men to indirectly express desire for one another and indulge their interests in watching one another in a setting that was increasingly sexualized.

This is not to say that the YMCA necessarily failed to shape men's consciousness in regard to their bodies and their sexuality. But it was much easier to shape men's consciousness than it was to control their desire, or to police all of their behavior in greatly expanded and ever more accessible public facilities. The YMCA's physical program heightened (homo)erotic tension by elevating the muscular male physique as an object of desire and employing a new discourse about male sexuality, while simultaneously intensifying the requirement for sexual self-control. Intensified control over sexuality was a prerequisite for the underground sexual economy that flourished in YMCA gyms, dormitories, and locker rooms. Continuing discomfort with same-sex sexual expression today hinders rational understanding of the same-sex sexual underground that is still a flourishing aspect of male (both gay and straight) culture in America. It is to the evolution of that underground and its implications for the YMCA which I will now turn.

chapter 7

CRUISING

The profoundest sociological fact of modern times is that the civilized world is leaving the country to live in the city. . . . The race is becoming urban. . . . The rise of the city . . . is the modern fact which occasioned the Young Men's Christian Association.—L. L. Doggett, 1916

I often feel quite Roman [at the YMCA] amid all those naked men.
—Donald Vining, Sloane House YMCA employee, c. 1959

The YMCA is the biggest Christian whorehouse in the world.
—Sam Steward, gay author, 1992

The YMCA was born out of young men's impulse to find male fellowship in the city. At its best, the Association succeeded in providing a nurturing emotional community, concrete resources, and helpful social services to men in transition. But the YMCA also actively sought to shape the identities of young men: to make them evangelical Christians, to inculcate in them a middle-class entrepreneurial work ethic, and, increasingly after 1890, to make them heterosexual. In a large sense, it was the YMCA's determination to shape men's physical and sexual lives which created the social space necessary for same-sex cruising. Its sex education program reshaped young men's consciousness in such a way as to focus more explicit attention on sexual behavior and sexual identity. Yet, even as the YMCA abhorred same-sex erotic inclinations in its sex education work, it heightened same-sex erotic desire through the gymnasium. It provided safe social spaces that encouraged men to connect sexually, through its ambitious urban building projects. This combination—sex education, physical education, and protected physical facilities—provided the key elements necessary for a dramatic flourishing of same-sex cruising. By the mid-twentieth century in certain downtown areas of large cities like San Francisco, New York, Los Angeles, and Chicago, as gay activist and archivist Jim Kepner noted in an interview, the Y became "gay turf," "almost as much as the [gay] bars." [1]

The thriving of a homosexual cruising scene in YMCA gyms and swimming pools, locker and shower rooms, and dormitories was not merely an embarrassing or ironic symbol of the YMCA's failure to guide young men's sexuality along the desired path. It was also indicative of the tragic failure of the new sexual consciousness promoted by the YMCA after 1890 to integrate or make room for the intense emotions and desires that drew men together under YMCA auspices in the city in the first place. Expressions of same-sex closeness and emotional interdependence that had once been openly celebrated and institutionalized were slowly cast under a pall of homophobic anxiety. Meanwhile, men could connect sexually, as long as they observed certain conventions and did not draw attention to what they were doing. But they could not openly integrate their sexuality into a sense of love for or commitment to other men. At its best, the same-sex cruising scene at the YMCA could produce some form of surreptitious community among YMCA clientele who came to identify themselves as gay; at its worst it hosted a form of sexual activity that was profoundly alienating, and, if publicly exposed, could result in a public wrath that literally destroyed men's families, relationships, livelihood, and lives.

A social history of homosexual cruising at the YMCA has never been written because of cultural blind spots, denials, and silences around sexuality. At a more profound level, the enduring spirit/body split has made the Christian agenda of the YMCA difficult to reconcile with the sexual community in which leaders and employees as well as more casual YMCA users participated on its premises. But those who see same-sex cruising as incompatible with the "C" in the YMCA understand little about how cruising inhabits urban spaces, how it depends on ambiguous situations and relationships. This ambiguity made it possible for men who were motivated by traditional Christian doctrine and who, I believe, were sincerely concerned about the welfare of young men, also to be involved in the cruising scene.

In 1912, a major sex scandal involving fifty men erupted at the Portland,

Oregon, YMCA. The subsequent trials of the men involved in this scandal and the scandal itself showed how large and widespread the cruising scene was by the end of the first decade of the twentieth century, and suggested that same-sex cruising had become a well-established feature of YMCAs all across the country. But testimony in the trials and the immediate fallout of the scandal also showed how interwoven cruising was in the social fabric of the YMCA. This fallout included numerous men's flight to evade the law and the attempted suicide of an upstanding member and leader of the Portland YMCA. The scandal touched the best and the most committed. Many contemporary observers were stunned by the implications of the scandal, refusing to believe what they were reading in the papers or attempting to silence public discussion of it. But the events of the scandal make sense in light of the social picture that was emerging in the YMCA as the result of two decades of sex education. Men were progressively being denied the means to make sense of powerful yearnings, even as proliferating sex discourse drew ever more explicit attention to these yearnings. Feelings that could once be interpreted as "the bonds of Christ" or "Christian brotherhood" were increasingly suspect. The ambiguous sexual environment of the locker rooms and dormitories had become one of the few places where men could experiment and test what they were feeling. It may or may not have permitted them to integrate what they were feeling into a broader identity and social network. This depended on their ability to successfully internalize a gay identity and connect with the emerging gay communities that were forming side by side with YMCAs in American cities at the turn of the century.

SCANDALS

Edward Irenaeus Prime Stevenson, an American expatriate homosexual who wrote under the pen name Xavier Mayne, commented in 1908 on the tendency of the American press to avoid commenting specifically on homosexuality. He found reference to homosexual scandals much more common in the German, French, and Italian presses, and noted that "in fact [homosexual incidents] seem to be the only personal scandals shunned by American journals."[2] Nevertheless, YMCAs in America were occasionally troubled by public scandal from at least the 1880s. In 1887, for instance, the Chicago Association was forced to act when knowledge surfaced that a YMCA member, a lawyer and former Reconstruction official, had been "encouraging immoral practices among boys at the gym." The board of managers made a public statement castigating the lawyer and disavowing his actions, expelled him from membership, and sent a circular to other associations warning them against him.[3]

The YMCA was publicly implicated in a homosexual scandal in 1919, during the Newport, Rhode Island, U.S. Navy trials. Numerous men were indicted for crimes against nature as the result of a Navy decoy operation, and two of the individuals involved were YMCA ministers.[4] While it is not clear in the 1887 Chicago scandal whether or not the individuals involved were part of an emergent gay subculture, in the 1919 trials there was abundant evidence of a gay underworld in Newport with its own jargon and with unique sexual roles and identities that structured the ways in which men interacted with one another. Noteworthy is that in both scandals, the YMCA was implicated by the actions of members or leaders who came from the YMCA's most traditional constituency. Also noteworthy was the perception on the part of YMCA leaders of the threat posed by such scandals to the very fabric of the organization: loving relationships among men and youth.[5]

A third scandal from this era, by far the most devastating to the YMCA's reputation, occurred at the Portland, Oregon, YMCA in 1912. This scandal not only implicated members of the YMCA's traditional constituency—middle-class, male Protestants of "high moral standards"—but it vividly brought to public attention the existence of a lively cruising scene on YMCA premises, and the existence of a gay subculture not only in Portland but in virtually every major city in America. Finally, the scandal cast a sinister light on "Christian brotherhood" and on men's involvement in charitable, youth-oriented religious organizations generally, just as the Newport scandal would seven years later. The nature of the scandal and the community's response to it reveal much about the relationship of the YMCA to the broader community, but also about common attitudes toward sexuality and the way these attitudes were shifting in response to a decade of "social hygiene" activism.[6]

In November 1912, in response to concerns expressed by juvenile court officers, police raided the Portland YMCA and arrested more than twenty men on charges of "indecent and degenerate conduct." As the men confessed to juvenile court authorities, they implicated others, and police began a hunt to track down as many members of this "ring" of "perverts" as they could. Eventually over fifty men were indicted. Many of the men who were implicated fled town when they heard of the police warrants for their arrest. One was in such a hurry that he left his packed bags in his room. Some were apprehended in flight. At least one of the men implicated, a member of the YMCA, attempted suicide. Most of the men, when apprehended, were so devastated that they immediately confessed, perhaps hoping for leniency. A juvenile officer was quoted as remarking, "They are coming through like little children. Not a man has balked."[7]

It seems likely that the confessions came so easily because so many of the men arrested came from Portland's respectable Protestant middle class, upheld middle-class values, and were profoundly ashamed of themselves. They included clerks, doctors, lawyers, and businessmen, "some of the most prominent in the city." Many were residents in the YMCA dormitories, and some were members of the YMCA. During the initial questioning, the accused were described as "well dressed, above the average in apparent intelligence, and with no outward signs of degeneracy. It was not a collection of bums or sots or street scourings. It was an orderly, solemn, quite respectable appearing aggregation."[8] Those who were initially arrested implicated others. Because so many of those implicated had high standing in the community, and because the scandal implicated the YMCA, an organization with strong business and church ties, some public controversy was occasioned over the fact that so many had successfully eluded arrest. The editor-in-chief of the *Portland News,* Dana Sleeth, who frequently championed working-class causes around the country, accused other papers of allowing their reporters to circulate the names of the accused so as to give them a chance to slip away quietly. He later also accused police of doing the same, under pressure from influential business and church circles.

Because the majority of the accused were from the YMCA's traditional constituency—white, middle-class Protestant businessmen and religious leaders—the lines of the public controversy were drawn by class. Sleeth denounced a general reticence on the part of the respectable classes of Portland to give proper attention to the scandal. While he gave daily, front-page coverage to the scandal, other papers hesitated to publish anything at all, and when they did, they avoided the front page. Indignant appeals to "decency" were the flag words of a middle-class business and religious community on the defensive. Leaders from business, church, and moral reform circles denounced Sleeth for sensationalism, and for exposing the public to news too indecent to print. Ministers and moral reformers rode to the rescue of the YMCA, trying to neutralize the scandalous charges with the invocation of "its past record, and . . . its present character, without a doubt the greatest single moral force in this city." The Reverend Delmar H. Trimble, a Methodist minister, fulminated in a sermon that the *News* "has struck a blow against the greatest agency for moral uplift in the city—a blow that has been felt not only by every Protestant church member of Portland, but by all reputable lovers of decency and fair play."[9]

The YMCA responded to the scandal with a public relations campaign that combined scapegoating, denial, and public posturing. Men who were implicated in the scandal were expelled from the Association rooms and denied membership. The YMCA publicized its cooperation with police authorities to track down the culprits. Finally, it held a community meeting to which it invited all of its traditional supporters, leaders from business, church, and moral reform circles, to present its side of the story and to denounce the *Portland News*. In a public statement, the YMCA disavowed responsibility for the actions of a minority of its members, publicly denying that any "officer, director, or employee of the Association" was involved.[10] Beyond this it attempted to maintain a dignified silence, hoping that its supporters in the community would defend it and that its reputation would stand it in good stead.

Because the YMCA had friends in high places, the *News* was in fact frequently on the defensive, having to justify at every turn what it had printed. Sleeth even quoted the Bible in his defense: "He that giveth answer before he heareth, the same shall be folly and shame to him," and "Poverty and shame shall be to him that refuseth correction." Sleeth claimed that YMCA officials were threatening to run the *News* out of business. Despite public rumblings against sleazy journalism, the YMCA never had grounds to sue for libel, since everything Sleeth printed about the YMCA was part of the public record. B. Lee Paget, a professional reformer, banker, and friend of the YMCA, demanded public retractions from the *News*. But in the November 2, 1912, issue, Sleeth printed a defiant challenge:

> The News invites any minister who wants to know the truth to ask Deputy Collier of the district attorney's office, to ask Judge Gatens, to ask Mr. Brick, who started this probe, to ask the Sheriff, to ask the grand jury. AND YOU HAD BETTER GET THE TRUTH BEFORE YOU RESOLUTE [*sic*] TOO MUCH, FOR THERE IS AN AWFUL AWAKENING GOING TO HIT SOME GOOD FOLKS WHO HAVE BEEN FOOLED BY THOSE TRYING TO COVER THEIR OWN GUILT. . . . CONFESSIONS IN THE HANDS OF THE LAW SHOW THAT THE LOWEST VICES WERE REPEATEDLY PRACTICED ON BOYS IN THE Y.M.C.A. . . . WOULD YOU KEEP STILL IF YOU WERE THE NEWS?

Sleeth was right when he accused his opponents of a conspiracy of silence to protect their own, of not wanting to know the truth. True, middle-class supporters of "social purity" had always debated how much publicity was appropriate in the struggle against vice. Many feared that too much publicity would result in the spreading of vice by planting impure thoughts where none had previously existed. But in this particular case, silence not only protected public decency, it also protected the reputations of middle-class friends and supporters of the YMCA who were implicated or whose husbands and fathers were implicated in the scandal and it protected the reputation of the YMCA itself. Official YMCA publications at the national level are conspicuous by the absence of any explicit response to the scandal, even though it began to have national repercussions. *Association Men* may have been responding indirectly in December 1912 when it published an editorial of Dr. Winfield S. Hall, a prominent social hygiene reformer in the Portland YMCA. Hall was probably responding to Sleeth's challenge to "ask Deputy Collier of the district attorney's office, to ask Judge Gatens, to ask Mr. Brick, who started this probe, to ask the Sheriff, to ask the grand jury." Sleeth had also encouraged concerned fathers of boys to go to the juvenile courts and to listen to the testimony. Hall's editorial in the pages of *Association Men* denied the usefulness of such "investigations":

> We have been told that in order effectively to deal with the problems of society we must know all that is to be known regarding the social evil, crime, degeneracy and delinquency. We must dredge the sewers of society and spread the dredge out before us to study their horrible content. . . . We must go to the police courts, see the victims brought before the magistrate and hear the testimony. . . . The writer maintains that it is not necessary. Moreover, not only is it unnecessary, but it is altogether unwise.[11]

The same issue of *Association Men* contained a notice commending the Portland YMCA on its work in the area of social hygiene, characterizing it as "to our minds the best put successful plan [*sic*] of promoting social purity that has ever been handled."[12]

Although the records of the confessions are no longer available, accounts from the *Portland News* reported that they conclusively proved that

> The Y.M.C.A. was one of the hotbeds of the practices, and the confessions of several men and boys shows that this institution has, to put it mildly, been woefully mismanaged. That the things confessed to have been continually and habitually . . . done in the association quarters is as stunning a blow to the cause of professional reform and orthodox piety as has been dealt in this town for years.

Court testimony revealed the existence of a vibrant gay subculture in Portland in 1912. This subculture had its own slang and included networks of men who knew each other by various effeminate nicknames like "Mother McAlister" and "Viola," and who had been acquainted with and participated in similar networks and subcultures in other American cities. Much like the gay underworld revealed in the Newport, Rhode Island, U.S. Navy trials described by George Chauncey, Jr., apparently two classes of people participated in this underworld. The "straights" were mostly young, working-class men who played the insertive role in the sex act and who claimed a masculine, "normal" identity. They clearly did not see themselves being effeminized by permitting "queers" to "go down on them." The "queers" or "queer parties" were viewed as effeminate because they actively sought sex with "real" men, and this class included many older, middle-class men (including lawyers, doctors, and businessmen). Many of these men had been leading double lives: one as prominent, respected husbands and fathers and as members of Portland's business, religious, and social elite, and the other as flamboyant queens (or "queans") in the gay sexual underworld. Sexual contacts in this subculture were made in many public, urban spaces, including parks, office buildings, and on the streets, although the YMCA was apparently one of the most reliable places to make assignations.[13]

George Chauncey, Jr., has already shown how the Newport trials in 1919 would in effect put "Christian brotherhood" on trial and YMCA officials on the defensive as their solicitous concern for the welfare of young men was publicly interpreted in the worst possible light. Similarly the 1912 scandal in Portland complicated same-sex male love. One of the pieces of evidence that clinched the case against E. S. J. McAlister (aka Mother McAlister) was a postcard he had sent to Roy Kadel during a business trip to Boston. The card mentioned no sexual improprieties, but damned McAlister because it was a mark of affection between two men. In another particularly tragic case, W. H. Allen, a member of the YMCA and one of the men named as having participated in the cruising, attempted suicide after his questioning by juvenile court officials. Allen was described as a "gray-haired business man," who, according to secretary Stone of the Portland YMCA, "was liked because of his many acts of kindness toward the boys. He was frequently known to sit up all night with sick persons in the building and was always ready to lend a hand wherever it was needed."[14] Allen's son told the press that the only reason his father had been accused was because of "his knowing so many of the young men involved, and his familiarity with them."[15] Whether or not Allen's denials were true, the scandal could only have a chilling effect on the dynamic that had sustained the YMCA from its foundation: men's love for other men. The *Portland News* sarcastically characterized men involved in the scandal as "nice, charitable, boy-loving men."[16]

A BRIEF HISTORY OF YMCA CRUISING, 1880–1950

The first available evidence documenting a gay culture in American cities dates back to the 1880s and 1890s.[17] Certain areas of the city— usually parks, particular streets, bath houses, gymnasiums, cheap hotels, and YMCAs—were sites of same-sex cruising activity. Doctors, psychiatrists, law enforcement officials, and social workers also began to comment on the existence of "cliques" or "networks" of "inverts" forming in certain clubs, theaters, cafes, and other places of leisure. The existence of male brothels and the organization of grand cross-dressing spectacles known as "drag balls" were other manifestations of early gay male cultures. Gay men identified themselves to one another through the use of certain coded terms, or through the wearing of certain kinds of clothing or certain styles of facial hair. There is evidence that homosexual cultures were divided along racial lines; black gay men more commonly socialized in private settings and at elaborate drag balls than their white gay counterparts, and developed their own social networks. Nevertheless, there were contexts in which men of all classes, races, and ethnicities interacted. Not all men who participated in the gay culture considered themselves to be "inverts." Furthermore, many of the places that were popular gathering places for men in search of same-sex sexual activity were also occupied by prostitutes and bohemians; there were many settings in which the gay world and the heterosexual world over-lapped, and many men who moved freely between same-sex and mixed-sex sexual settings. By the first decade of the twentieth century, gay cultures could be found in virtually every major American city and in every region of the country.

The emergence of new same-sex sexual communities coincided with in-tensifying American urbanization and industrialization, and with mass movements of people. Growing cities attracted a large, young, single male workforce from the American countryside as well as from abroad. Further-more, urban areas offered public spaces where individuals could meet and interact anonymously, where church and family no longer afforded guide-lines or restraints. These two developments were prerequisites for the emer-gence of gay cultures and of public cruising scenes, and were also, not co-incidentally, cited as the primary reasons for the YMCA's existence. The YMCA deliberately positioned itself at the city's points of entry, and delib-erately created public spaces for men to meet each other, in the hopes that it could shape young men before they could be exposed to bad influences.

Often, young men coming to the city for the first time from rural areas stopped at the YMCA first. The main character of the novel *Scarlet Pansy*, a gay novel of the 1920s set in the Baltimore YMCA, arrived from the country in the train station at Baltimore. After explaining to a police officer that he had just arrived from the farm he was pointed to the YMCA.[18] Interviews with older gay men who were involved in the YMCA through the 1930s confirm that the YMCA continued to play this role well into the twentieth century, and that the YMCA actually served as a point of entry for many rural young men into an urban homosexual subculture. Martin Block re-called that "people from small towns had no place else to go—a lot of coun-try boys [stayed at the Y]." Block, born in 1919, recalled knowing a gay couple in the 1930s who lived in a tenement district in New York City and worked for the city as garbage collectors, one of whom had had his first sexual experience at the YMCA in the 1890s. He had had other friends who told him about having their first sexual experiences at the YMCA during or just before World War I. The Y, he recalled, was a "nice, religious place" where "they'll take care of you." [19] Harry Hay stayed at the Reno and San Francisco YMCAs in the late 1920s when he was with the IWW, and recalled that most of the men staying there were "lower middle-class farming men, sent to the Y by Sunday School teachers or ministers." [20] William Billings believed that YMCAs, like the Oklahoma City YMCA that he frequented, were "very important" as sexual meeting grounds in the rural Midwest in particular, since they were one of the only available options. [21]

Besides simply being a natural stop in the transition from country to city life, the YMCA's physical culture movement and its single-sex emphasis also attracted men who were interested in experimenting with male eroticism. Gay narrator Paul Hardman was attracted to the YMCA by "all the muscular trappings—the sports." [22] A biography of homosexual musician Charles T. Griffes described how in the late 1890s and early 1900s "so great was his need to be with boys, that though his home contained two pianos, he chose to practice on a public instrument at the Y, and his favorite hour was the time when players were coming and going from their games." [23] Dorr Legg was convinced that homosexuals were drawn to the YMCA because it was a "one-sex thing." "It goes with the territory," he speculated, calling the YMCA "a safe refuge to single/homosexual men." He had a lifelong bachelor uncle who lived in a YMCA residence hall from about 1900 through the 1930s, though he had no idea whether his uncle ever had sex with men. But he also knew of other "bachelors [in the residence halls] who've opted out of two-sex society." [24] Paul Hardman recalled that unlike at many hotels, at the YMCA "young men could share a room without suspicion." [25]

YMCAs quickly developed a reputation as a sexual meeting place within the gay subculture. As word spread, the process of creating public, anonymous sexual communities in YMCA space was intensified, since men actively went to YMCAs seeking sex. Information about where male sex could be found was easily had in the emerging gay subculture, but it was by no means the only place where such information was passed on. Even condemnation of purported cruising activity was an effective means of spreading the word to the sexually curious. Testimony from the Portland sex scandal in 1912 confirmed that YMCAs across the country housed flourishing sexual communities in the years before World War I. [26] When Martin Block chose to stay at the YMCA during a trip to Washington, DC, in 1936 and 1937, he had already heard since the 1920s about its reputation as a place where sex could easily be found. In the 1930s, he knew that the 63rd Street YMCA in New York was "notorious," though he found sex easier to obtain at the Sloane House.[27] Paul Hardman first went to the YMCA in search of sex "as a kid" in the late 1920s, when he had heard about what was going on from friends.[28]

All evidence about the nature of cruising indicates that many, perhaps a majority of, participants were men who did not themselves identify as gay. Gay men knew about and participated in the cruising scene, but they were not solely responsible for creating it. Early public cruising provided a necessary prerequisite for the emergence of a self-conscious gay subculture, but it was never synonymous with it. On the other hand cruising was closely connected to the gay community. Discovering the public cruising scene could be a first step toward learning about the existence of a gay subculture, and a first step toward internalizing a new homosexual identity. The *Scarlet Pansy*'s main character, Fay Etrange, was portrayed as being initiated into Baltimore's gay subculture in the years before World War I at the YMCA. On the other hand, entry into the gay community through other means made one aware of public cruising's availability as a form of sexual release. Furthermore, the sexual interaction of "queers" with "normal" men as "trade" became an important part of emerging sexual identities and patterns of male-male sexual interaction.

YMCAs were not the only places for male erotic interaction. Public parks and street corners, saloons, and houses of male prostitution also offered erotic possibilities. But these places were more dangerous. One risked becoming the victim of crime or police harassment. YMCAs were protected by their middle-class, Christian aura, even as they offered all the advantages of other public spaces for male-male erotic interaction. William Billings recalled that in spite of the occasional "witch-hunt," "men could feel relatively safe at the Y."[29] Martin Block recalled a "police friend" in the 1940s who went to the YMCA for sex because it was the one place his fellow officers never raided.[30] Harry Hay recalled that in the 1930s, there were two places to go for public sex, "the Y or the park," and recalled that sex at the Y was always more leisurely since one did not have to fear police intervention.[31]

The YMCA cruising scene was intensified during World War I by the boom in YMCA army and navy work. Armed services work had the effect of bringing a huge influx of men into YMCA dormitories and gymnasiums. The effect of armed services work on the YMCA cruising scene was even more dramatic during World War II, and initiated what could be called the golden age of YMCA cruising. Paul Hardman recalled that "World War II opened the floodgates [of cruising at the YMCA], though before then, the gates leaked a lot."[32] William Billings recalled that "there was a lot of activity . . . particularly since World War II."[33] As Alan Bérubé has demonstrated in *Coming Out under Fire*, a study of homosexuality in the armed services during World War II, psychological screening had the effect of spreading popular awareness of homosexuality, while the concentration of men and women in coastal military cities gave individuals opportunities to explore their sexuality and connect with already existing gay communities.[34]

AMBIGUITY AND THE YMCA'S CHRISTIAN AURA

Laud Humphries's classic (and controversial) study, *Tea Room Trade*, identifies ambiguity—situations where more than one interpretation can be put on any given action—as the essential stuff of which cruising is made.[35] This is the key to understanding how the YMCA could tolerate cruising on its premises. When the Portland sex scandal broke in 1912, one of the questions that repeatedly surfaced was how much the YMCA actually knew about what had been going on. Dana Sleeth repeatedly accused the YMCA of a cover-up. He blamed the YMCA for knowing what had been going on for a long time before social workers uncovered it. In its turn the Portland YMCA denied any knowledge, and claimed to have taken the precautions necessary to prevent its recurrence. There is some evidence, however, that in the decade before the scandal YMCA leaders, both local and national, did know that YMCA buildings were being used as sexual meeting places. An occasional article in official YMCA publications expressed concern about homosexuality on YMCA premises, like this editorial appearing in the March 1906 *Association Men*: "Another danger, more serious than is understood, is that effeminate, moral degenerates, men who may move in the higher circles, cultured, refined and devilish, often musical and affecting spirituality, may come and bring their unmentionable immoralities [into the dormitories]."[36] Instructions in YMCA manuals about the need to maintain adequate supervision of key access points to Association buildings and of the locker rooms and toilets may also have reflected the growing awareness of what was happening.

Donald Vining's diary from the 1940s and older gay men's recollections of the cruising scene at YMCAs from the 1920s through the 1960s suggest that despite the public humiliation caused by the Portland sex scandal, YMCAs took virtually no precautions to prevent cruising, at least none that lasted beyond World War I.[37] Indeed the opposite appears to have occurred. YMCA building managements more or less capitulated and let cruising be, so long as it did not become so conspicuous as to threaten public exposure and embarrassment. If YMCAs were lackadaisical in their responses to cruising after Portland in 1912 and after Newport in 1919, it seems unreasonable to believe that they had ever been very vigilant. As documented in the preceding chapter, YMCA buildings were more understaffed in the decades before World War I than they were in the decades after. Even if there had been some will to control the cruising situation, it appears that the manpower for necessary supervision was lacking. Oral history sources strongly indicate that cruising was popular at the YMCA after the 1920s precisely because it had always been tolerated before the 1920s.

A unanimous refrain of narrators and documentary sources was that the YMCA management after the 1920s knew of the cruising scene and did nothing to stop it. Members of the YMCA's 1964 committee on homosexuality acknowledged that the existence of cruising had been common knowledge among YMCA leaders and staff at least since the early 1920s, perhaps earlier.[38] Occasionally, an individual who was too brazen might be thrown out of the building. Sporadic witch-hunts occurred, but they were extremely rare and were usually, as in 1912, only a response to public pressure. "The management of the Embarcadero [YMCA] was very well aware of what was going on," recalled Harry Hay; "most of the clerks knew what was going on."[39] Martin Block recalled that the managements of the Sloane House and 63rd Street YMCAs in New York in the 1940s "had an attitude of pretending it didn't exist, except [the] clerks which were flaming queens."[40] Jim Kepner remembered that some YMCA desk clerks even funneled potential cruisers to different locker rooms to avoid causing a fuss: "The clerk at the desk would sort of size people up, and suggest that they go either upstairs or downstairs to the locker room." Sometimes they gave "knowing advice," warning men to "close the door if you're having fun."[41] George Mendenhall witnessed a similar response on the part of YMCA desk clerks: "If they suspected you were gay they would assign you to an upper floor."[42] Despite the rampant sex going on at the 63rd Street YMCA, Wayne Flottman recalled that "no great efforts were made . . . to stop [it]." He was occasionally asked to show that he had a key, to prove that he was staying there, but that was the only precaution he knew of taken by the management. James Dawson recalled occasional attempts on the part of YMCA management to curtail cruising activity in the late fifties and early sixties. He recalled that in one Y, staircase doors were occasionally locked to prevent easy passage between floors, though YMCA patrons responded by propping them open. But, he recalled, these attempts to curtail cruising were made only by "some segment of the management." "Some were less straight-laced than others," he recalled, and even suspected that some managers were gay.[43] Hal Call remembered that the YMCA "had a reputation of being tolerant of gays if they weren't too flamboyant or outrageous."[44]

There were a number of reasons why YMCAs would be reluctant to take serious, punitive measures against individuals involved in the cruising scene. First of all, involving police authorities would have risked creating negative publicity for the YMCA. The response to the 1912 Portland scandal was typical. Once the scandal had broken into the press, the YMCA cooperated with police and social workers to bring the "culprits" out into the open. But most of what the YMCA did in response to the scandal was geared toward reducing bad publicity. Confessions and court testimony during the trial suggested that YMCA officials had known about cruising before it came to the attention of the public and did little or nothing to stop it. The lack of official response to the scandals in YMCA publications like *Association Men* suggest that what the YMCA feared most in this regard was continuing public discussion of the problem. A vigilant and consistently punitive response would have been too strong and too public an acknowledgment that cruising existed in the first place, and the YMCA's official stance throughout the scandal was that this was an aberration.

It is also reasonable to believe that most YMCA leaders had sincere concern about men's welfare, and would not have wanted to destroy their reputations by publicly exposing homosexual behavior. Quiet warnings, counseling, or expelling "troublemakers" from the premises would have been more likely responses to flagrant situations. But there is also reason to believe that the most common response was to look the other way.

Another reason for the YMCA's failure to do anything about the cruising scene, at least after the 1920s, also appears to be that desk staffs were sometimes completely infiltrated by gay men. Larry Littlejohn recalled that at the Sloane House YMCA "you could [always] spot the queen" among the lobby clerks.[45] When narrators described YMCA desk clerks as "flaming queens," perhaps they were referring to behavior like that described in Donald Vining's diary. Vining was a gay male employee of the YMCA, and referred to the behavior of a gay desk clerk coworker: "[Andy] really embarrasses me when he does things like yelling, when a plain soldier turns away from the window, 'Oh, Christ, why don't we get some attractive customers?'"[46] George Mendenhall had a gay YMCA clerk friend, who would help out his friends by assigning them to desirable dormitory rooms.[47] Sam Steward also recalled cruising at YMCAs where "control . . . fell into the hands of homosexual clerks."[48] But Donald Vining's diary shows that gay clerks were not the only ones who tolerated the cruising, and that the presence of gay clerks in the management was known and tolerated by straight people in the management.

Donald Vining's diary confirms that at least in the Sloane House YMCA in the 1940s, nongay employees and management generally knew about the cruising but looked the other way. When Bob, a YMCA desk clerk, tried to turn in a resident who had passed a note soliciting sex, another (presumably straight) desk clerk "threw [the note] away without getting the house man to check on the guy who wrote it." It appears that even if he had turned the man in, nothing might have come of it, since in another incident, "One sailor came down . . . and said the guy with whom he had taken a room made a pass at him and would somebody go up for his clothes, as he was leaving. . . . The protection officer . . . did nothing about it and made the sailor go get his own clothes." The only antihomosexual witch-hunt that occurred there was prosecuted by a closeted gay man, and straight employees at the Sloane House sided against him: "Henry and Vernon are even more furious than I. Mr. Henry, whose language is ordinarily quite decorous, kept spitting 'The son-of-a-bitch, trying to make trouble for other people. We've never in the history of the house had anyone who hounded people that way.'" Vining's straight coworkers knew that he and a number of other clerks were gay. Not only did it not seem to bother them, but they occasionally discussed their social lives with their gay coworkers in a friendly manner: "Mr. Henry, trying to sound us out, said 'I don't know but what I better arrange for you two to have the same nite off together.'" At one point, a coworker openly acknowledged her support for the gay men on the YMCA desk staff: "Mae delighted me when she said [regarding the witch-hunt], . . . 'They don't even have the guts to speak out and go ahead like you and Andy do.' That's the closest she's ever come to putting her cards on the table in admitting she understands tho we've each known she really did for some time."[49]

IN PRETENDING NOT to know what was going on, YMCA building managements helped create the aura of ambiguity that is one of the central elements of most public cruising scenes. Public cruising has always thrived best in situations where men's intentions could remain uncertain for as long as possible, where one couldn't know for certain that their purpose in being there was for sex. In that sense, the YMCA was an ideal place for cruising not in spite of its Christian reputation but because of it. It is not merely that the YMCA provided an effective cover for homosexuals (although it might possibly have done that). New awareness of the existence of homosexual behavior in the first half of the twentieth century simultaneously exposed men to a disturbing (and possibly desirable) option, and made it possible or even necessary for them to reinvent their personalities and appropriate an identity as a "real man" or "normal,"; or as "queer," or as a "fairy." But adoption of a new sexual identity was not easy or immediate. Sometimes it required time and experimentation. Cruising at the YMCA offered men a number of denial strategies without eliminating the possibility of sexual experimentation and without having to embrace a homosexual identity. One might be "upright," "Christian," and "disapprove" of "perversion," and deny knowledge of its existence. One might disapprove, but maintain the Christlike need to "help" those who have gone astray. Unlike going to a gay bar, a notorious park, or a house of male prostitution, going to the YMCA might offer evidence of desire for self-improvement and uprightness. Yet it was easy to put one-self in situations there where sex might happen, even while denying to oneself that that was the goal. Then, if sex happened, one could dismiss it merely as "blowing off steam" or as a "slip up." The YMCA cruising scene permitted men to slip into whichever role or denial strategy seemed appropriate, and also to occasionally experiment sexually without having to surrender one's masculinity.

Perhaps the most dramatic example of this role "slippage" appears in Donald Vining's diary. Vining recalled having a crush on "Bob," a fellow YMCA desk clerk who was presumably straight. At one point, Bob invited Vining to shower with him. Though nothing sexual came of it, Bob invited him to "do this every morning." Later, after an incident in which a YMCA resident was "asked to leave after . . . going from room to room with open door and going down on the fellows," Bob "vehemently declared himself disgusted by such things and said he'd have poked [hit] him, etc." Later, when he found a note soliciting sex, Bob tried to turn in the offender, though another YMCA staff person prevented him. Two years later, however, a chance encounter between Vining and Bob in a YMCA swimming pool led to "horsing around," and later on to sex in a YMCA dorm room. Bob later became so actively involved in the cruising scene at the YMCA that he risked being caught.[50] The anecdote with Bob also clearly suggests that building staff might choose not to be overly vigilant about cruising because they themselves were implicated in it.

The adoption of "queer" and "normal" roles was a way of ritualizing and acknowledging the reality of role slippage at the YMCA. For this reason, the YMCA acquired a reputation as a popular cruising place, because it suppos-edly attracted straight types. The YMCA's Christian mission actually helped shape the erotic system that evolved on its premises. One reason Jim Kepner enjoyed cruising at the YMCA was because the men he could pick up there were more "religious."[51] Other gay narrators recounted that it was easier to connect with "real" (that is, straight) men and rural men there. Some also were attracted to the kind of virility that was implied by the YMCA's physical program, and by its outreach to working-class men and army and navy ser-vicemen. Paul McGuinness had a preference for "men who were really men, not just a bunch of faggots running around." At the YMCA, he recalled, it was easy to meet and have sex with "straight" men. He was attracted to the YMCA because he could find "soldiers, marines on leave, truck driver, construction-worker types."[52] The Embarcadero YMCA, George Mendenhall recalled, was where people went if they were looking for "straight trade." "Every-body hoped they would connect with servicemen," he recalled. Mendenhall preferred "construction workers" himself. "I was very much into straight guys."[53] Bob Basker remembered getting presumably straight trade in YMCA shower rooms in the late 1930s and early 1940s. "Most of the men I had sex with considered themselves completely straight," he recalled.[54]

YMCA executives and ordained ministers also participated in the YMCA cruising scene, though they were more likely to use their religious creden-tials as a cover. Despite the greater risks run by men in these positions, and thus the need for extreme discretion and secrecy, gay men who participated in the cruising scene were aware of such individuals who cruised just like everybody else. Martin Block knew of Christian ministers who stayed at YMCAs and had sex there in the 1930s and 1940s.[55] Dorr Legg remembered one particular high-level YMCA executive who had sex with men but "used wife and family as a front."[56] One narrator, who requested anonymity, was an ordained Christian minister who cruised for sex at YMCAs in the early 1960s. He was introduced to the Young Men's Christian Association through its Student Christian Association in the mid-1950s. He recalled hearing about the YMCA's reputation for cruising at McCormick Seminary.[57] The participation of YMCA secretaries and ministers, as well as traditional con-stituents and members in the homosexual cruising scene, was most dra-matically brought to the public eye in the 1912 Portland, Oregon, sex scan-dal and the 1919 Newport, Rhode Island, navy trials, in which two YMCA ministers were entrapped by navy decoys. As one might expect, YMCA leaders publicly denied and the public generally refused to believe that ministers could possibly be implicated in this kind of activity.[58]

CRUISING AND THE CHANGING AMERICAN SEXUAL LANDSCAPE

YMCAs may not have been willing or able to do a lot to curtail cruising, but awareness of cruising and of homosexuality generally had an impact on the social and emotional texture of YMCA community life and leadership. As I have already argued in preceding chapters, the YMCA changed its single-sex membership basis and pressured YMCA leaders to marry in re-sponse to such concerns. Ironically, accusations of homosexual perversion against the YMCA were particularly shattering because of the success of the YMCA's own sex hygiene campaigns. It is perhaps no coincidence that national YMCA leaders for some years before the Portland sex scandal had considered the Portland YMCA's sex hygiene program to be one of the most effective in the country. It had promoted sex education and striven to create a climate of open discussion about sexuality. In the years before the scandal, the Portland YMCA had formed a Social Hygiene Society that cooperated with the Oregon State Board of Health to develop a sex education curriculum. Among other things, the society held meetings with parents, issued publications for youth, and held sex education conferences. Its pamphlet "The Social Emergency" was disseminated through YMCAs across the country. In 1911, under its aegis, Dr. Winfield S. Hall had "visited fifty-one educational institutions" to talk about sex education.[59]

The scandal forced to the surface some of the hidden implications of the sex hygiene work that the YMCA had been doing. It forced YMCA leaders to acknowledge the potential dangers of intense relationships among men which had always been the mortar of the organization. It also rendered precarious the YMCA's latest and most popular new venture: boys' work. The *Portland News*'s most damaging attack on the YMCA was that the permissive sexual environment there was destroying Portland's youth. The image of innocent boys being spoiled by ruthless perverts caused an intense emotional reaction, and was invoked as permission for the most paranoid extremism. Then, as today, it was harder to rally public indignation against acts performed between consenting adults, so the antihomosexual crusade was clothed in rhetoric about the protection of young boys. Editor Dana Sleeth made emotional appeals to "fathers of boys" and to mothers. In one typical appeal, he declaimed: "But chiefly, the News is proud of the support given it by the women who are mothers and who prefer their boys' safety to a sickish, sentimental, prudish covering of nastiness."[60] The YMCA found itself on the defensive, and at pains to show that men and boys were kept separate on its premises.[61]

Again, the chief irony in this is that the YMCA had for some years been promoting boys' work particularly because of new sexual developmental theories that stressed the importance and the vulnerability of childhood. In its sex education curriculums, the YMCA drew particular attention to child-rearing, and the formative impact of boyhood experiences on adult male sexuality. The YMCA's official philosophy of physical work as expressed in publications like *Physical Education* and *Physical Training* was not only that it should be coordinated with efforts to develop the mind and spirit, but that it should attend to diet, sleep, and sexual development as well as physical exercise. Dr. Luther Gulick, the preeminent leader of the YMCA's physical work, advocated frank discussion of sexuality with boys from an early age combined with efforts to prevent masturbation and keep them away from pornography.⁶² Many of the YMCA's early physical programs were infused with this emphasis, and physical directors cooperated closely with social hygiene efforts. Much of the impetus given to boys' work in the early twentieth century was due to the growing conviction among YMCA educators that boyhood was an important formative period.

It was significant that the Portland sex scandal broke because of concerns raised by juvenile protection officers to the police. The existence of juvenile protection workers was itself a result of Progressive Era concern about youth as a formative and vulnerable time. YMCA leaders had helped to promote such a view, and in their sex education work cooperated with social workers and teachers in their outreach to youth. It was also for the sake of protecting boys and in the name of sex education that the *Portland News* raised the alarm against "perversion" being practiced in the rooms of the YMCA. Dana Sleeth went so far as to suggest the existence of a national trafficking in boys that was a homosexual counterpart to the "white slave trade." Ironically, the YMCA had heightened parents' belief in boys' sexual vulnerability and broken down the atmosphere of censorship and silence on sexual issues, creating a public more receptive to Sleeth's antiperversion grandstanding in the *Portland News*.

THE LATE NINETEENTH century and the early twentieth century were a period of transformation in American history. Family structures and sexual relationships were transformed by changes in the economy, and by a shift in population from the country to the city. If, as historians of sexuality have suggested, this was a period when sexual identities were being reforged, then one might expect to find an arena like YMCA cruising, where new kinds of social relations could be tested. Homosexual cruising was a way for men to explore their relationship to their bodies and their masculinity. Unlike prostitution, which might be viewed as an arena for men to affirm their social superiority to women, the erotic interaction between "queers" and "real men" was a way for "straight" men to affirm their desirability and power. New definitions of masculinity centering on (hetero)sexual prowess and the muscular male body, oddly enough, were affirmed through the creation of (homo)erotic hierarchies in gyms, dormitories, and locker rooms.

The tendency to dismiss cruising as a marginal activity, engaged in by a minuscule, perverse minority says more about American anxieties than it says about cruising or its relationship to the YMCA. Most of those who were indicted and convicted in the Portland sex scandal of 1912 were the kinds of men who, since the 1850s, had formed the core constituency of the Association. They were middle-class clerks, businessmen, doctors, and lawyers, who supported and were involved in respected religious and ethical institutions.

Court testimony confirmed that "most of these degenerates are masked behind a religious or charitable institution." The editor of the *Portland News* of course questioned their motives for being involved in such institutions, implying that their sole purpose in joining was to find opportunities to perpetrate unsuspected vice.[63] This interpretation was clearly an overreaction. While some in the late 1910s may have joined the YMCA specifically for the purpose of connecting sexually with other men, many who participated in the cruising scene probably supported and sincerely believed in the religious mission of the organization.

If there was religious hypocrisy in the behavior of men who engaged in same-sex sexual activity at YMCAs after the turn of the century, it was a hypocrisy analogous to that practiced by contemporaries who upheld Victorian virtues of chastity and simultaneously made use of (heterosexual) prostitution for the purpose of "protecting" marriage. Turn-of-the-century writers—both heterosexual, like Luther Gulick and Max Exner, and homosexual, like John Addington Symonds and Xavier Mayne—idealized male love, and attributed to it the basis of civilization's greatest achievements. They all—homosexual and heterosexual—viewed physical expressions of male-male love as selfish and debasing. This was analogous to the Victorian mistrust of heterosexual lust, and emphasis on self-control in the relationships between men and women. But the fact that homosexual writers like Symonds also engaged in promiscuous sexual activity in urban gay underworlds testifies to yet another value that they shared with their contemporaries: that sexual self-gratification was more acceptable in a working-class underworld than in an idealized relationship governed by the strictures of romantic love.[64]

That more liberating and less hypocritical views of human sexuality were possible is illustrated in the interesting, if exceptional, case of Walt Whitman. Whitman illustrates the potential overlap between the worlds of idealized male love and the gay sexual underworld. Whitman proclaimed a much more positive view of the role of human sexuality than most of his contemporaries, a view that he celebrated in his poetry, his personal life, and his correspondence. Despite his disregard for what he characterized as the narrow evangelistic aims of the Young Men's Christian Association, and despite the suspicion with which some YMCA workers regarded him, Whitman volunteered for Civil War service under the aegis of the YMCA's Christian Commission because of his intense love for and desire to serve young men in arms. In this regard, at least, he likely fit in well with other Christian Commission workers. In April 1920, *Association Men* published an excerpt from the writings of Walt Whitman about his war service as a typical example of YMCA war work. Whitman's quoted expression of a love that did not discriminate between black or white, South or North, was obviously part of a tradition the YMCA was proud to claim.⁶⁵ Whitman expressed his love for the men he nursed through physical tokens of affection—embraces, kisses, bedside vigils, and hand-holding. Numerous letters attest to the intense gratitude and bonds of affection felt by the men to whom he ministered. Historical evidence is inconclusive as to whether Whitman was overtly sexual with any men in this context, but a preponderance of historical evidence supports the now generally accepted fact of Whitman's same-sex sexuality, both within and outside a series of intense relationships with younger men, which he pursued until his death in 1892.⁶⁶ Whitman, in his poetry, celebrated manly love as a force that would democratize civilization by breaking down barriers of class and race. It seems possible that he interpreted his same-sex acts of physical love as expressions of an ennobling love that motivated him in other nonsexual acts of charitable service to and friendship with men.

Such an integration of same-sex sexuality with a philosophy of generalized love for mankind would have been inconceivable for the evangelical Protestant middle-class men who were the main constituency of the YMCA. Many who participated in the thriving gay cruising scene in the YMCA did so in a way that left their sexual lives completely unintegrated with other aspects of male-male social relations. Sexual relationships could not appropriately be entertained in the context of intense loving bonds between "Christian gentlemen." Many faced this dilemma by leading double lives in a gay sexual underworld and in the respectable world of business and the church. The exposure of the gay world drove men to suicide or left them running for their lives. Those unfortunate enough not to elude detection or to escape the hands of the law were subjected to humiliating public trials, the publication of their names in all of the papers, merciless denunciation from every pulpit, prison sentences, and the permanent ruin of their reputations and careers. Since the mainstream American cultural response to homoeroticism was denial that it could play any positive role in friendship, the ideal of manly Christian love was salvageable to the extent that social condemnation of same-sex sexuality was fierce and unrelenting.

But the social cost of exacting such punishments consistently, of maintaining constant vigilance against perversion, was too great. After all, those who experienced the full wrath of a self-righteous middle-class Protestant society were its own sons, brothers, and fathers. That is likely why the vice was ignored, shushed up, and tolerated in virtually every YMCA in every major American city. For those who participated in it as well as for those who did not participate but tolerated it, the existence of and easy access to a gay sexual underworld provided a context in which the "filth" could at least be contained. It touched only those fleeting relationships that existed in the context of the underworld, and left men free to enjoy Christian fellowship and community respect in another context, but only so long as the two contexts remained radically separate.

If anything is clear from the Portland scandal, it is that the context for viewing the sexual underworld was shifting. Double standards and secret sex lives were becoming increasingly unacceptable. And the YMCA had played no small role in making them unacceptable. Furthermore, shifting understandings of the nature of sex and of human sexual development were casting suspicion even on nonsexual romantic friendship. Despite glaring evidence in the scandal that marriage was no proof of heterosexual purity, the assumption that certain men were "capable" of perversion and others were not was beginning to transform the symbolic power of marriage. Increasingly, the bachelor secretary who devoted his life in sacrificial love to the welfare of young men, and the single-sex organization that specialized in a work exclusively for young men would be viewed as outdated and even embarrassing.

EPILOGUE

From the 1940s through the 1960s, the cruising scene at the YMCA reached the peak of its activity and flagrancy. During this period, as a result of the war and the McCarthy era "pink scare" more individuals than ever had embraced a gay identity, though it was still a period when relatively few gay community institutions provided social outlets. Public homophobic paranoia and police raids made involvement in the few existing gay community institutions (mainly the bars) more dangerous than ever. In the late 1960s, Wayne Flottman made regular business trips to New York City, and stayed at the 63rd Street YMCA. "That place there was always something happening—a continuous sexual scene. If I went to the Y I might not make it to the village [because there was so much sex going on]. . . . It was almost like the bathhouses of the '70s."[1] A new sexual revolution in the late sixties led to years of the most wild activity at the YMCA. Paul McGuinness recalled that the Embarcadero YMCA in the 1970s was "like a sex place," "a sexual frenzy." He recalled "people masturbating naked, people tied up, people in uniforms, cowboys, a man wearing a leash like a dog." There were "some men who just lived on the toilet seats." He recalled that it was hard to sleep there at nights because of the noise of men having sex coming from adjoining rooms.[2]

But the emergence of a public, militant gay rights movement in the late 1960s signaled the beginning of the end of the golden era of YMCA cruising. As early successes of the gay rights movement and a waning of McCarthyism made coming out less dangerous, participation in gay community institutions became more attractive to those who had accepted a gay identity, and many resorted to the bars in search of "relationships." Paul Hardman, who cruised YMCAs in the 1940s, recounted that the "wild" sex scene at the YMCA declined after the "gay movement."[3] Paul McGuinness recalled that after he met his lover Ken in the early 1970s, he stopped going to the YMCA.[4] Jim Dawson also stopped going to the YMCA in the early 1970s.[5] William Billings did not feel that it was "necessary to go to the Y now— so much more [is] available."[6] Fear of the AIDS epidemic in the 1980s appears to have had a dampening effect on the public cruising scene as well. McGuinness returned to the Embarcadero YMCA in the 1980s, only to learn that the scene "had totally changed." "The whole thing died out."[7]

Shifts in the YMCA's constituency and focus after the 1920s would eventually have an impact on the cruising scene. Even though the YMCA revised its constitution to grant women full membership in 1933, women did not flock to join the YMCA at first. Women's participation rates remained relatively stable until after World War II, when YMCAs began to move to the suburbs and family memberships became a common membership marketing tool. Although cruising persisted in many of the downtown and central urban YMCAs, which continued to cater to a disproportionately male constituency, cruising in the newer suburban YMCAs was virtually nonexistent. The YMCA's committee on homosexuality in the 1960s noted that the "family-oriented" YMCA had been a deterrent to cruising, and favored increasing the "heterogeneity" of the organization.[8]

YMCA cruising continued to be an important field of erotic interaction between "straight" and "gay" men, however, and was still one of the few relatively safe sexual releases for men who did not accept a gay identity or who were still afraid to come out. But in some sense, the success of the gay rights movement made the YMCA less safe, as public awareness of YMCA cruising increased. Serious attempts on the part of YMCAs to curtail cruising began only in the 1960s and 1970s as their image began to suffer under accusations that they were soft on homosexuality and that they were unsafe for children. Though the Sloane House had once been jokingly dubbed "the French Embassy" by gay men, by the 1970s, Dorr Legg recalled, the cruising scene there had practically become nonexistent because of heightened YMCA security.[9] Some YMCAs even considered the use of closed-circuit television monitoring to put an end to cruising.[10] Tightening up by the YMCA led to the first clashes between gay rights activists and the Y. The YMCA's decision in the early 1970s to end its long policy of nude bathing led to accusations of homophobia. The downtown Minneapolis YMCA's decision to close its steam room as recently as 1991 led to similar accusations, and to a consultative meeting between YMCA administrators and the local Gay and Lesbian Community Action Council to iron out differences.

Changes in the psychiatric establishment's attitude toward homosexuality brought on by the work of individuals like Alfred Kinsey, Wardell Pomeroy, and Evelyn Hooker also provided a rationale for more liberal attitudes toward homosexuality in the Y. In the mid-1960s, the YMCA's National Council appointed a committee to study the issue of homosexuality, and to find positive ways to deal with cruising. The committee's deliberations included a meeting with Wardell Pomeroy, and resulted in a report extremely progressive for its time. The report affirmed the importance of treating homosexuals with dignity. The committee concluded that the most effective long-term way to decrease cruising was to win greater social acceptance for gay and lesbian persons. Though the progressive report was initially tabled and the committee disbanded because "some people [at the national headquarters] got scared," interest in the report of the committee revived in the early seventies in the wake of gay rights protests against the YMCA.[11]

Despite the immense changes in attitudes toward sexuality and toward men's relationships with one another, "Christian brotherhood" has not died out as a phenomenon. Unfortunately, it has been sustained most successfully in religious circles that encourage intense homophobia. Apparently a disgruntled conservative Christian YMCA member in the 1960s told one of the members of the YMCA's committee on homosexuality to ask the committee, "What do you call two men who love each other?" His rhetorical answer: "They are Christians." My own involvement in right-wing evangelical and fundamentalist groups as a college student offered me emotional satisfaction. Though I first acknowledged to myself my feelings of physical attraction for men when I was fourteen years old, coming from a conservative religious background I could not reconcile those feelings with my religious life and sought to repress them. The intimate and intense relationships I sustained with friends from Bible study and prayer groups included physical affection like hugging, touching, and in two cases, even sleeping together. Although this sleeping together did not involve overt sexual acts, it did involve caressing and holding. Though we were satisfied that such expressions were merely manifestations of our love for one another "in Christ," our relationships could be maintained only through intense denial of homosexuality in ourselves and extreme condemnation of homosexuality as a form of Satanic possession. In later years of spiritual exploration, I discovered similar patterns of emotional and physical intimacy within the walls of a Roman Catholic monastery. My spiritual wanderings since then have led to a more Whitmanesque acceptance of sexuality and active participation in the gay rights movement.

Today American churches are engaged in serious—sometimes schismatic—debate over sexual morality. Many Christian liberals now believe that the cultural sexual reforms sought in the 1920s and 1960s failed partly because traditional moral leaders and organized religious institutions simply abdicated their role in the realm of sexuality. They viscerally condemned any change in sexual morality and refused to submit their assumptions to the careful, prayerful exegesis that difficult moral issues demand. American capitalism and the lust for profit stepped into the moral void. Denomination-wide studies by the Presbyterian Church, U.S.A., and the Evangelical Lutheran Church in America in the early 1990s are only two of the most recent examples of the new direction sought by significant— if minority—constituencies within Protestant churches. While upholding marriage as a sacred institution, the reports also affirmed the validity of nonmarital relationships, withheld condemnation of masturbation, and sought normalization and acceptance of same-sex sexual relationships. These reconsiderations of traditional Christian sexual morality were offered in the hope of developing a less restrictive, more holistic view of sexuality, but also of acknowledging the presence of Christian values in realms of human experience where the possibility of faithfulness to God had been denied by an earlier generation. While such views remain minority views in most Protestant denominations, at least one mainline denomination, the United Church of Christ, has adopted policies emphasizing the wholeness and equality of all people regardless of sexual orientation. (Significantly, the UCC is the modern-day successor of nineteenth-century Congregationalism, a religious tradition that played a central role in the founding and growth of the YMCA.)

As more complete views of same-sex love and intimacy inform discussions of spirituality and ethics, it will become more possible to appreciate, and perhaps learn from, the ironies and tragedies in the history of the YMCA and other single-sex organizations and movements in the history of Christianity—from medieval monasticism to early Methodism—where intense friendship and same-sex love played central roles. Perhaps the final irony for the YMCA is that just as a spiritual ferment in the churches is bringing such issues to the forefront of theological deliberation, the YMCA is more distant from the churches than ever in its history. Christianity is still a force in the organization, but many who honor the YMCA's spiritual heritage find themselves asking how the organization could become so thoroughly secularized, so removed from the spirituality that was once its foundation. Ironically, much of the spiritual vitality and communitarian ethos of the early organization flowed out of the passionate commitments between men which were once celebrated and later eschewed by the YMCA. In discernible ways, the YMCA of men loving men has left a palpable heritage to this day. It has persisted to the extent that "Christian Brotherhood" was able to hold its own against homophobic anxiety. But in another very real sense, a valuable piece of the YMCA heritage was relinquished in the elusive search for "scientific man-making." YMCA leaders were never sophisticated theologians; they always prided themselves more in simplicity and piety than in theological hairsplitting. Yet, an enriched debate in the 1920s and 1930s over the appropriate role of same-sex love within Christianity might have shifted the terms of a debate that was eventually won by those who favored a heterosexualized, social-service-oriented YMCA dominated by physical education. Only as the YMCA continues in the present to grapple with the problems of institutionalized homophobia is it beginning to re-integrate some of the pieces that were shattered by the campaign against perversion.

ANALYSIS OF QUANTITATIVE SOURCES ON

YMCA SECRETARIAL MARITAL STATUS

The main source on the marital status of nineteenth-century
YMCA secretaries is the YMCA's official register of secretaries
and employed officers from 1879 to 1900. Although the title
imprinted on the register indicates that the record-taking began in 1879, it appears that the register was printed and began
to be used in 1882, the earliest year indicated as a date of
entry. Nevertheless, the register contains information on all
YMCA secretaries who entered service from 1862 through
1899, some 6,000 employees. I have also relied on the considerable biographical materials available at the YMCA of the
USA Archives to assemble some ninety or so biographical profiles of prominent secretaries and supporters of the YMCA. Re-
searching the marital status of YMCA secretaries using qualitative rather than quantitative sources was an arduous task. It
was rendered no less difficult by the fact that wives were
mentioned so rarely as to make them virtually invisible. It
was not uncommon for autobiographies and biographies of
YMCA figures who were married to make no reference to their
spouses. Fortunately, the marital status of YMCA secretaries
was considered important enough to include on all official

personnel records. In fact, it was one of the few items of information that was virtually never missing in the main register, compared with information about previous careers or place of birth (which was missing about 2 percent of the time) or information about subsequent careers (which was provided in only about a third of the cases). Later, twentieth-century YMCA personnel records asked for the name of the wife, and also asked for names of children, but the nineteenth-century register requested only two kinds of information from an employee: was he married? And if not, did he subsequently marry? This spare concern, reflected in these two terse questions, is indicative of what other sources already show. Marriage was considered a mark of stability, and the employer's main concern was whether or not his employee was married.[1]

In calculating marital statistics for YMCA secretaries, I took a sample of about 1,600 secretaries (or roughly one in four) from the YMCA employee registers for the nineteenth century, which I entered by hand into machine-readable format. I chose an alphabetical rather than a purely random sampling technique because of the way the data was arranged in the register. For example, there was a page for last names beginning with the letters Bo, then Br, then Bu, and so forth. On each page, entries were listed not in perfect alphabetical order, but rather according to the date they were entered, with the earliest entries first. Not all entries were made at the time an individual entered YMCA service, however: sometimes an individual might be overlooked, only to be entered later. If the page or pages allotted for a particular alphabetical section filled up, entries were continued on blank pages at the end of the register with a note indicating where the entries continued. There were typically only a handful of entries for the years before 1882. Most space in the register was taken up by individuals who entered YMCA service after the mid-1880s. For the purposes of my study, I felt that it was crucial to make sure that the early cases were not over- or underrepresented. It seemed that the easiest way to sample the records in a way that proportionately represented all years of entry into YMCA service was to sample alphabetically. Although there is some danger of ethnic bias in this sampling technique (since different nationalities may favor certain letters of the alphabet in last names), I believe that the benefits of having a sample that maintains the proportion of early YMCA employees to later YMCA employees—like allowing more confidence in chronological analysis and generalizations—outweigh the slight possibility of ethnic bias in the sample. At any rate, I already knew this sample to be overwhelmingly white Protestant men of northern and western European origin. For this study I simply used all the cases listed for the letters A, B, C, D, E, and F. Since there were so few secretaries before the early 1880s, I created a separate sample that included all secretaries who entered YMCA service before 1884. I was able to supplement this data with a collection of some sixty applications for the position of YMCA secretary for the years 1879 and 1880.

Data on the YMCA workforce for the earliest years is not as reliable as for later years, when regular bookkeeping was established. For example, about 20 percent of the cases for the years through 1882 contain no information about place of birth, compared to about 2 percent for the general sample. About 2 percent of the cases for early years are missing information on marital status, compared to 0.2 percent in the general sample. It is hard to know whether or not entire cases are missing. The haphazard manner in which a few were entered suggests that some may be missing and, if so, the cases most likely to have been excluded were those whose service in the organization was most ephemeral. However, that secretaries were included whose service had already ended by the time the YMCA began to keep records (1882) indicates that at least some attempt was made to keep a record of all secretaries whom the organization had employed from the beginning. Because the total number of secretaries on whom records were kept through 1883 is relatively small (449), it was realistic to analyze all of the material and evaluate this period with attention to the impact that a relatively small group of individuals had on the Association in its formative years.

In making comparisons with the general population, I used census data from 1880 and 1890. Tabulated data is not currently available for any year prior to 1880, though 1880 and 1890 are adequate years for comparison since approximately 90 percent of the paid workforce of the YMCA in the nineteenth century entered service after 1883. My sources for 1890 included: U.S. Department of Commerce, Bureau of the Census, *Historical Statistics of the United States* (Washington, D.C.: U.S. Bureau of the Census, 1975), pt. 1, p. 21; and U.S. Bureau of the Census, Current Population Reports, ser. P–20, publ. #242, "Marital Status and Living Arrangements," p. 2. The University of Minnesota Census Project has created machine-readable public use samples of the 1880 census, which I was able to use to tabulate comparable marriage statistics for 1880. The standard means of estimating the percentage never married is to calculate the percentage never married among those between the ages of forty-five and fifty-four. In the U.S., the percentage never married rose slightly at the end of the nineteenth century, peaked in 1890, and then steadily decreased throughout the first half of the twentieth century. In 1880, 8 percent of men never married; in 1890, approximately 9 percent.

The nature of the information in the YMCA employee registers made it easy to check directly whether or not a secretary ever married, either prior to or during his service. The marital status of the typical secretary, and the average age at marriage, were more difficult to ascertain and required more indirect means to estimate.

Because of the differing lengths of service, straightforward averages or percentages describing various characteristics of YMCA secretaries do not give a very accurate picture of how the YMCA employed staff typically looked. Only 8 percent of secretaries gave fifteen or more years of service, but this 8 percent constituted about 28 percent of the YMCA's entire paid staff in any given year. Even though 63 percent of the men who served in the YMCA served for less than five years, because of the ephemerity of their service, in any given year they constituted only between one-quarter and one-third of the Association's paid staff. So in order to provide a truer picture of what the YMCA secretarial force looked like, I have calculated most of my overall averages and statistics by weighting individual cases by the length of their service to the YMCA. I have also done a year-by-year analysis of the YMCA secretarial force from 1873 to 1899, selecting for each year only those secretaries who were in service for that year. This latter method of analysis allows for some sense of changes that may have taken place in the secretarial staff over time, and requires no special weighting to account for length of service. The former method of analysis allows more statistically sound generalizations for the entire nineteenth century since it relies on a larger number of cases but gives little sense of what variation may have existed over time. Use of these two methods together gives a good sense of the evolution of the YMCA secretaryship throughout the nineteenth century.

Ideally, in order to calculate average age at marriage, one should have the age at marriage of all YMCA secretaries. Occasionally the keeper of the register scrawled the date of a secretary's marriage into its margin, but such information was provided so inconsistently and in so few cases that it was useless for the purpose of ascertaining averages or making generalizations. There are, however, several pieces of information that could be used to estimate the average age of marriage indirectly. The register indicates the date of the entry, the age of the individual in question at the date of entry, and whether or not the individual was married at the time the entry was made. It also indicates what year the secretary left YMCA service, and whether the secretary married during the course of his service. With this information, it is possible to construct two artificial cohorts, one allowing us to estimate the average age at marriage of men during the year they were entered into the register (which is in most cases the same year they entered YMCA service) and the other allowing us to estimate the average age at marriage of men during the year they left YMCA service. Once I had constructed these artificial cohorts, I could then ascertain the age at which as close as possible to 45 percent of the men were married for each cohort. This is a technique typically used by demographers to estimate the average age at marriage from artificial cohorts.[2]

Using this procedure, it was possible to estimate that the average age at marriage among men entering YMCA service was about 31.5, and the average age at marriage among men leaving YMCA service was about 33.0. The disparate average ages at marriage between the two cohorts suggests that we are measuring two different groups of men, which in fact we are. The average length of service for YMCA secretaries for this period was about five years, although about half of all YMCA secretaries served for three years or less. The median age of YMCA secretaries entering service was 24. Thus, a typical YMCA secretary in the nineteenth century might enter YMCA service in his early twenties, serve for one, two, or three years, and then leave. One can correctly assume, given these figures, that the majority of YMCA secretaries were young and probably unmarried. These men, who left service well below the average age at marriage, would not affect the estimate of average age at marriage among the cohort of men leaving YMCA service. This estimate would be more heavily affected by the men who committed more than three years of service to the YMCA, whose service was long enough to have the possibility of marrying during the service.

The lack of information about when secretaries actually married also requires an indirect estimate of the percentage of the secretarial force that was typically unmarried. Two-thirds (66.5 percent) of all YMCA secretaries remained unmarried throughout the entire period of their YMCA service, though many of these were young secretaries with short terms of service. When this number is weighted by length of service, the figure falls to slightly more than half (52.7 percent). The percentage of secretaries who were listed as having married during their term of service (weighted by length of service) was 22.3. We have no way of knowing how long into their service these men married. We know that as a group, they probably married on average later than the general population, since none of them were married when they entered YMCA service. The most reasonable guess that we can make on the basis of available data is that they married halfway through their YMCA service; or that in any given year, half of this group would have been married and the other half unmarried. Of course this was not true, but if we use this as a basis for guessing how many secretaries were unmarried at any given time, we will not be far off. We know for certain that at least a bit more than half were unmarried; and we know that not more than 75 percent were unmarried; a little less than two-thirds (64 percent) is probably a reasonable overall estimate.

When estimating what percentage of YMCA secretaries never married, we must keep in mind that we can estimate this only for those who remained in YMCA service until they were old enough for us to conclude with some certainty that they never married. Among YMCA secretaries, the percentage of never married levels off at about age fifty, at roughly 15 percent. This is significantly higher than for men in the general population at this time period, where about 8–9 percent never married. Finally, when we weight the cases by length of service in order to estimate for a typical year the proportion of YMCA workers who never married, it rises to slightly more than one-fifth (21.3 percent). Never-married secretaries in the fifty-and-older age group gave on average 20.8 years of service to the YMCA, compared with an average of 15.7 years among married secretaries of comparable age.

METHODOLOGICAL PROBLEMS:
SILENCES, THE SPIRIT/BODY SPLIT,
AND THE DENIAL OF CRUISING

Despite my knowledge of the YMCA's reputation and the apparently long history of cruising on its premises, and despite the fact that one focus of my study was the history of male sexuality, I resisted examining cruising at the YMCA until the late stages of my research. My decision not to investigate cruising stemmed from more than just embarrassment about the topic, or the fear that it might ruffle feathers both in the YMCA and in the historical profession. At the time I believed that there was an unbridgeable abyss between the historic Christian mission of the YMCA—which was, after all, the central organizing principle of my research—and the sexual behavior that occurred on its premises seemingly in spite of that Christian mission. I assumed that the YMCA either did not know about what was happening on its property, or if it did know, that it did not approve and that it surely attempted to curb or stop it. I also assumed that cruising was engaged in only by non-Christian or nominally Christian men who made opportunistic use of YMCA facilities and who had no

interest in the YMCA's Christian mission, and certainly not by respected
YMCA leaders, YMCA employees, or committed Christian YMCA members.
If all these assumptions were true, then even if a social history of YMCA
cruising might make a very interesting chapter in the history of American
sexuality, it belonged in some other book, not in a study that took seriously
the Christian mission of the Association. It seemed pointless to include a
chapter about cruising in a book on the YMCA only so I could show how the
institution officially disapproved of and discouraged the practice. I was content to write about romantic friendship in the YMCA fellowship, and leave
it at that. As it turns out, however, I was mistaken on most of my assumptions and premises. I knew little about the nature of cruising, or the way it
inhabits the social spaces in which it takes place.

My ignorance was abetted by the spirit/body split, a cultural bias that
encourages us to see sexuality and spirituality as mutually exclusive phe-
nomena, and by persistent, insistent lying about men's sexual behavior.[1]
Few people want to believe the truth about cruising, even when it hits them
squarely on the nose, partly because the spirit/body split is so fundamental
to our way of understanding the world that we would be confused without
it. A letter to the editor of the *L.A. Times* responding to the Walter Jenkins
scandal in 1964 was typical: despite the evidence that Jenkins had a long
history of cruising at the Y (including a previous, 1959 arrest at the same
YMCA) the letter-writer could only believe that the incident had somehow been rigged by Goldwater Republicans. One factor in her disbelief was
her conviction that such goings on could not possibly occur at the Young
Men's Christian Association.[2] In 1962, Dr. Roy R. Grinker suggested in a
YMCA Midwest Counseling Workshop that "based on my studies of George
Williams [College] people over several years" there was considerable evidence of "latent homosexuality" among YMCA leaders and employees. In
the question-and-answer session that followed, the only interest anyone
showed in the data was to find out the best way to purge homosexuality from
the organization. Grinker himself backed away from his own conclusions:
"Don't draw any conclusions from that—I don't say that this means they
are latent homosexuals. There may be other reasons."[3] The vast silence in
YMCA sources about sexuality reinforces the myth that it just doesn't happen in the Association, and that if it does it could not possibly have any real
significance for how the organization operates or how men in the organization relate to each other.

For obvious reasons, sources on the history of YMCA cruising were difficult to come by. Not only has the YMCA historically had an interest in
denying the existence of cruising, but the phenomenon under study is by its

nature furtive and ephemeral. I have relied on two sets of sources for information about the YMCA's cruising scene. One set offers perspectives on how the public and the YMCA reacted to homosexual cruising. This set consists of references to the phenomenon in newspapers and YMCA publications, court records and judicial reports from sex scandals, and records from the first official studies of homosexuality conducted by the YMCA's National Council in the mid-1960s. The second set provides understanding of how the men who participated in the cruising scene viewed it and understood their participation in it. Besides the above mentioned artistic and literary sources (which document the YMCA cruising scene at least back to the 1920s), this set includes the court testimony of men caught in sex scandals, interviews conducted with gay men in the early 1930s published in George Henry's *Sex Variants*, Donald Vining's diary, which recounts his experiences as a YMCA employee in the 1940s, and oral histories of nineteen gay men in their sixties, seventies, eighties, and nineties who experienced the cruising scene at YMCAs as early as the 1920s, and who knew, through acquaintances in the urban gay subculture, of cruising activity that had gone on at YMCAs in the decades before then.

Understanding the perspective of the men who participated in the scene is crucial to understanding how and why it developed where it did and in the way it did. Yet, unfortunately, there is little data from this perspective before 1930: what data exists consists mostly of court testimony and medical research, both settings that were not friendly to the men giving testimony and which naturally biased the kind of information offered. Yet I believe that evidence from the years after 1930 can give relevant insight into the period before 1930. Despite enormous changes that took place in attitudes toward sexuality during the twenties, same-sex sex acts continued to be intensely stigmatized. While the "sexual revolution" of the 1920s allowed certain forms of heterosocial leisure and heterosexual interaction to begin to move out of the Victorian sexual underworld and into popular culture, resulting, among other things, in a decline in prostitution and an increase in premarital sex, there was no corresponding lightening of attitudes toward homosexuality. If anything, homosexuality was even more stigmatized as popularized Freudian psychology spread the perception of homosexuality as a disease and threat to society and the family. Evidence about both homosexual and heterosexual underworlds in the nineteenth and early twentieth centuries suggests that stigmatization of certain forms of sexual behavior was the key reason for the existence of these underworlds. Thus, the continuing stigmatization of homosexuality suggests a key area of continuity in the homosexual underworld through the 1920s. The fact that the homosexual underworlds of American cities were exposed to psychiatric and medical discourse about homosexuality much earlier than the general population—as early as the 1880s and 1890s, when American homosexual subcultures first began to form—similarly suggests more continuity in homosexual experience after 1930 than there would be for heterosexual experience. Thus, while shifts in sexual categories that occurred in the 1920s are crucial to understanding "heterosexual" responses to the homosexual subculture, this suggests that the periodization of men's experience within that subculture should be somewhat different, that there was no major transformation of identities and roles until the rise of an organized, national gay rights movement in the 1950s and 1960s.

I compiled the oral histories used in this study during research in Los Angeles and San Francisco in the summer of 1992. Jim Kepner, the director of the International Lesbian and Gay Archives, West Hollywood, California, put me in contact with a number of older gay men whom he knew to have been involved in the cruising scene at the YMCA, who in turn referred me to friends of theirs who were willing to talk about their YMCA cruising experiences. In San Francisco, Allan Bérubé helped put me in contact with more men. All agreed to be quoted in print, and only one objected to having his real name used. I interviewed nineteen men, on the following dates, either by phone or in person: Jim Kepner, Los Angeles, August 20 and 24, 1992; Howard Warren, Los Angeles, August 21, 1992; Dorr Legg, telephone conversation, August 21 and 22, 1992; James Dawson, Los Angeles, August 25, 1992; Wayne Flottman, Los Angeles, August 25, 1992; Martin Block, telephone conversation, August 27, 1992; Harry Hay, with Jim Kepner, Los Angeles, August 29, 1992; Paul Hardman, Los Angeles, August 31, 1992; Tony Raffo, telephone conversation, August 31, 1992; William Billings, Los Angeles, August 31, 1992; Larry Littlejohn, telephone conversation, August 31, 1992; George Mendenhall, San Francisco, September 2, 1992; Sam Steward, telephone conversation, September 2, 1992; Hal Call, San Francisco, September 2, 1992; Bob Basker, telephone conversation, September 3, 1992; Paul M. McGuinness, Los Angeles, September 11, 1992; Morris Kight, Los Angeles, September 12, 1992; Randy Alfred, Los Angeles, no date; Fred Morrison (pseudonym), telephone conversation, no date. Although all of the men interviewed currently live in California, I was satisfied with the sample since almost all of them were originally from other parts of the country, and had had experiences in YMCAs across the country, from San Francisco to New York, from Chicago to Denver, and from Kansas City to Miami.

Before meeting with any of the narrators, I prepared a set of questions that I posed to each narrator, in the same order:

What brought you to the YMCA?

How did you know there was sex going on at the Y?

What kinds of activity were going on there?

What years did you go to the Y? Which Y's did you patronize?

How long do you think cruising had been going on there?

Did the YMCA management know what was going on?

Were there attempts to stop what was going on? [If yes,] What kind of attempts?

Did the police ever get involved in attempts to control YMCA cruising?

What kind of men patronized the Y?

What kind of men came looking for sex?

Were there particular types who were sought after?

Why do you think the Y had such a cruisy reputation?

The last four questions were aimed at trying to get some sense of the interplay of class, race, gender, and sexual identity. Sometimes the narrators discussed their own preferences and experiences, and sometimes they described what they had observed. When appropriate, I probed further with additional questions that arose in response to their answers to the above questions, although they were usually only of a clarifying nature. I did not tape any of the interviews, but simply took down the responses with pen and paper, since I have in the past found the use of a tape recorder awkward and occasionally intimidating to the narrator. In recording responses, I tried to record information in the exact words of the narrator as much as possible. I also received permission from all of the narrators to follow up the interviews with later questions should I need future clarification of my notes.

NOTES

Introduction

Unless otherwise noted, all manuscript collections and unpublished documents are located in the YMCA of the USA Archives (YMCA Archives), St. Paul, MN.

1. For those who are unfamiliar with the field of lesbian and gay history, the following works have played an important role in my understanding of the field for late-nineteenth- and early-twentieth-century America: Jonathan Ned Katz, *The Invention of Heterosexuality* (New York: Dutton, 1995); George Chauncey, *Gay New York: Gender, Urban Culture, and the Making of the Gay Male World, 1890–1940* (New York: Basic Books, 1994); Elizabeth Lapovsky Kennedy and Madeline D. Davis, *Boots of Leather, Slippers of Gold: The History of a Lesbian Community* (New York: Routledge, 1993); Edward J. Tejirian, *Sexuality and the Devil: Symbols of Love, Power, and Fear in Male Psychology* (New York: Routledge, 1990); Eve Kosofsky Sedgwick, *Epistemology of the Closet* (Berkeley: University of California Press, 1990); Martin Bauml Duberman, Martha Vicinius, and George Chauncey, Jr., eds., *Hidden from History: Reclaiming the Gay and Lesbian Past* (New York: Meridian, 1989); E. Anthony Rotundo, "Romantic Friendship: Male Intimacy and Middle-Class Youth in the Northern United States, 1802–1900," *Journal of Social History* 23 (Fall 1989): 1–25; Allan Bérubé, *Coming Out under Fire: Gay Americans and the Military in World War II* (New York: Free Press, 1989); Christina Simmons, "Modern Sexuality and the Myth of Victorian

Repression," in Kathy Peiss, Christina Simmons, and Robert Padgug, eds., *Passion and Power: Sexuality in History* (Philadelphia: Temple University Press, 1989), pp. 157–177; Bert Hansen, "American Physicians' Earliest Writings about Homosexuals, 1880–1900," *Milbank Quarterly* 67 (1989): 92–108; David F. Greenberg, *The Construction of Homosexuality* (Chicago: University of Chicago Press, 1988); John D'Emilio and Estelle Freedman, *Intimate Matters: A History of Sexuality in America* (New York: Harper and Row, 1988); Gloria T. Hull, *Color, Sex, and Poetry: Three Women Writers of the Harlem Renaissance* (Bloomington: Indiana University Press, 1987); John W. Crowley, "Howells, Stoddard, and Male Homosexual Attachment in Victorian America," in Harry Brod, ed., *The Making of Masculinities: The New Men's Studies* (Boston: Allen and Unwin, 1987), pp. 301–324; Martin Duberman, *About Time: Exploring the Gay Past* (New York: Gay Presses of New York, 1986); Henry L. Minton, "Femininity in Men and Masculinity in Women: American Psychiatry and Psychology Portray Homosexuality in the 1930s," *Journal of Homosexuality* 13 (1986): 1–21; Michael Lynch, "'Here Is Adhesiveness': From Friendship to Homosexuality," *Victorian Studies* 29 (1985): 67–96; George Chauncey, Jr., "Christian Brotherhood or Sexual Perversion? Homosexual Identities and the Construction of Sexual Boundaries in the World War I Era," *Journal of Social History* 19 (1985): 189–212; Gregory Sprague, "Male Homosexuality in Western Culture: The Dilemma of Identity and Subculture in Historical Research," *Journal of Homosexuality* 10 (1984): 29–44; Esther Newton, "The Mythic Mannish Lesbian: Radclyffe Hall and the New Woman," *Signs* 9 (1984); Michel Foucault, *Histoire de la sexualité*, 3 vols. (Paris: Galimard, 1978–1984); Jonathan Ned Katz, *Gay/Lesbian Almanac: A New Documentary* (New York: Harper and Row, Publishers, 1983); John D'Emilio, *Sexual Politics, Sexual Communities: The Making of a Sexual Minority in the United States* (Chicago: University of Chicago Press, 1983); Terry L. Chapman, "'An Oscar Wilde Type': 'The Abominable Crime of Buggery' in Western Canada, 1890–1920," *Criminal Justice History* 4 (1983): 97–118; Eric Garber, "'T'Ain't Nobody's Bizness': Homosexuality in 1920's Harlem," in Michael Smith, ed., *Black Men/White Men* (San Francisco: Gay Sunshine Press, 1983); Lillian Faderman, *Surpassing the Love of Men: Romantic Friendship and Love between Women from the Renaissance to the Present* (New York: Morrow, 1981); Blanche Wiesen Cook, "The Historical Denial of Lesbianism," *Radical History Review* (1979): 60–65; Nancy Sahli, "'Smashing': Women's Relationships before the Fall," *Chrysalis* 8 (1979): 17–27; Jonathan Ned Katz, *Gay American History: Lesbians and Gay Men in the U.S.A., A Documentary* (New York: Thomas Y. Crowell Co., 1976); Carroll Smith-Rosenberg, "The Female World of Love and Ritual: Relations between Women in Nineteenth Century America" *Signs* 1 (1975): 1–29; John Burnham, "Early References to Homosexual Communities in American Medical Writings," *Human Sexuality* 7 (1973): 34–49; Vern Bullough and Martha Vogt, "Homosexuality and Its Confusion with the 'Secret Sin' in Pre-Freudian America," *Journal of the History of Medicine* 28 (1973): 143–154; Mary McIntosh, "The Homosexual Role," *Social Problems* 16 (1968): 182–192.

2. Smith-Rosenberg's "The Female World of Love and Ritual" has been seminal in studies of female relationships and intimacy. It showed that physical and sexual intimacy could be part of the spectrum of female friendship in the nineteenth century,

but it has also been used to prove that passionate expressions of love between women which seem lesbian to twentieth-century readers were physically chaste. Adrienne Rich, in "Compulsory Heterosexuality and Lesbian Existence," *Signs* 5 (1980): 631–660, complicated discussions of female sexuality by offering a definition of lesbians as "women-oriented women"—a definition based on female solidarity rather than sexual behavior. Much of the controversy about historical analysis of women's relationships has revolved around biographies which tended to downplay intense relationships between women, or which sought to deny evidence that the relationships were in fact lesbian: Anna Mary Wells, *Miss Marks and Miss Woolley* (Boston: Houghton Mifflin, 1978); Doris Faber, *The Life of Lorena Hickok: E.R.'s Friend* (New York: William Morrow, 1980); and Marjorie Housepian Dobkin, *The Making of a Feminist: Early Journals and Letters of M. Carey Thomas* (Kent, Ohio: Kent State University Press, 1980). A classic statement critiquing denials of possible lesbianism in intense female friendships was made by Blanche Wiesen Cook in "The Historical Denial of Lesbianism," a review of Wells's biography of Mary Woolley, former president of Mount Holyoke. Cook has since written her own biography of Eleanor Roosevelt (*Eleanor Roosevelt* [New York: Viking, 1992]), revisiting the denials in the Hickok biography. Another influential critique of efforts to deny lesbianism was Gerda Lerner, "Where Biographers Fear to Tread," *Women's Review of Books* 11 (1987): 11–12. Cook's and Lerner's critiques claimed as lesbian many of the most influential female reformers of the nineteenth and early twentieth centuries: Jane Addams, Susan B. Anthony, Carrie Chapman Catt, Anna Dickinson, Alice Paul, Mary Rozet Smith, Lillian Wald, and Frances Willard. Arguments about whether historical individuals or relationships could be classified as lesbian or not have not, however, depended on whether relationships were believed to include a sexual component. Lillian Faderman, in *Surpassing the Love of Men,* took for granted that these relationships were in fact chaste, though they were clearly viewed as in continuity with modern lesbian relationships. Rich's analysis also saw the verifiable presence of a sexual component in women's relationships as irrelevant to the question of whether the relationship could be described as lesbian. For an interesting interpretation of the debate, see Leila Rupp, "'Imagine My Surprise': Women's Relationships in Mid-Twentieth Century America," in Bauml Duberman, Vicinus, and Chauncey, eds., *Hidden From History.* The issues continue to resurface. Trisha Franzen, *Spinsters and Lesbians: Independent Womanhood in the United States* (New York: New York University Press, 1996) is a recent book which virtually claims all nineteenth-century spinsters as lesbians. A new take on the subject appears in Esther D. Rothblum and Kathleen A. Brehony, eds., *Boston Marriages: Romantic but Asexual Relationships among Contemporary Lesbians* (Amherst: University of Massachusetts Press, 1994). *Boston Marriages*, based on interviews with modern lesbian couples, argues that among modern lesbians passion and romance define their relationships more than actual sex.

3. See Bérubé, *Coming Out under Fire.*

4. See John Spurlock, *Free Love: Marriage and Middle-Class Radicalism in America, 1820–1860* (New York: New York University Press, 1988); Linda Gordon, "Voluntary Motherhood: The Beginnings of Feminist Birth Control Ideas in the United

States," in Mary S. Hartman and Lois Banner, eds., *Clio's Consciousness Raised* (New York: Harper and Row, 1974), pp. 54–64; Victoria Woodhull, *The Scare Crows of Sexual Slavery* (New York: Woodhull and Claflin, 1874).

5. I use the term "cruising," common in modern gay parlance, to describe the practice of men meeting each other in public settings for casual sex.

Chapter One

1. The following outline of YMCA history in the British Isles and North America is based on institutional histories of the YMCA. All agree on the broad outlines of the Association's founding, early growth, and development: Elmer Johnson, *The History of YMCA Physical Education* (Chicago: Follett Publishing Co., 1979); Clifford M. Drury, *San Francisco YMCA: 100 Years by the Golden Gate, 1853–1953* (Glendale, CA: Arthur H. Clark Co., 1963); Emmett Dedmon, *Great Enterprises: 100 Years of the YMCA of Metropolitan Chicago* (New York: Rand McNally, 1957); William B. Whiteside, *The Boston YMCA and Community Need* (New York: Association Press, 1951); Galen M. Fisher, *Public Affairs and the YMCA, 1844–1944* (New York: Association Press, 1948); Mary Ross Hall and Helen Firman Sweet, *Women in the YMCA Record* (New York: Association Press, 1947); S. Wirt Wiley, *The History of YMCA-Church Relations in the United States* (New York: Association Press, 1944); Paul M. Limbert, *Christian Emphasis in YMCA Program* (New York: Association Press, 1944); S. Wirt Wiley and Florence Lehman, *Builders of Men: A History of the Minneapolis YMCA, 1866–1936* (Minneapolis, MN: Association, 1938); Clarence P. Shedd, *Two Centuries of Student Christian Movements: Their Origin and Intercollegiate Life* (New York: Association Press, 1934); Paul Super, *Formative Ideas in the YMCA* (New York: Association Press, 1929); Laurence L. Doggett, *History of the YMCA* (New York: Association Press, 1896); *The Verdict of Time: Fifty Years—Philadelphia YMCA* (Philadelphia: YMCA, 1905); Henry J. McCoy, et al., *San Francisco, Five Decades: 1853–1903 Historical Record* (San Francisco: YMCA, 1903); W. H. H. Smith, et al., *The Record of Fifty Years and a Look Ahead* (N.p., 1902); L. L. Doggett, *History of the Boston YMCA* (Boston, YMCA, 1901); Russell Thompson, *The YMCA of Cleveland* (Cleveland: Association, 1901); *Then and Now, 1881–1891: The Progress of a Decade of Years in the YMCA, Newburgh, N.Y.* (Newburgh, NY: Association, 1891); *The Story of Twenty Years in the Life of the YMCA of Dayton, Ohio* (Dayton: Association, 1890); Robert R. McBurney, *Historical Sketch of the YMCA* (St. Louis: State Executive Committee, 1884). The most reliable and comprehensive history of the YMCA in North America is C. Howard Hopkins, *History of the YMCA in North America* (New York: Association Press, 1951). Hopkins was a professional historian who specialized in the study of social welfare movements in America, and was commissioned by the YMCA to write this comprehensive history using institutional sources. This study is based on many of the same archival sources that Hopkins used in his work.

2. The following works have been influential in my understanding of nineteenth-century American religion, and can provide a useful cultural and social context for the American "layman's revival" of the 1850s that led to the establishment of the

YMCA and the growth of the YMCA movement in the nineteenth century: Martin E. Marty, *Righteous Empire: The Protestant Experience in America* (New York: Dial Press, 1970), especially pp. 90–110, 121, 148–155, 163–182; Martin E. Marty, *Pilgrims in Their Own Land* (Boston: Little, Brown, 1984); Martin E. Marty, *Religion and Republic* (Boston: Becson Press, 1987); Jon Butler, *Awash in a Sea of Faith: Christianizing the American People* (Cambridge: Harvard University Press, 1990); see also Winthrop S. Hudson, *Religion in America*, 2nd ed. (New York: Charles Scribner's Sons, 1973); Henry F. May, *Protestant Churches and Industrial America* (New York: Harper, 1949); Aaron Ignatius Abell, *The Urban Impact on American Protestantism, 1865–1900* (Cambridge: Harvard University Press, 1943).

3. Among others, the YMCA recruited the good services of Walt Whitman as part of its Christian Commission outreach efforts. Charley Shively has examined Whitman's same-sex attractions as a motivation in his YMCA service during the Civil War. Charley Shively, *Drum Beats: Walt Whitman's Civil War Boy Lovers* (San Francisco: Gay Sunshine Press, 1989); and *Calamus Lovers: Walt Whitman's Working-Class Camerados* (San Francisco: Gay Sunshine Press, 1987).

4. The term "British Provinces" referred to Canada.

5. The Portland Convention of 1869 defined evangelical churches as "those . . . which, maintaining the Holy Scriptures to be the only infallible rule of faith and practice, do believe in the Lord Jesus Christ (the only begotten of the Father, King of Kings, and Lord of Lords, in whom dwelleth the fullness of the Godhead bodily, and who was made sin for us, though knowing no sin, bearing our sins in His own body on the tree), as the only name under heaven given among men whereby we must be saved from everlasting punishment." *YMCA Annual Report* (New York: International Committee, 1869), pp. 51, 101, cited in Hopkins, *History of the YMCA*, p. 366.

6. See Hopkins, *History of the YMCA*, pp. 426–427.

7. See Ibid., pp. 444–446.

8. The best study to date of the "Colored" associations is Nina Mjagkij, *Light in the Darkness: African Americans and the YMCA, 1852–1946* (Lexington: University of Kentucky Press, 1994). See also Hopkins, *History of the YMCA*, pp. 180, 210–221, 472–475, 540–543, 580–82, for discussions of YMCA work among African Americans, Native Americans, and Chinese. For a discussion of the physical plant and resources available to black associations in Hopkins, see pp. 156, 458, 580, and 582.

9. The term "physical work" was used by YMCA leaders as a synonym for their physical education program. The YMCA used the term "work" to refer to different program emphases, e.g., "college work," "Colored work" (segregated programming for blacks), "army work."

See Hopkins, *History of the YMCA,* for an overview of the early growth and development of the YMCA; because of Robert Weidensall's role as first field secretary, the Robert Weidensall Papers (YMCA of the s, St. Paul, MN) are an invaluable primary source on the International Committee's role in establishing early associations, the first "railroad work," early "college work," "county work" (YMCA rural outreach), and the establishment of YMCA training schools. See especially Robert Weidensall, "Early History of the College Work of Young Men's Christian Associations" (typescript, 1911); Robert Weidensall, comp., "Letters: Cephas Brainerd to Robert Weidensall, 1868–1893" (typecript, 1911); Robert Weidensall, "The First Field Work and Early Development of the YMCA Movement as Conducted under the International Committee and Its First Employed Agent" (manuscript, 1912).

10. Hopkins, *History of the YMCA,* has the best overall discussion of the evolution of the organization's mission and program; for a more detailed discussion of the role played by the "evangelical test" (the requirement that voting members of the YMCA be members of evangelical churches) and the fourfold plan in YMCA-church relations, see S. Wirt Wiley, *History of YMCA-Church Relations in the United States* (New York: Association Press, 1944) and Owen E. Pence, *Present-Day YMCA-Church Relations in the United States* (New York: Association Press, 1948).

11. See Bruce Haley, *The Healthy Body and Victorian Culture* (Cambridge: Harvard University Press, 1978).

12. See, for instance, Emmett A. Rice, *A Brief History of Physical Education* (New York: A. S. Barnes and Co., 1929), chap. 20, esp. p. 191. L. L. Doggett, YMCA historian and first president of the YMCA's training school in Springfield was a wholehearted advocate of the "liberal" approach to Christian manhood and of physical education. He wrote:

> In its plan of operations it embodied the modern religious ideal of development as contrasted with the ascetic ideal. It recognized that all human powers should be developed to their utmost capacity and consecrated to God's service. It agreed with modern science in denying the separation between the sacred and the secular, and it recognized with the new psychology the unity of man in body, mind, and spirit. (Doggett, *History of the Boston YMCA*, p. 72.)

13. Robert Weidensall, *Man's Needs and Their Supplies* (New York: Association Press, 1919), pp. 242–243.

14. Cited in Emmett Dedmon, *Great Enterprises: 100 Years of the YMCA of Metropolitan Chicago* (New York: Rand McNally, 1957), p. 42.

15. Richard C. Morse, Report to Milwaukee Convention, 1883 Annual Report.

16. Mention or accounts of "breakdowns" popped up in the correspondence of several leading YMCA international secretaries. See Robert Weidensall Papers; Robert Weidensall, "Letters: Cephas Brainerd to Robert Weidensall"; C. K. Ober Papers; L. D. Wishard Papers; and R. C. Morse Papers. One example can be found in a series of correspondence between Robert Weidensall and John R. Boardman (in the Weidensall Papers: Boardman to Weidensall, September 19, 1904; November 18, 1905; January 29, 1907; and March 18, 1910; Weidensall to Boardman, April 4, 1907). Boardman was clearly showing signs of stress in his correspondence, which included vows to "absolutely . . . give every moment of my time to field work that is possible." In 1907 he confessed that a "nervous breakdown" had "knocked [him] square out of business."

17. See Kathy Peiss, *Cheap Amusements: Working Women and Leisure in Turn-of-the-Century New York* (Philadelphia: Temple University Press, 1986); Kevin White, *The First Sexual Revolution: The Emergence of Male Heterosexuality in Modern America* (New York: New York University Press, 1993).

18. Samuel M. Sayford, *Personal Work* (New York: International Committee, 1899), p. 112.

19. From the 1863–1864 San Francisco YMCA Annual Report, cited in Drury, *San Francisco YMCA*, p. 41.

20. Cited in Drury, *San Francisco YMCA*, p. 81.

21. George J. Fisher, "The Story of the Association's Physical Work," *Association Men* 38 (1912): 1.

22. William Blaikie, "Physical Training in the Young Men's Christian Association," *Association Men* 27, no. 6 (March 1902): 236.

23. Doggett, *History of the Boston YMCA*, p. 50.

24. Charles Helmick, untitled article, *Kansas Pilgrim*, no. 1 (January 1891).

25. Frank M. Gates, "The Future of the Physical Department in Kansas," *Kansas Pilgrim,* no. 3 (March 16, 1891).

26. Letter, W. A. Holmes to Thomas Cochran, February 6, 1892, Kansas Sudan Movement Papers.

27. Circular letter from George S. Fisher, December 31, 1890.

28. George S. Fisher, untitled speech, *Kansas Pilgrim,* no. 1 (January 1891).

29. E. E. Helms, "Why Do Associations Fail?" *Kansas Pilgrim*, no. 3 (March 1891).

30. Letter, Walter T. Hart to Chris Hall, April 13, 1897, Messer Papers, Chicago Historical Society, Chicago, IL.

31. Letter, L. W. Messer to J. F. Oates, March 4, 1897, Messer Papers.

32. "Personal Purity," *Boston Globe* (1891?), Newspaper clipping, Samuel M. Sayford Papers.

33. Article, Philadelphia, December 18, 1893, Samuel M. Sayford Papers.

34. Undated newspaper clipping, Samuel M. Sayford Papers.

35. Letter, Edward H. Bosworth to L. W. Messer, December 16, 1912, Messer Papers.

36. Letter, L. W. Messer to F. B. Barnes, July 28, 1897, Messer Papers.

37. "From the Viewpoint of Association Men," *Association Men* 38, no. 1 (October 1912): 23–24.

38. Ibid.

39. From a Kansas-Sudan Mission tract; *Kansas Pilgrim*, nos. 3 and 4 (March and April, 1891).

40. Morse Family League letter, February 18, 1903, Morse Papers.

41. Charles Conrad Hamilton, "Journal, 1892–93" (manuscript), pp. 66, 80, 96, 109, 127, 129, 137; Frank H. Wood to R. C. Morse, December 15, 1892, India Files.

42. Cited in Edwin Burritt Smith, et al., *Historical Sketch of the YMCA of Chicago 1858–1898* (Chicago: Association, 1898).

43. See Mayer N. Zald, *Organizational Change: The Political Economy of the YMCA* (Chicago: University of Chicago Press, 1970). This study documents the YMCA's shift from a mission-driven evangelical organization to a service organization that sold memberships. As a result, the YMCA was forced to become more attentive to the market. For a more general discussion of changes in how physical education is provided, see Michael J. Ellis, *The Business of Physical Education* (Champaign, IL: Human Kinetics Books, 1988), esp. pp. 86–87, for a discussion of

the YMCA's increasing attentiveness to (and success in) shaping its program to market forces since the 1920s.

44. R. A. Allen, M.D., "Moral and Religious Opportunities in the Physical Department," *Physical Training* 19 (December 1921).

45. R. C. Cubbon, "The Physical Department's Religious Opportunity," *Association Men* 38 (October 1912): 28.

46. Laurence L. Doggett, *A Man and a School: Pioneering in Higher Education at Springfield College* (New York: Association Press, 1943), pp. 40–43.

47. For general accounts of the development of the YMCA's physical program, see Hopkins, *History of the* YMCA, pp. 245–270; Johnson, *The History of YMCA Physical Education*; Rice, *A Brief History of Physical Education*; Fred Eugene Leonard, *A Guide to the History of Physical Education* (Philadelphia: Lea and Febiger, 1947); Physical Directors' Society of the Young Men's Christian Associations of North America, *Physical Education in the Young Men's Christian Associations of North America* (New York: Association Press, 1920); see also Mabel Lee, *A History of Physical Education and Sports in the U.S.A.* (New York: Wiley, 1983); Betty Mary Spears, *History of Sport and Physical Activity in the United States* (Dubuque, IA: William C. Brown Co., 1978); and Earle E. Zeigler, *A History of Physical Education and Sport in the United States and Canada* (Champaign, IL: Stipes Publishing Co., 1975).

Emmett Rice's history of physical education (1929 ed.) contrasted the YMCA's "modern" Christianity with earlier "ascetic" views. Before the YMCA's development of a holistic mind-body-spirit philosophy, Christians would have found it difficult to accept the kind of physical program promoted by the YMCA (p. 191). Rice's analysis probably reflected the tension still existing in some quarters in the 1920s over the proper role of physical education in the YMCA's broader mission.

48. Doggett, *Man and a School*, pp. 43–44.

49. Luther Gulick's January 1888 circular, "The Real Work of the YMCA," quoted in Doggett, *Man and a School*, p. 50.

50. *Triangle* 1, no. 2 (March 1891): 34.

51. Luther Halsey Gulick, "Unity and Symmetry," *Triangle* 1, no. 3 (April 1891).

52. Luther Halsey Gulick, "Why Every Christian Worker Should Take Systematic Physical Exercise," *Triangle* 1, no. 1 (February 1891): 5.

53. Doggett, *Man and a School*, pp. 56–57.

54. Ethel J. Dorgan, *Luther Halsey Gulick, 1865–1918* (New York: Bureau of Publications, Teachers College, Columbia University, 1934), pp. 17, 58.

55. Luther H. Gulick, *The Dynamic of Manhood* (New York: Association Press, 1917), pp. 121–124.

56. Gulick was appointed as the YMCA International Committee's first secretary for physical work in 1889, but he began training physical directors for the YMCA as early as 1887. When the YMCA training school was established in Springfield, Massachusetts, in 1894, Gulick held the chair of history and philosophy of physical training, and oversaw the training school's program for physical directors until 1906. Gulick was succeeded as the International Committee's secretary for physical work in 1903 by George J. Fisher. Fisher was succeeded by Martin I. Foss. John Brown, Jr.

served as international secretary in the 1920s. *Triangle*, 1891–92; *Physical Education*, 1892–96; *Physical Training*, 1901–1928.

57. Fisher, "The Story of the Association's Physical Work," p. 1.

58. Cubbon, "Religious Opportunity," p. 28.

59. Samuel M. Sayford, undated sermon, Samuel M. Sayford Papers. Compare with his criticism of athletics in *Personal Work*, p. 112.

60. *Triangle* 1, no. 2 (March 1891): 34.

61. See John D'Emilio and Estelle B. Freedman, *Intimate Matters: A History of Sexuality in America* (New York: Harper and Row, 1988), pp. 266–268; Michael Gordon, "From an Unfortunate Necessity to a Cult of Mutual Orgasm: Sex in American Marital Education Literature, 1830–1940," in James Henslin and Edward Sagarin, eds., *The Sociology of Sex: An Introductory Reader*, rev. ed. (New York: Schocken,1978); Dennis Brissett and Lionel Lewis, "Guidelines for Marital Sex: An Analysis of Fifteen Popular Marriage Manuals," *Family Coordinator* 19 (January 1970): 41–48; Christina Simmons, "Marriage in the Modern Manner: Sexual Radicalism and Reform in America, 1914–1941" (Ph.D. diss., Brown University, 1982); Christina Simmons, "Modern Sexuality and the Myth of Victorian Repression," in Kathy Peiss and Christina Simmons, with Robert Padgug, eds., *Passion and Power: Sexuality in History* (Philadelphia: Temple University Press, 1989), 157–177.

62. Cephas Brainerd recalled that "the first arrests and the first convictions under that law were obtained by members of the Board of Directors of the New York Association, who performed the parts of detective and prosecutor." From a privately printed transcript of a memorial dinner for Brainerd on the occasion of his retirement from the International Committee: *A Tribute to Twenty-five Years of Successful Leadership in Work for Young Men* (New York: 1893), pp. 29–30.

63. See Hopkins, *History of the YMCA*, p. 385: "[The White Cross Army's] opponents, who included Weidensall and several leading city secretaries, declared that the pledge violated Association principle and that the program was 'simply a moral reform' and as such had no place in the Association. 'No man's heart is pure unless made so by the acceptance of Jesus Christ as a personal Saviour and the work of the Holy Spirit,' wrote Weidensall; 'No pledges without Christ can do it'"; citations from *Watchman* 11 (1885): 161, 200, 258, 260, 284.

64. Hopkins, *History*, pp. 383–386.

65. H. S. Ninde, J. T. Bowne, and Erskine Uhl, eds., *A Hand-Book of the History, Organization, and Methods of Work of Young Men's Christian Associations* (New York: International Committee of Young Men's Christian Associations, 1892), p. 321.

66. James W. McCandless, *Association Administration: A Study of the Professional Task of Operating a Young Men's Christian Association* (New York: Association Press, 1925), p. 25; See also Paul Super, *Training a Staff: A Manual for Young Men's Christian Association Executives* (New York: Association Press, 1920); and the General Board of the Young Men's Christian Associations, *Men Working: The YMCA Program and the Present Needs of Youth* (New York: Association Press, 1936), which discuss sex education as an accepted part of the standard YMCA program.

67. See Gulick, *Dynamic of Manhood*.

68. Dorgan, *Gulick*, p. 5.

69. "A Physical Department Policy," *Association Men* 38 (October 1912): 38.

70. William Blaikie, "Physical Training in the Young Men's Christian Association," *Association Men* 27 (March 1902): 234.

71. George J. Fisher, "Prolonging Life at Least Ten Years," *Association Men* 38 (October 1912): 3.

72. Introduction, R. C. Morse, "How a Man of Seventy Keeps in Form," *Association Men* 38 (October 1912): 4.

73. "From the Viewpoint of Association Men," *Association Men* 38 (October 1912): 25.

74. "Revelations of the Examining Room," *Association Men* 38 (October 1912): 16–17.

75. Ninde, et al., eds., *HandBook*, pp. 304–305.

76. See YMCA *Yearbooks,* 1870–1940.

77. Medical doctors who shaped the YMCA's physical work included (of course) Luther H. Gulick, George J. Fisher (his successor as international physical work secretary), James H. McCurdy (Gulick's successor at the Springfield Training School), George Poole, William G. Anderson, Henry F. Kallenberg, J. Gardner Smith, W. B. Newhall, A. E. Garland, John Brown, Jr., and not least, Max J. Exner.

78. Some social hygiene writers in the YMCA discussed race survival in terms that clearly carried racist connotations, that is, they were concerned about the success of Western civilization over against the other "darker" races and civilizations of Asia, Africa, and indigenous America. But rarely was this type of social Darwinist rhetoric emphasized in YMCA circles. "Race survival" was also discussed in contexts where the term clearly connoted the progress of the human race as a whole.

79. For discussion of Progressive Era attitudes toward sex education, see D'Emilio and Freedman, *Intimate Matters*, pp. 205–208; Simmons, "Modern Sexuality and the Myth of Victorian Repression."

80. David J. Pivar, *Purity Crusade: Sexual Morality and Social Control, 1868–1900* (Westport, CT: Greenwood Press, 1973); Mark Thomas Connelly, *The Response to Prostitution in the Progressive Era* (Chapel Hill: University of North Carolina Press, 1980); Judith R. Walkowitz, *Prostitution and Victorian Society: Women, Class, and the State* (New York, Cambridge University Press, 1980)

81. Hopkins, *History of the YMCA*, p. 386.

82. Johnson, *The History of YMCA Physical Education*, pp. 67–68.

83. Dorgan, *Gulick*, p. 58.

84. Fisher, "Prolonging Life," p. 3.

85. Fisher, "The Story of the Association's Physical Work," p. 2.

86. See Orrin G. Cocks, *Engagement and Marriage: Talks with Young Men,* Sex Education Series Study no. 4 (New York: Association Press, 1913).

87. Karl Reiland, "Sex," *Association Men* 53 (January 1928): 202.

88. There has been a debate in recent years among historians of nineteenth-century America about whether Victorians were prudes or not, and how important a role heterosexual romance and sexuality played in family life and society. Revisionists like Peter Gay, Ellen Rothman, and Karen Lystra have argued that Victorians were

much more sex-positive than they have historically been given credit for. These historians have essentially argued that Victorians enjoyed sex in private, though they were guarded about speaking of it in public. Most Victorian doctors viewed sex as a necessary and central part of a healthy life. Revisionists have dismissed the plethora of medical writings about the dangers of sex as the scribblings of a fanatical minority of "sexual restrictionists" who did not represent mainstream views. They have also downplayed the importance of same-sex "romantic friendship" and have argued that heterosexual romance in Victorian culture was an antidote to the exclusion of women from participation in the public worlds of law, politics, and business. Heterosexuality promoted closeness and equality between the sexes. The characterization of Victorians as sex-negative, and of Victorian male-female relationships as cold, distant, and unequal was a myth created by twentieth-century progressives whose social agenda was served by unfavorable comparisons of the nineteenth century with the modern era. Much of the debate over Victorian revisionism has focused on the representativity of sexual advice literature, and on the social meanings attached to the private sexual behavior documented in love letters and diaries.

I have found considerable continuity between sexual purity discourse and sex education discourse in the YMCA, and agree with revisionists that the stereotype of the sex-negative Victorian has been overdrawn. But I believe that the revisionists have largely failed to draw sufficient attention to the function of Victorian sexual ideology: to defend and expand the privileges and power of the white middle class, its familial constellations, and its gender roles. Recent scholarship has pointed out that sex-negative messages in Victorian America were directed at certain constituencies, and used as rationales for social repression, while sexual ideologies of moderation and the fundamental healthiness and goodness of sex shielded the respectable white middle class—especially men—from sexual scrutiny or criticism. See, for instance, Gail Bederman, *Manliness and Civilization: A Cultural History of Gender and Race in the United States, 1880–1917* (Chicago: University of Chicago Press, 1995); Linda Mahood and Barbara Littlewood, "The 'Vicious' Girl and the 'Street-Corner' Boy: Sexuality and the Gendered Delinquent in the Scottish Child-Saving Movement, 1850–1940," *Journal of the History of Sexuality* 4 (1994): 549–578; Margaret Morganroth Gullette, "Male Midlife Sexuality in a Gerontocratic Economy: The Privileged Stage of the Long Midlife in Nineteenth-Century Age-Ideology," *Journal of the History of Sexuality* 5 (1994): 58–89; Lesley A. Hall, "Forbidden by God, Despised by Men: Masturbation, Medical Warnings, Moral Panic, and Manhood in Great Britain, 1850–1950," *Journal of the History of Sexuality* 2 (1992): 365–387; Hall, *Hidden Anxieties*; see also Christina Simmons, "African Americans and Sexual Victorianism in the Social Hygiene Movement, 1910–40," *Journal of the History of Sexuality* 4 (1993): 51–75. The relative sexual freedom, pleasure, and closeness experienced by white, middle-class married couples was secured against a backdrop of lynchings of black men accused of lusting after white women, campaigns against working-class "urban vice" and "amusements," raillery against and mockery of "spinsters," the torment of youth through masturbation paranoia, and the incarceration or institutionalization of sodomites and "inverts." The middle-class construction of a realm of privacy where sexual pleasure was enjoyed free from public knowledge or scrutiny, which was sacrosanct and undiscussable in public, provides a shocking contrast with Victorian openness in publicly discussing the sex lives of stigmatized others: Mormon polygamists, prostitutes, urban perverts and inverts, youthful masturbators, black rapists, and the degenerate heathen of Africa and Asia.

Steven Seidman has argued that Karen Lystra's division of Victorian sex writers into "restrictionist," "moderate," and "enthusiast" camps is not "credible" and ignores certain fundamental similarities among all of them (*Romantic Longings: Love in America, 1830–1980* [New York: Routledge, 1991]). It is revealing that Lystra's analysis of the historiography of sexuality segregates "Minority Sexuality/Sexual Minorities" as a separate category, where she dumps gay history, black history, working-class history, and the history of prostitutes. Works that she lists dealing with "Sexual Politics," "Sexual Ideology/Sexual Advice," and "Private Behavior" all deal with the white (heterosexual) middle class. Apparently homosexuals, blacks, and the working class didn't have a sexual politics, didn't deal with Victorian sexual ideology, and didn't have private behavior (Lystra, *Searching the Heart: Women, Men, and Romantic Love in Nineteenth-Century America* [New York: Oxford University Press, 1989], pp. 276–278, n. 7).

89. Dr. Charles D. Scudder, *A Handbook for Young Men on Personal Purity* (New York: New York YMCA, White Cross Committee, n.d.); Sylvanus Stall, *What a Young Man Ought to Know* (Philadelphia: Vir Publishing Co., 1897); Sylvanus Stall, *What a Young Husband Ought to Know* (Philadelphia: Vir Publishing Co., 1899); Sylvanus Stall, *What a Man of Forty-five Ought to Know* (Philadelphia, Vir Publishing Co., 1901); Sylvanus Stall, *What a Young Boy Ought to Know* (Philadelphia: Vir Publishing Co., 1897); Lyman E. Sperry, *Confidential Talks with Young Men* (New York, 1907); H. Northcote, *Christianity and the Sex Problem* (New York, 1907); Dr. Winfield S. Hall, *Reproduction and Sex Hygiene* (New York, Association Press, 1907); Dr. Winfield S. Hall, *Youth: Its Education, Regimen, and Hygiene* (New York, Association Press, 1907); Dr. Winfield S. Hall, *Developing into Manhood* (New York, Association Press, 1913); Dr. Winfield S. Hall, *Life's Beginnings* (New York, Association Press, 1913); Max J. Exner, *The Rational Sex Life for Men* (New York: Association Press, 1914); Max J. Exner, *Physician's Answer* (N.p., n.d.); F. N. Seerley, *Suggested Methods for Instruction in Sexual Hygiene* (N.p., 1913); *Better Than a Fortune* (Pamphlet, 1918); Max J. Exner, *Friend or Enemy* (N.p., 1918); *Nurse and the Knight* (Pamphlet, 1918).

90. I use the term "progressive" throughout this chapter to describe the views and program of early-twentieth-century sex educators who encouraged open discussion of sexuality. These innovators generally saw themselves as forward-looking, scientific, and compassionate, and often used the term "progressive" to describe themselves. Their agenda, however, was not necessarily what many today would characterize as progressive, because of their emphasis on sexual repression and abstinence.

91. For discussions of the effects of Progressive Era sex education on attitudes toward homosexuality, see Lillian Faderman, *Odd Girls and Twilight Lovers: A History of Lesbian Life in Twentieth-Century America* (New York: Columbia University

Press, 1991), pp. 88–92; Simmons, "Modern Sexuality and the Myth of Victorian Repression"; Nancy Sahli, "'Smashing': Women's Relationships before the Fall," *Chrysalis* 8 (1979): 17–27; Lisa Duggan, "The Social Enforcement of Heterosexuality and Lesbian Resistance in the 1920s," in Amy Swerdlow and Hanna Lessinger, eds., *Class, Race, and Sex: The Dynamics of Control* (Boston: G. K. Hall, 1983); Rayna Rapp and Ellen Ross, "The Twenties Backlash: Compulsory Heterosexuality, the Consumer Family, and the Waning of Feminism," in Ann Snitow, Christine Stansell, and Sharon Thompson, eds., *Powers of Desire: The Politics of Sexuality* (New York: Monthly Review Press, 1983); Christina Simmons, "Companionate Marriage and the Lesbian Threat," *Frontiers* 4 (1979).

92. L. L. Doggett, William H. Ball, H. M. Burr, and William Knowles Cooper, *Life Problems: Studies in the Native Interests of Young Men* (New York: International Committee, 1905), pp. 39–43.

93. A. Herbert Gray, *Men, Women, and God: A Discussion of Sex Questions from the Christian Point of View* (New York: Association Press, 1923), p. 17.

94. Ibid., pp. 26–27.

95. Max J. Exner, "The Question of 'Petting,'" *Association Men* 51 (March 1926): 317–318, 349.

96. "The Dormitory: Some Real Questions," *Association Men* (March 1906): 259.

97. "From the Viewpoint of Association Men," *Association Men* (June 1909): 473.

98. See White, *The First Sexual Revolution*; Mark C. Carnes and Clyde Griffen, eds., *Meanings for Manhood: Constructions of Masculinity in Victorian America* (Chicago: University of Chicago Press, 1990); Mark C. Carnes, *Secret Ritual and Manhood in Victorian America* (New Haven: Yale University Press, 1989); James Eli Adams, *Dandies and Desert Saints: Styles of Victorian Masculinity* (Ithaca, NY: Cornell University Press, 1995); Steven Mintz and Susan Kellogg, *Domestic Revolutions: A Social History of American Family Life* (New York: Free Press, 1988); Carroll Smith-Rosenberg, *Disorderly Conduct: Visions of Gender in Victorian America* (New York: Knopf, 1985); Steven Mintz, *A Prison of Expectations: The Family in Victorian Culture* (New York: New York University Press, 1983); Barbara Welter, "The Cult of True Womanhood, 1820–1860," *American Quarterly* 18, no. 2, pt. 1 (1966): 151–74; G. J. Barker-Benfield, *Horrors of the Half-Known Life: Male Attitudes toward Women and Sexuality in Nineteenth-Century America* (New York: Harper and Row, 1976); Peter Filene, *Him/Her/Self* (New York: Harcourt Brace Jovanovich, 1975); Peter N. Stearns, *Be a Man! Males in Modern Society* (New York: Holmes and Meier, 1979); Carl Degler, *At Odds: Woman and the Family in America from the Revolution to the Present* (New York: Oxford University Press, 1980); Ann Douglas, *The Feminization of American Culture* (New York: Knopf, 1977); John S. Haller, Jr., and Robin M. Haller, *The Physician and Sexuality in Victorian America* (Urbana: University of Illinois Press, 1974); Lesley A. Hall, *Hidden Anxieties: Male Sexuality 1900–1950* (Cambridge: Polity, 1991); and Betty A. DeBerg, *Ungodly Women: Gender and the First Wave of American Fundamentalism* (Minneapolis: Fortress Press, 1990).

99. Luther Halsey Gulick, "Vitality and Modern Life," *Physical Education* 5 (May 1896): 21–25; and (June 1896): 1–3; Dorgan, *Gulick*, p. 41.

100. George M. Martin, "Does the Size of the Muscle Indicate Health?" *Association Men* 38 (October 1912): 5.

101. Doggett, *A Man and a School*, pp. 122–123.

102. John Brown, Jr., M.D., "Rural Health and Recreation," *Association Men* 38 (October 1912):10–12.

103. Other recent studies have examined gender and sports: White, *The First Sexual Revolution*; Susan Cahn, *Coming On Strong: Gender and Sexuality in Twentieth-Century Women's Sport* (New York: Free Press, 1994); Michael A. Messerer and Donald F. Sabo, eds., *Sport, Men, and the Gender Order: Critical Feminist Perspectives* (Champaign, IL: Human Kinetics, 1990); Jennifer Hargreaves, *Sporting Females: Critical Issues in the History and Sociology of Women's Sports* (New York: Routledge, 1994). The association between masculinity and competitive sports has been so strong that women attempting to participate have faced enormous institutional and cultural obstacles. Resistance to the integration of sports has been particularly strong, both because sports became one of the few modern arenas in which men could "prove" their masculinity, and also because crossing gender boundaries in sports undermines the biological assumptions that make the gender system seem natural.

104. Steven Marcus, *The Other Victorians: A Study of Sexuality and Pornography in Mid-Nineteenth-Century England* (New York: Basic Books, 1964). Other interpretations that stress the repressiveness of Victorian culture include: Barker-Benfield, *Horrors of the Half-Known Life*; Ronald Pearsall, *Public Purity, Private Shame: Victorian Sexual Hypocrisy Exposed* (London : Weidenfeld and Nicolson, 1976); Howard Gadlin, "Private Lives and Public Order: A Critical View of the History of Intimate Relations in the U.S.," *Massachusetts Review* 17 (Summer 1976): 304–330; Haller and Haller, *The Physician and Sexuality*; Ronald G. Walters, *Primers for Prudery: Sexual Advice to Victorian America* (Englewood Cliffs, NJ: Prentice-Hall, 1974); Barbara Welter, "The Cult of True Womanhood, 1820–1860," *American Quarterly* 18, no. 2, pt. 1 (1966): 151–74; Duncan Crow, *The Victorian Woman* (New York: Stein and Day, 1972).

105. Peter Gay, *The Bourgeois Experience: Victoria to Freud,* vol. 1, *Education of the Senses* (New York: Oxford University Press, 1984); and vol. 2, *The Tender Passion* (New York: Oxford University Press, 1986); Karen Lystra, *Searching the Heart*; and Ellen K. Rothman, *Hands and Hearts: A History of Courtship in America* (New York: Basic Books, 1984); other recent revisionist interpretations include John Maynard, *Victorian Discourses on Sexuality and Religion* (Cambridge: Cambridge University Press, 1993); and Michael Mason, *The Making of Victorian Sexual Attitudes* (New York: Oxford University Press, 1994). See also Linda M. Shires, ed., *Rewriting the Victorians: Theory, History, and the Politics of Gender* (New York: Routledge, 1992). Classic revisionist arguments interpreted Victorian sexual restraint and social purity campaigns as early expressions of domestic and public feminism. Daniel Scott Smith, in "Family Limitation, Sexual Control, and Domestic Feminism in Victorian America," in Mary S. Hartman and Lois Banner, eds., *Clio's Consciousness Raised* (New York: Harper and Row, 1974), pp. 126–133; and Nancy Cott, in "Passionlessness: An Interpretation of Victorian Sexual Ideology, 1790–1850," *Signs* 15 (1978):

219–236, argued that Victorian sexual restraint was the result of women's efforts to assert greater control over pregnancy. Carroll Smith-Rosenberg, in *Disorderly Conduct* and "Beauty, the Beast, and the Militant Woman: A Case Study in Sex Roles and Social Stress in Jacksonian America," *American Quarterly* 23 (1971): 562–584, argues that moral purity crusades were a manifestation of women's dissatisfaction with social inequality and a desire to play a more public role. In "From an Unfortunate Necessity to a Cult of Mutual Orgasm," Michael Gordon shows that nineteenth-century marital manuals did not portray women as "passionless."

106. See Seidman, *Romantic Longings*. For more about Seidman's perspective on the history of American sexuality, see *Embattled Eros: Sexual Politics and Ethics in Contemporary America* (New York: Routledge, 1992). Karen Lystra's views on the relationship between public expression and private attitudes are problematic, to say the least. In Foucauldian fashion, she argues that censorship actually heightened desire. But this is not the same thing as saying that censorship could contribute to a positive view of sexuality; desire and healthy integration of desire into one's life are not necessarily the same thing. Furthermore, Lystra interprets the antimasturbation "mania" of the nineteenth century "as a dominant symbol of the secrecy and opportunity for non-conformity which the ethic of privacy allowed." But this would seem to seriously undermine her argument about privacy creating a realm in which sex could be appreciated free of shame. It arguably would heighten fear and anxiety, especially for sexual minorities or others who fail to conform to Victorian sexual ideology. (Lystra, *Searching the Heart*, pp. 290–291.)

Chapter Two

1. Laurence L. Doggett, *History of the YMCA* (New York: Association Press, 1922), pp. 55–56. The "third great aim" refers to the fact that YMCAs sought to develop young men spiritually, intellectually, and "socially."

2. Anthony E. Rotundo, "Romantic Friendship: Male Intimacy and Middle-Class Youth in the Northeastern United States, 1802–1900," *Journal of Social History* 23 (1989): 1–25. Donald Yacovone documents the commonness of same-sex love among religious abolitionists in "Abolitionists and the 'Language of Fraternal Love,'" in Mark C. Carnes and Clyde Griffen, eds., *Meanings for Manhood: Constructions of Masculinity in Victorian America* (Chicago: University of Chicago Press, 1990). Henry Abelove takes a look at early Methodism in *The Evangelist of Desire: John Wesley and the Methodists* (Stanford: Stanford University Press, 1990). David Hilliard studies "manly love" in Anglo-Catholicism in "UnEnglish and Unmanly: Anglo-Catholicism and Homosexuality," *Victorian Studies* 25 (1982): 181–210. Peter Gay, in *The Bourgeois Experience: Victoria to Freud*, vol. 2, *The Tender Passion* (New York: Oxford University Press, 1986), saw "intense Christianity" as a "refuge to which the troubled and effete might repair in the nineteenth century," attractive to homosexuals.

3. Unlike ancient Greece or premodern Europe, North America has evolved a culture in which there is a fine line separating same-sex "friendship" and "homosexuality." (See Michel Foucault, *History of Sexuality*, 3 vols., trans. Robert Hurley [New

York: Vintage Books, 1978–1988]; David M. Halperin, *One Hundred Years of Homo-sexuality and Other Essays on Greek Love* [New York: Routledge, 1990]; and David F. Greenberg, *The Construction of Homosexuality* [Chicago: University of Chicago Press, 1988].) Same-sex sexual relationships, David Greenberg has noted in his *Construction of Homosexuality*, in almost every other case outside the modern West have followed two patterns: a transgenerational pattern, in which one partner was considerably older, had higher social status, and could serve as a mentor to the younger partner, or a transgenderal pattern, in which one partner played a traditional male role while the other partner played a female or other-gendered role. Curiously, little evidence of "egalitarian homosexuality"—in which both partners are of similar age and social status and play the same gender role—exists outside the modern West. The search for the origins and meaning of modern Western homosexuality has thus appropriately turned to the institution of friendship, to look at instances where both male and female egalitarian relationships became emotionally intense or erotically charged.

In significant ways, modern gay male relationships have more in common with straight "male bonding" than they do with heterosexual marriage. If Carroll Smith-Rosenberg, in her study "The Female World of Love and Ritual: Relations between Women in Nineteenth-Century America," *Signs* 1 (1975): 1–29, found it difficult to find a break in the continuum between platonic (nonsexual) friendship and friend-ship that included eroticism and sex play, it is because all the relationships she stud-ied along the sexual continuum shared the same meaning: they upheld social rela-tions in the all-women's spheres of childbearing and homemaking. Similarly, Martin Bauml Duberman, in "'Writhing Bedfellows,' 1826: Two Young Men from Antebel-lum South Carolina's Ruling Elite Share 'Extravagant Delight,'" *Journal of Homo-sexuality* 6 (1980/81): 85–101, found that the overtly sexual relationship of two mem-bers of South Carolina's ruling elite could be openly joked about and celebrated in correspondence because, far from interfering with their roles as slave-owning patri-archs and southern aristocrats, it intensified their bonds as up-and-coming wielders of social power.

There has been something of a backlash among some historians against the view of intense same-sex friendship in the preindustrial age developed by lesbian and gay historians. One recent effort to dissociate male romantic friendship from homo-eroticism appears in Yacovone, "Abolitionists and the 'Language of Fraternal Love.'" While Yacovone grants that "for some individuals . . . there may indeed have been ambivalent, disturbed, or incomprehensible sexual drives behind their friendships," he presents no evidence that these relationships were not erotic. He simply asserts that they could not have been, given nineteenth-century Protestant strictures against sodomy. His positing of "incomprehensible sexual drives" is itself an imposition of post-Freudian categories on a pre-Freudian era, in its assumption that true homo-sexuals masked their feelings in the language of romantic friendship. His work seems aimed at preserving a certain notion of heterosexuality in the past from the "taint" of homoeroticism. However, if it is historically inaccurate to claim same-sex romantic friendships as gay relationships, it is also inaccurate to portray them as a form of heterosexual male bonding. Though no one, not even lesbian and gay historians in search of a "usable past" as Yacovone puts it, claims that these relationships were gay, romantic friendships clearly did provide a model for later lesbian and gay relationships and many of these relationships included erotic elements. The main source of confusion is that definitions of the erotic have shifted. As historians of sexuality have demonstrated, physical intimacy and even arousal could be dissociated from "sex" so long as no penetration occurred. Such expressions of affection might or might not induce guilt among romantic friends. See Duberman, "'Writhing Bedfellows'"; Smith-Rosenberg, "The Female World of Love and Ritual."

4. Friendship plays an important role in maintaining social power. See Mary Ann Clawson, *Constructing Brotherhood: Class, Gender, and Fraternalism* (Princeton, NJ: Princeton University Press, 1989); Peggy Sanday, *Female Power and Male Dominance: On the Origins of Sexual Inequality* (Cambridge: Cambridge University Press, 1981); and Marilyn Frye, *The Politics of Reality: Essays in Feminist Theory* (Freedom, CA: Crossing Press, 1983), pp. 128–151. This was arguably a key role played by friendship in the early YMCA. Early YMCA fellowships generally consisted of upwardly mobile, urban young men, usually young, white, Anglo-Protestant clerks and entrepreneurs. YMCAs were supported financially and led by successful businessmen, and one of their major roles was to assist young men in their early careers through job placement and by connecting them socially to urban business leaders. Sociologist Graham A. Allan has argued, in *Friendship: Developing a Sociological Perspective* (New York: Harvester Wheatsheaf, 1989), that insufficient attention has been played to the social role of friendship because, unlike marriage, it is not institutionalized or ritualized in our society (p. 4).

5. Graham Allan argues that "informal relations of a friendship type help to oil the more formal channels of communication and command" (*Friendship*, p. 3).

6. Samuel M. Sayford, *Personal Work* (New York: International Committee, 1899), p. 85.

7. Doggett, *History of the YMCA*, p. 36.

8. Letter of Dwight L. Moody to John V. Farwell, February 25, 1876; and letter of Alex Kerr to Dwight L. Moody, February 25, 1876, as quoted in John V. Farwell, *Early Recollections of Dwight L. Moody* (Chicago: Winona Publishing Co., 1907), p. 145. For examples of other conversion stories involving male couples, see Second Annual Report of the London YMCA, November 1846, p. 15, quoted in Doggett, *History of the YMCA*, p. 59; and A. K. Spence, address delivered at the 1877 International Convention of the YMCAs of the United States and British Provinces, Louisville, Kentucky, quoted in Robert Weidensall, "Early History of the College Work of Young Men's Christian Associations" (typescript, 1911), p. 21.

9. Richard C. Morse, "Robert R. McBurney: A Memorial," 1899, Robert R. McBurney Papers.

10. Anonymous biographical sketch, "Robert R. McBurney," [1898?], McBurney Papers.

11. See Robert Weidensall, "The First Field Work and Early Development of the Young Men's Christian Association Movement as Conducted under the International Committee and Its First Employed Agent" (manuscript, 1912), Robert Weidensall Papers.

12. In a letter (likely written in the mid-1920s) to the Richard C. Morse Octave of Senior High School, Trenton, New Jersey, Morse wrote of his late adolescence: "At that time—as a lad—I very seriously doubted whether I could develop capacity enough to write sermons and occupy the pulpit and pastorate acceptably." Morse Papers.

13. See Richard C. Morse, *My Life with Young Men* (New York: Association Press, 1918), pp. 29, 40–41, 106.

14. Ibid., pp. 40, 59, 68–69.

15. Letter, R. C. Morse to P. A. Wieting, June 25, 1916, Morse Papers.

16. Speech given at Morse's twenty-fifth anniversary of YMCA service, February 20, 1895, Morse Papers.

17. Sermons by Robert R. McBurney, McBurney Papers.

18. Robert Weidensall, "The First Field Work," Weidensall Papers.

19. Sayford, *Personal Work*, pp. 26–28.

20. Letter, Chas. F. Rogers to Abraham Bowers, July 10, 1911, Messer Papers, Chicago Historical Society, Chicago, IL.

21. Prof. Chase, speech delivered at the 1877 International Convention, Kalamazoo, Michigan, quoted in Weidensall, "Early History of the College Work," p. 42.

22. George A. Warburton, *George Alonzo Hall: A Tribute to a Consecrated Personality* (New York: International Committee of Young Men's Christian Associations, 1905), pp. 16–17, 19, 71.

23. Doggett, *History of the YMCA*, pp. 31, 36.

24. Testimonial of the Rev. Dr. McBryde, Ober Papers.

25. Doggett, *History of the YMCA*, p. 31.

26. Sayford, *Personal Work*, p. 90.

27. Doggett, *History of the YMCA*, pp. 38, 52.

28. Sayford, *Personal Work*, p. 11.

29. Ibid., p. 59.

30. Quoted in Morse, *My Life,* p. 92.

31. From an unmarked newspaper clipping describing a public speech of Robert Weidensall, St. Joseph, Missouri, October 1877, Weidensall Papers.

32. Sayford, *Personal Work*, pp. 13, 14, 16, 69. Emphasis in original.

33. Farwell, *Moody*, pp. 10, 13, 14.

34. Charles Conrad Hamilton, Journal (manuscript, 1892–1893), pp. 131, 135, 136.

35. Ibid., pp. 66, 80, 96, 109, 127, 129, 137.

36. Sayford, *Personal Work*, p. 115.

37. Yacovone, "Abolitionists and the 'Language of Fraternal Love.'"

38. Robert Weidensall, *Visitation 'Round-the-World by Robert Weidensall to Young Men's Christian Associations* (N.p., 1911), pp. 94, 109–110.

39. John Wesley did marry once, a woman by the name of Mary Vaizelle. Wesley taught that God had commanded believers to remain celibate, and he publicly declared to his followers that he had married Vaizelle only to stop rumors about his unmarried status. He demanded that "helpers" and "preachers" who labored

under his supervision remain celibate, and he attempted to keep his followers sex-segregated and single. Wesley and Vaizelle remained childless, and in 1758, after seven years of marriage, she left him. Wesley never remarried. See Abelove, *The Evangelist of Desire*.

40. Letter, Robert Weidensall to Cephas Brainerd, June 21, 1876, Robert Weidensall Papers.

41. Letter, Robert Weidensall to Dr. J. V. Conzett, June 25, 1898, Business Series, Weidensall Papers.

42. Letter, J. W. Dean to Robert Weidensall, March 2, 1880, Business Series, Weidensall Papers.

43. Letter, J. P. Dummett to Robert Weidensall, January 22, 1900, Business Series, Weidensall Papers.

44. Letter, John R. Boardman to Robert Weidensall, June 10, 1904, Business Series, Weidensall Papers.

45. Letter, Robert Weidensall to John R. Boardman, December 31, 1904, Business Series, Weidensall Papers.

46. Letter, Curtis D. Thorpe to L. D. Wishard, July 26, 1893, Richard C. Morse Papers.

47. Letter, "Jai" to L. D. Wishard, September 27, 1887, Luther D. Wishard Papers.

48. Luther D. Wishard, "The Beginning of the Students' Era in Christian History" (typescript, 1917), p. 59.

49. Ibid., p. 100.

50. Richard C. Morse, "The New Internationalism in France," 1919, Morse Papers.

51. From a speech of John F. Moore at Morse's fiftieth anniversary of YMCA service, Morse Papers. A memorandum with the transcript of the speech explained that the speech had been dictated from memory, and that the original speech had been impromptu. Nevertheless, it seems logical to assume that unusual metaphors, such as the one here cited, would be more likely to be remembered, so the passage cited is likely reliable.

52. Letter, L. D. Wishard to Robert Weidensall, April 16, 1886, Business Series, Weidensall Papers.

53. Hamilton, Journal, p. 105.

54. Letter, John R. Boardman to Robert Weidensall, June 10, 1894, Business Series, Weidensall Papers.

55. Letter, Robert Weidensall to John R. Boardman, December 31, 1904, Business Series, Weidensall Papers.

56. Weidensall, *Visitation 'Round-the-World,* pp. 94, 109–110.

57. Quoted in Doggett, *Man and a School*, p. 31.

58. Letter, C. W. Jerome to C. K. Ober, October 20, 1888, "College Associations," C. K. Ober Papers.

59. "Out of the Life of Men," *Association Men* 38, no. 1 (October 1912): 21.

60. Quoted in Doggett, *Man and a School*, p. 31.

61. H. S. Ninde, Jacob T. Bowne, and Erskine Uhl, eds., *A HandBook of the History, Organization, and Methods of Work of Young Men's Christian Associations*

(New York: International Committee of Young Men's Christian Associations, 1892), p. 125.

62. See Foucault, *History of Sexuality*, vol. 2; Halperin, *One Hundred Years of Homosexuality*.

63. Nolan Rice Best, *Two Y Men: David A. Sinclair and Edwin L. Shuey* (New York: Association Press, 1925), p. 22.

64. "Mr. Bowne was eminently successful in recognizing the dynamic kind of student he needed and in training him for his specialized work." Doggett, *Man and a School*, p. 31.

65. See for example, letter, Samuel M. Sayford to C. K. Ober, February 12, 1889, Ober Papers.

66. Wishard, "Students' Era," pp. 34–37.

67. Excerpt from an account by David McConaughy, quoted in Ober, *Wishard*, pp. 156–157.

68. Letter, R. C. Morse to P. A. Wieting, December 29, 1915, Morse Papers.

69. Letter, R. C. Morse to Jennie Van Cott Morse, May 7, 1907, Morse Family League letters, Morse Papers.

70. Rotundo, "Romantic Friendship." For other discussions of American entrepreneurial capitalism and the havoc it wrought on male-male friendship, see G. J. Barker-Benfield, *Horrors of the Half-Known Life: Male Attitudes toward Women and Sexuality in Nineteenth-Century America* (New York: Harper and Row, 1976); and David Leverenz, *Manhood and the American Renaissance* (Ithaca: Cornell University Press, 1989).

71. Yacovone documents the commonness of same-sex love among religious abolitionists in "Abolitionists and the 'Language of Fraternal Love.'" Abelove takes a look at early Methodism in *The Evangelist of Desire*. Hilliard studies "manly love" in Anglo-Catholicism in "UnEnglish and Unmanly."

72. Ninde et al., eds., *Hand-Book*, pp. 129, 138.

73. Judson J. McKim, *The Operation and Management of the Local Young Men's Christian Association* (New York: Association Press, 1927), pp. 112–114.

74. James W. McCandless, *Association Administration: A Study of the Professional Task of Operating a Young Men's Christian Association* (New York: Association Press, 1925). See also, Paul Super, *Training a Staff: A Manual for Young Men's Christian Association Executives* (New York: Association Press, 1920).

75. Luther Gulick, *The Dynamic of Manhood* (New York: Association Press, 1917).

76. Max J. Exner, M.D., "Let the Man Learn First," *Association Men* 51 (November 1925): 110–111, 129.

77. Grace Loucks Elliott and Harry Bone, *The Sex Life of Youth* (New York: Association Press, 1929), pp. 49–52.

78. Arthur Gordon, "Friendship," *Association Men* (July 1920): 498–527.

79. See Allan, *Friendship*, pp. 71–72; J. H. Pleck, "Man to Man: Is Brotherhood Possible?" in N. Glazer-Malbin, ed., *Old Family/New Family: Interpersonal Relationships* (New York: Van Nostrand, 1976). Sociological studies of male friendship since

the 1960s suggest that while certain romantic ideals of friendship persist, men rarely live up to these ideals in their relationships with each other. Pleck distinguished between "sociability" and "intimacy" in friendship, and found that men's relationships tended to score high in sociability and low in intimacy. This is in contrast with women's relationships, which score higher in intimacy. Neither study considers the impact that homophobia has had on male friendship since the 1920s. See also Lillian B. Rubin, *Intimate Strangers: Men and Women Together* (New York: Harper and Row, 1983), pp. 129–140, which discusses the difficulty men experience relating intimately to one another.

80. Victor Murdock, "The Need of Nearness," *Association Men* 45 (November 1919): 141.

Chapter Three

1. See Jackie M. Blount, "Manly Men and Womanly Women: Deviance, Gender Role Polarization, and the Shift in Women's School Employment, 1900–1976," *Harvard Educational Review* 66:2 (Summer 1996): 318–338, which documents a parallel phenomenon in female public school administration.

2. Ellen K. Rothman, *Hands and Hearts: A History of Courtship in America* (New York: Basic Books, 1984), p. 105.

3. See John M. Robson, *Marriage or Celibacy? The "Daily Telegraph" on a Victorian Dilemma* (Toronto: University of Toronto Press, 1995). This analysis of lower-middle-class and middle-class Victorian Londoners' attitudes toward marriage and sexuality found overwhelmingly negative attitudes toward male singleness. Single men's uncontrolled sexuality was seen as the primary cause of prostitution (pp. 23–25). "The overwhelming weight of opinion was that marriage, with children, is the 'natural' state. As a necessary corollary, the celibate state is incomplete" (p. 139). The choice not to marry was seen as selfish. Men who so chose were presumed to do so because they preferred financial comfort over the duty of supporting a wife and raising a family (p. 146ff.).

4. Luther D. Wishard, "The Beginning of the Students' Era in Christian History" (typescript, 1917), p. 138.

5. From a transcript of the proceedings of R. C. Morse's twenty-fifth anniversary of YMCA service, February 20, 1895, R. C. Morse Papers.

6. Morse Family League Letter, May 2, 1884, Morse Papers.

7. Charles Conrad Hamilton, Journal, 1892–1893 (manuscript), p. 79.

8. Letter, John B. Brandt to W. W. Vanarsdale, April 14, 1886, Business Series, Robert Weidensall Papers.

9. There were two versions of the letter in the Weidensall papers, one handwritten, and another typewritten. The handwritten version contained a bracket in the margins next to the above quoted passage with the word "omit." The typewritten copy omitted the passage without any indication (such as ellipses) that any portion of the original text was missing. Weidensall apparently considered most of the letter

important for historical preservation, but did not want any reference to his unmarried status. Much of Weidensall's correspondence was copied in typewritten format and the originals destroyed. This original was apparently accidentally preserved, affording intriguing insight into the preservation of his YMCA papers. See John D. Wrathall, "Provenance as Text: Reading the Silences around Sexuality in Manuscript Collections," *Journal of American History* 79, no. 1 (June 1992): 165–178.

10. Letter, David McConaughy to L. D. Wishard, July 13, 1892, India Files.

11. Letter, David McConaughy to Robert R. McBurney, November 17, 1892, India Files.

12. Letter, David McConaughy to L. D. Wishard, February 21, 1893, India Files. Emphasis is original.

13. Frank Wood resigned, under a cloud of scandal, owing to a self-professed "loss of faith." He no longer believed he could proclaim the Christian message, since he entertained too many doubts as to its truthfulness. A close reading of the correspondence of Frank Wood with the International Committee reveals a more complex picture, however. Wood's "loss of faith" took place in the context of his deteriorating relationship with his senior mission companion, David McConaughy. Wood felt intense admiration and love for McConaughy, and at the same time experienced considerable "self doubt." McConaughy, on the other hand, did not seem particularly to like Wood, and expressed mistrust of his abilities from the beginning—largely because of his prejudice that marriage should be a prerequisite for missionary service. Wood wanted to stay by McConaughy's side in Madras, and strongly expressed this preference to the International Committee. McConaughy's ambitions for expansion of the YMCA work in India—and personal conflict with Wood—led him to demand that Wood be transferred to Calcutta. In his letters to the International Committee Wood expressed a desire to remain close to McConaughy, but was transferred to Calcutta over his vehement protests. He anticipated the transfer to solitary service in Calcutta as a form of exile, leading to such anguish that he literally entertained thoughts of suicide. When he arrived in Calcutta, he eluded the men waiting to greet him at the train station, wrote his resignation letter to New York, and took the first possible ship back to America. Despite Wood's apostasy, however, he was eventually won back to Christ after being surrounded by the "warmth" of the YMCA fellowship back in America. The incident reinforces the argument, developed above, that intense friendship played an integral role in young men's sense of self and the development of their faith. For a more detailed account of the Wood scandal, see John D. Wrathall, "American Manhood and the YMCA, 1869–1920" (Ph.D. diss., University of Minnesota, 1994), pp. 29–33. See correspondence of Frank H. Wood and David McConaughy in the India Files; see also the letter of L. D. Wishard to R. C. Morse, March 10, 1893, Luther D. Wishard Papers.

14. Letter, L. W. Messer to L. E. Buell, July 14, 1897, Messer Papers, Chicago Historical Society, Chicago, IL.

15. Letter, Thomas Kirby Cree to the "Dear Misses Cree," July 15, 1890, Thomas K. Cree, Bio B Files.

16. Cited in Mary Ross Hall and Helen Firman Sweet, *Women in the YMCA Record* (New York: Association Press, 1947), pp. 32–33.

17. See for instance the broadside of Louis Dwight, April 25, 1826, reprinted in Jonathan Ned Katz, *Gay American History: Lesbians and Gay Men in the U.S.A.* (New York: Meridian, 1992), pp. 27–28.

18. U.S. Department of Commerce, Bureau of the Census, *Historical Statistics of the United States* (Washington, DC: U.S. Bureau of the Census, 1975) , pt. 1, p. 21; U.S. Bureau of the Census, Current Population Reports, ser. P–20, publ. #242, "Marital Status and Living Arrangements," p. 2; Miriam L. King, Steven Ruggles, Russell R. Menard, eds., "America at 1880: A View from the Census," typescript, Department of History, University of Minnesota, 1994, pp. 99–100; and the 1880 Census Public Use Sample.

19. There is no direct information on the average age at marriage of YMCA secretaries in the nineteenth century. But using data on whether or not YMCA secretaries were married when they entered YMCA service, what their age was on entering service, and their age and whether they were married when they left service allows us to make a rough estimate. See Appendix 1 for a complete discussion of statistical methods and analysis of nineteenth-century YMCA personnel records.

20. C. Howard Hopkins, *History of the YMCA in North America* (New York: Association Press, 1951), p. 161.

21. Roberts was actually employed as a clerk in the Boston YMCA from 1869 to 1870. But it was not until 1875 that he was hired again as the Boston Association's physical director, with dramatic results for the physical program of the YMCA as a whole.

22. Other names of influential YMCA secretaries who entered service during this period include: I. G. Jenkins (1871), D. A. Sinclair (1871), S. A. Taggart (1871), H. S. Ninde (1872), Robert A. Orr (1872), Erskine Uhl (1872), W. W. Vanarsdale (1872), Thomas S. Cole (1873), D. A. Budge (1874), Edwin Ingersoll (1874), L. W. Munhall (1875), James McConaughy (1875), Walter C. Douglass (1876), Oliver Morse (1876), S. M. Sayford (1876), C. B. Willis (1878), A. T. Hemingway (1879), H. F. Williams (1879), Philip Augustus Wieting (1879), Henry E. Brown (1880), I. E. Brown (1880), George A. Warburton (1880), George T. Coxhead (1881), Frank and Charles Ober (1882), Henry O. Williams (1882), F. C. Child (1883), and Charles Sumner Ward (1883).

23. Most large cities operated on the metropolitan system. YMCAs throughout the city were all under a unified administration that was generally overseen by the general secretary of the central branch. Branch YMCAs were semiautonomous but financially dependent on the central organization.

24. From a personal recollection of Wayne Hanson, Thomas S. McPheeters, Bio A Files.

25. David I. McCleod, *Building Character in the American Boy: The Boy Scouts, YMCA, and Their Forerunners, 1870–1920* (Madison: University of Wisconsin Press, 1983), p. 142. Baden-Powell biographer Tim Jeal believes that the founder of Boy

Scouting was homosexual (though he doubts that his love for other men was ever consummated). Baden-Powell's devotion to his Boy Scouts was likely motivated by his same-sex sexual attraction. Tim Jeal, *The Boy-Man: The Life of Lord Baden-Powell* (New York: William Morrow, 1990).

26. Paul S. Boyer, *Urban Masses and Moral Order in America, 1820–1920* (Cambridge: Harvard University Press, 1978), pp. 111–112; see also Mary P. Ryan, *Cradle of the Middle Class* (New York: Cambridge University Press, 1981).

27. Robert Weidensall, *Man's Needs and Their Supplies* (New York: Association Press, 1919), p. 13, 35–36.

28. Ethel Josephine Dorgan, *Luther Halsey Gulick, 1865–1918* (New York: Bureau of Publications, Teachers College, Columbia University, 1934), p. 8.

29. Luther H. Gulick, *The Dynamic of Manhood* (New York: Association Press, 1917), pp. 4, 15, 73, 77–79, 87, 113.

30. The title of the newsletter conjured images of the expected role of the YMCA wife, to serve as an ever-ready hostess for anyone who might be invited into the welcoming home of the secretary.

31. This is probably because it was easier to preserve complete, centralized records for an era when the total number of YMCA secretaries was considerably smaller and the quantity of records was easily managed.

32. The foreign service files contained information on a total of 692 secretaries. Of those, 523 contained information about marital status. Twenty-two of those listed were unmarried. Only 16 secretaries were listed entering the foreign service before 1900, of which 2 were unmarried. I left this small number of secretaries out of the sample, since I was trying to ascertain marital statistics only for the twentieth century from this sample.

33. Foreign Service Files; Herbert Shenton, "Reconnaissance Study: YMCA-YWCA Relations in the Field in the United States of America," report, 1930. See p. 379 for marital statistics.

34. For information about the survey methods used in the study see Shenton, "Reconnaissance Study," pp. 23–24. Since only 3.9 percent of secretaries in the Foreign Service Files were unmarried and only 2.3 percent of those responding to the survey reported that they were unmarried, it seems safe to estimate that the number of never-married secretaries serving in the YMCA in this period was between 2 and 4 percent. By comparison, only 8 percent of men in the general population at this time were never married. U.S. Department of Commerce, Bureau of the Census, *Historical Statistics,* pt. 1, p. 21; U.S. Bureau of the Census, Current Population Reports, ser. P–20, publ. #242, "Marital Status and Living Arrangements," p. 2.

35. H. S. Ninde, J. T. Bowne, and Erskine Uhl, eds., *A Hand-book of the History, Organization, and Methods of Work of Young Men's Christian Associations* (New York: International Committee of Young Men's Christian Associations, 1892), pp. 126–128, 150.

36. Judson J. McKim, *The Operation and Management of the Local Young Men's Christian Association* (New York: Association Press, 1927), p. 60.

37. James W. McCandless, *Association Administration: A Study of the Profes-*

sional Task of Operating a Young Men's Christian Association (New York: Association Press, 1925), p. 170.

Chapter Four

1. For a good synthesis of sociohistorical research on "companionate marriage" and its relationship to the history of heterosexual marriage in the United States, see Steven Mintz and Susan Kellogg, *Domestic Revolutions: A Social History of American Family Life* (New York: Free Press, 1988).

2. Letter, R. C. Morse to Shipton, August 20, 1884, Morse Papers.

3. See Morse Family League Letters, March 4, March 31, June 2, July 7, 1883.

4. Morse's marriage was performed at the bride's family homestead.

5. See Ellen K. Rothman, *Hands and Hearts: A History of Courtship in America* (New York: Basic Books, 1984), esp. p. 78; and Karen Lystra, *Searching the Heart: Women, Men, and Romantic Love in Nineteenth-Century America* (New York: Oxford University Press, 1989). In his personal memoirs, Lucien C. Warner described his own marriage, in which "great pains were taken to keep secret the fact of the engagement as well as the date of the intended marriage." He mentioned this, however, only because he thought it was of interest given that this practice was "so different from the present usages, and yet so characteristic of the country village at that time." *Personal Memoirs of Lucien Calvin Warner, During Seventy-three Eventful Years, 1841–1914* (New York: Association Press, 1915), pp. 63–66.

6. Richard C. Morse, *My Life with Young Men* (New York: Association Press, 1918), p. 167.

7. See Morse's description of his wedding in his memoirs: ibid., pp. 196–198.

8. Luther D. Wishard, "The Beginning of the Students' Era in Christian History" (typescript, 1917), p. 93.

9. Many published biographies of YMCA leaders—employed and lay—do not discuss their wives at all: George A. Warburton, *George Alonzo Hall: A Tribute to a Consecrated Personality* (New York: International Committee of Young Men's Christian Associations, 1905); Allen Folger, *Twenty-five Years as an Evangelist* (Boston: James H. Earle and Co., 1905); Ward Adair, *Memories of George Warburton* (New York: J. J. Little and Ives Co., n.d.); Frank W. Ober, ed., *James Stokes: Pioneer of Young Men's Christian Associations* (New York: Association Press, 1921); Herbert Adam Gibbons, *John Wanamaker*, 2 vols. (New York: Harper and Brothers, 1926); Ward Adair, *The Road to New York* (New York: Association Press, 1936); Ethan T. Colton, *Forty Years with Russians* (New York: Association Press, 1940); and Clarence J. Hicks, *My Life in Industrial Relations: Fifty Years in the Growth of a Profession* (New York: Harper and Brothers, 1941). All of these biographies and autobiographies include details about childhood, growing up, parentage, and personal life, but do not discuss married life. The two books authored by Ward Adair (the biography of George Warburton and Adair's autobiography) include entire chapters detailing the individuals' love of outdoor life, but never mention their wives! Adair's autobiography has a picture of him with his dog (caption: "My faithful pal") but no pictures of his wife.

Sherwood Eddy's autobiography, *A Pilgrimage of Ideas, or The Re-education of Sherwood Eddy* (New York: Farrar and Rinehart, 1934), revealingly mentions his wife only in a section where he describes "asceticism" as "dangerous" and "extreme." Some of these biographies are dedicated to wives, which is usually the only evidence that they even existed. In those autobiographies that do include discussion of the wife or married life, it is circumscribed in the extreme. Sometimes, as in Fletcher S. Brockman, *I Discover the Orient* (New York: Harper and Brothers, 1935), Mrs. Brockman exists only as a phantom companion: "Mrs. Brockman and I . . . sailed for China" (p. 29); "Mrs. Brockman and I took a river steamer for Nanking" (p. 33). Otherwise, she never says anything, never does anything, never really has any significant relationship with her husband. Other biographies have a brief section (between one and three paragraphs) or sometimes even a chapter summarizing the courtship and marriage, and perhaps offering a few details about home life: Wayne C. Williams, *Sweet of Colorado* (New York: Association Press, 1943); Aaron G. Knebel, *Four Decades with Men and Boys* (New York: Association Press, 1936); Robert Dollar, *Memoirs of Robert Dollar* (San Francisco: privately printed, 1925); Louis A. Bowman, *The Life of Isaac Eddy Brown* (New York: Association Press, 1926); Warner, *Personal Memoirs of Lucien Calvin Warner*; Robert Ellis Thompson, ed., *The Life of George H. Stuart, Written by Himself* (Philadelphia: J. M. Stoddard and Co., 1890); William Adams Brown, *Morris Ketchum Jesup: A Character Sketch* (New York: Charles Scribner's Sons, 1910); J. Wilbur Chapman, D.D., *The Life and Work of Dwight C. Moody* (Philadelphia: International Publishing Co., 1900). There are a few significant exceptions. Some biographies that went into greater detail about marriage and family life were actually written by the wife or daughter: Addie W. Hunton, *William Alphaeus Hunton: A Pioneer Prophet of Young Men* (New York: Association Press, 1938); [Mrs. Frederick Morgan Harris], *Frederick Morgan Harris: A Little of His Life and Some of His Letters* (Chicago: privately printed, 1929). Authorship by a family member, however, was no guarantee that family would receive significant attention. Ruth Wilder Braisted's biography of her father *In This Generation: The Story of Robert P. Wilder* (New York: Association Press, 1941) briefly described her parents' courtship and marriage, and made occasional mention of her mother but was generally as silent about this aspect of her father's life as most other biographies.

10. See Morse Family League letter, April 1, 1895. Morse's correspondence with his wife during their brief separation in 1907 filled eighty-six pages, and contained numerous expressions of tender affection. See Morse Family League letter, July 4, 1907; letters, R. C. Morse to Jennie V. C. Morse, May 7, May 12, and May 31, 1907, Morse Papers. See also May 11, and May 25, 1910.

11. Rothman, *Hands and Hearts;* Lystra, *Searching the Heart.*

12. Morse Family League letter, May 20, 1917, Morse Papers.

13. Morse Family League letter, May 20, 1917, Morse Papers.

14. Letter, Richard C. Morse to P. A. Wieting, May 28, 1917, Morse Papers.

15. Letter, Morse Family League, November 16, 1915, Morse Papers.

16. See Morse, *Life*, pp. 196–198.

17. Ibid., p. 167.

18. Ibid.

19. Morse later celebrated a similar milestone: "Mr. & Mrs. Stebbins with their family of four dined with us one day—the first time in our long friendship when I have been able to extend this hospitality to him and his" (Morse Family League letter, May 1, 1886, Morse Papers). Obviously the extension of this hospitality to the Stebbins children was also a status milestone. This is logical, since besides marriage, siring children was the final expectation of men, the requirement that made them fully men. Acknowledgment of Stebbins's fatherhood would be an important mark of their friendship. Of course, despite his marriage, Morse was never able to fulfill this requirement, since he and his wife remained childless throughout their thirty-four-year marriage.

20. Morse Family League letter, October 31, 1885, Morse Papers.

21. Letter, Samuel M. Sayford to C. K. Ober, April 15, 1890, Ober Papers.

22. Letter, R. C. Morse to L. D. Wishard, September 10, 1889, Luther D. Wishard Papers.

23. Morse Family League letter, April 1, 1890, Morse Papers.

24. Morse Family League letter, October 31, 1885, Morse Papers.

25. Letter, R. C. Morse to J. V. C. Morse, May 11, 1910, Morse Papers.

26. Letter, R. C. Morse to J. V. C. Morse, May 25, 1910, Morse Papers.

27. Report of the Conference to the Session of the Secretaries' Association, in *Proceedings of the First Conference of Wives of Secretaries of the Young Men's Christian Associations of North America* (New York, 1900), p. 27.

28. Mrs. C. B. Willis, Speech, in *Proceedings of the First Conference of Wives*, pp. 16–17.

29. Mrs. W. M. Danner, Speech, in *Proceedings of the First Conference of Wives*, p. 12.

30. Mrs. E. C. Brownell, Speech, in *Proceedings of the First Conference of Wives*, p. 19. Emphasis is original.

31. Letter, to the wives of foreign secretaries from "The Secretaries' Wives," in *Proceedings of the First Conference of Wives*, pp. 26–27.

32. Letter of Cornelia S. Mills to W. B. Smith, May 13, 1920.

33. Letter of Edith L. Brown to W. B. Smith, March 18, 1920.

34. Letter of Julia H. Trueman to W. B. Smith, May 30, 1920.

35. Letter of Anna White Stewart to W. B. Smith, April 27, 1920.

36. Charlotte Oliver Wiley, "An Old Wife's Tale," *Open Door* 3 (June 1944): 8–9.

37. Doris Hall, "Why a 'Y' Wife?" *Open Door* 7 (Spring 1948): 9.

38. *Open Door* 3, no. 2 (June 1944): 9.

39. Esther McCaslin, "It Happened at Lake Geneva," *Open Door* 8, no. 3 (Autumn 1949): 8.

40. Hall, "Why?" p. 9.

41. Thomas P. Pearman, "Y-Wives Must Be Partners," *Open Door* 3 (February 1944): 17–18.

42. *Addresses and Papers of John R. Mott* (New York: Association Press, 1946–1947), vol. 4, p. 990; cited in C. Howard Hopkins, *John R. Mott, 1865–1955: A Biography* (Grand Rapids, MI: William B. Eerdmans Publishing Co., 1979), p. 9.

43. Hopkins, *Mott*, pp. 18–19, 44. Subsequent references will appear as page numbers in the text.

44. Marc Boegner, *The Long Road to Unity* (London: Collins, 1970), pp. 33–34.

45. Hopkins, *Mott*, p. 23. Subsequent references will appear as page numbers in the text.

46. Bruce Benton, "The Greatest Y Man," *American Magazine* (Oct. 1918): 9–10, 100.

47. Hopkins, *Mott*, pp. 95–97.

48. Ibid., pp. 283–285, 469.

49. Letter, John R. Mott to Leila White Mott, New Year's Eve, 1906, quoted in Hopkins, *Mott*, p. 306.

50. Letter, John R. Mott to Leila White Mott, March 15, 1907, quoted in Hopkins, *Mott*, p. 313.

51. Eugene E. Barnett, "As I Look Back: Recollections of Growing Up in America's Southland and of Twenty-six Years in Pre-Communist China, 1888–1936" (typescript, 1963), p. 2. Subsequent references to "As I Look Back" are cited by page number in the text.

52. Eugene Epperson Barnett, "Memoirs of Eugene Epperson Barnett" (typescript, edited by Committee on YMCA Historical Resources, National Board of Young Men's Christian Associations of the U.S., 1968), p. 20.

53. Ibid.

54. Ibid., p. 167.

55. Letter, Bertha Barnett to W. B. Smith, August 23, 1920.

56. Morse Papers. Emphasis is original.

Chapter Five

1. Mary Ross Hall and Helen Firman Sweet, *Women in the YMCA Record* (New York: Association Press, 1947), p. 15.

2. L. L. Doggett, *History of the Boston Young Men's Christian Association* (Boston: YMCA, 1901); Hall and Sweet, *Women*, pp. 15–16.

3. Clifford M. Drury, *San Francisco YMCA: 100 Years by the Golden Gate, 1853–1953* (Glendale, CA: Arthur H. Clark Co., 1963), p. 128.

4. Laurence L. Doggett, *A Man and a School: Pioneering in Higher Education at Springfield College* (New York: Association Press, 1943), pp. 146, 156.

5. Richard C. Morse, "The International Committee and Its Work," an address at the graduating class of Springfield Training School, March 16, 1910, Richard C. Morse Papers.

6. Luther D. Wishard, "The Beginning of the Students' Era in Christian History" (typescript, 1917), pp. 83, 232.

7. *The Verdict of Time: Fifty Years—Philadelphia YMCA* (Philadelphia: YMCA, 1905), pp. 99, 101.

8. Doggett, *Man and a School*, pp. 146, 156.

9. Cited in Hall and Sweet, *Women*, p. 51.

10. Ibid., p. 9.

11. "Those Women," *Portage La Prairie YMCA Bulletin,* July 1883. Emphasis is original.

12. Hall and Sweet, *Women*, p. 15.

13. Letter, Robert Weidensall to Burgess, June 9, 1915, Robert Weidensall Papers.

14. Robert Weidensall, "Settled Principles in the Work of the Young Men's Christian Association," February 7, 1896, Weidensall Papers.

15. "'I Live Not Yet I [*sic*] for Christ Liveth in Me': Masculinity in the Salvation Army, 1865–1890," in Michael Roper and John Tosh, eds., *Manful Assertions: Masculinities in Britain since 1800* (New York: Routledge, 1991).

16. Mary P. Ryan, *Cradle of the Middle Class* (New York: Cambridge University Press, 1981); Ann Douglas, *The Feminization of American Culture* (New York: Knopf, 1977); Barbara Welter, "The Feminization of American Religion, 1800–1860," in Mary S. Hartman and Lois Banner, eds., *Clio's Consciousness Raised* (New York: Harper and Row, 1974), pp. 137–157. For a discussion of the numerical preponderance of women in American churches in the nineteenth century, see Douglas, *Feminization*, pp. 7–8.

17. "Those Women."

18. Cited in Hall and Sweet, *Women*, p. 50.

19. Cited in Robert Weidensall, "Early History of the College Work of Young Men's Christian Associations" (typescript, 1911), pp. 9–10.

20. Samuel M. Sayford, *Personal Work* (New York: International Committee, 1899), pp. 88–89.

21. Weidensall, "Early History of the College Work," p. 92.

22. Thomas Hughes, a nineteenth-century observer of the YMCA, believed that the Association was "effete," too effeminate to reach working-class men. See Thomas Hughes, *The Manliness of Christ* (Boston: Houghton Mifflin and Co., 1879). Mary Ann Clawson's study of male fraternities in the nineteenth century, *Constructing Brotherhood: Class, Gender, and Fraternalism* (Princeton, NJ: Princeton University Press, 1989), p. 186, suggests that there was skepticism about the ability of an all-male organization free of feminine influence to uplift the morals of men.

23. Hall and Sweet, *Women*, p. 53.

24. Cited in ibid., p. 53.

25. Ibid., p. 5.

26. Drury, *San Francisco YMCA*, pp. 71–76; Hall and Sweet, *Women*, p. 33.

27. Drury, *San Francisco YMCA*, p. 89.

28. Cited in Hall and Sweet, *Women*, p. 51.

29. Drury, *San Francisco YMCA*, p. 77.

30. Hall and Sweet, *Women*, p. 51.

31. Doggett, *Man and a School*, p. 29. Ellen Brown was also a lifelong "spinster."

32. Cited in Hall and Sweet, *Women*, pp. 15–16.

33. William B. Whiteside, *The Boston YMCA and Community Need* (New York: Association Press, 1951), p. 31.

34. Hall and Sweet, *Women*, pp. 30–31, 34.

35. Quoted in C. K. Ober, *Luther D. Wishard: Projector of World Movements* (New York: Association Press, 1927), p. 67.

36. Drury, *San Francisco YMCA*, p. 76.

37. Emmett Dedmon, *Great Enterprises: 100 Years of the YMCA of Metropolitan Chicago* (New York: Rand McNally, 1957), p. 108.

38. Edwin Burritt Smith et al., *Historical Sketch of the YMCA of Chicago, 1858–1898* (Chicago: Association, 1898), p. 16.

39. Drury, *San Francisco YMCA*, pp. 31–32, 35, 44, 71.

40. Minutes, San Francisco YMCA, February 20, 1894, cited in Drury, *San Francisco YMCA*, p. 105.

41. Wishard, "Students' Era," p. 139.

42. Ober, *Wishard*, p. 69.

43. Historical sketch, inventory, Chicago YMCA Archives, Chicago Historical Society.

44. Hall and Sweet, *Women*, pp. 35, 52.

45. Mrs. L. W. Messer, "Robert Weidensall and the Young Women's Christian Association," Weidensall Papers.

46. Cited in Drury, *San Francisco YMCA*, p. 57.

47. Wishard, "Students' Era," p. 138.

48. Cited in Hall and Sweet, *Women*, p. 52.

49. Wishard, "Students' Era," p. 141.

50. Ibid., p. 144.

51. Ibid., p. 140–141.

52. Ibid., p. 141.

53. Letter, R. C. Morse to C. K. Ober, December 27, 1884, Morse Papers. Emphasis is original.

54. Paula Fass, in *The Damned and the Beautiful: American Youth in the 1920s* (Oxford: Oxford University Press, 1977), shows how dating norms became more sexually permissive in the 1920s. YMCA leaders sought to fight this by providing controlled environments where young men and women could meet.

55. Hedley S. Dimock, "Implications of the U.S.O. Experience for Group Work" (U.S.O. pamphlet, 1944), cited in Hall and Sweet, *Women*, p. 135.

56. Cited in Hall and Sweet, *Women*, p. 119.

57. Fass (*The Damned and the Beautiful*) argues that the expectation of a more sexually integrated social life and the rise of dating made the defense of traditional masculine camaraderie problematic. Fass's analysis and a broad reading of YMCA sources from this period suggest that some of the pressure to "heterosocialize" may have come from YMCA youth themselves.

58. It is significant, though it should not be surprising, that YWCA protests against

YMCA mixed work and work for women and girls received almost no attention in official YMCA publications. An article by Rhoda E. McCulloch entitled "Mabel Cratty: 'Explorer of the Hearts of Women, Discovering Them to Themselves,'" *Association Men* 53, no. 8 (April 1928): 350, gave the impression of warm reciprocal relations between the YW and the YM, despite the fact that Cratty, who was being eulogized, had been one of the most vocal voices of protest against YMCA policies. Another article published in *Association Men* by Cratty's successor, Emma Bailey Speer, addressed conflicts between the YM and the YW only indirectly. See Emma Bailey Speer, "What *Does* the Woman Want?" *Association Men* 53, no. 10 (June 1928): 443 – 444.

59. Letter, Emma Bailey Speer to Francis S. Harmon, June 10, 1931, reprinted in "A Letter to the YMCA concerning the Proposed Amendment to Its Constitution," *Woman's Press*, July 1931, newspaper clipping, YMCA-YWCA Relations Papers.

60. "Relationships with the Young Men's Christian Association," February 23, 1928, published in the biennial report of the National Board of the YWCA, box 1195.

61. Memo of Mildred Corbett to the Town Department, YWCA, 192[?].

62. Sub-committee on Methods and Procedure in Connection with Immediate Situations, "Synopsis of Case Histories of YMCA and YWCA Relationships," Appointed by YMCA Commission and YWCA Commission, March 15, 1926.

63. See William A. McGarry, "The YMCA in Philadelphia," *Association Men* 49, no. 1 (September 1923): 23 – 24; William A. McGarry, "Breaking Precedent at Ardmore," *Association Men* 51, no. 1 (September 1925): 13 – 14.

64. Herbert Shenton, Project Director, "Reconnaissance Study: YMCA-YWCA Relations in the Field in the United States of America" report, 1930, p. 390.

65. Paul Super, *Outline Studies of Some Fundamental Principles and Tested Policies of the North American YMCAs* (New York: Association Press, 1920), pp. 13–14.

66. See George W. Broden, "Outline of Questionnaire on Work for Women and Girls," *Physical Training* (October 1920); "The Women and Girls Question: A Variety of Opinions on the Significance of This Problem to the YMCA," *Association Forum* (January 1931); "Poll of Boys' Work Committeemen on Policy for Supervision of Young Girls' Work"; Shenton, "Reconnaissance Study," pp. 269–332.

67. See Letter, J. A. Urice to Mildred Corbett, February 16, 1927.

68. Letter, J. A. Urice to Robert R. Vernon, February 25, 1928.

69. Memo, Henry Israel to Jay Urice, November 26, 1927.

70. Circular memo, entitled "Cooperation with the YMCA from September 1931 to March 1932, as Related to the Work of the National Services Division" (n.d.); Shenton, "Reconnaissance Study," p. 262.

71. Memorandum, Herbert Shenton, director of the reconnaissance study, to the National Council of the YMCA, about a proposed amendment to the constitution and by-laws of the National Council, January 26, 1931.

72. See Nina Mjagkij, *Light in the Darkness: African Americans and the YMCA, 1852–1946* (Lexington: University of Kentucky Press, 1994), esp. pp. 116–127, for a more complete discussion of segregation in the YMCA and the means by which it was brought to an end.

73. See also Jodi Vandenberg-Daves, "The Manly Pursuit of a Partnership between the Sexes: The Debate over YMCA Programs for Women and Girls, 1914–1933," *Journal of American History* 78 (March 1992): 1324–1346.

74. "Relationships with the Young Men's Christian Association."

75. Chambers, Gimsel, Murry, Brown, and Wilson, "Activities That Unite Young Men and Young Women," Study Conference YMCA, April 26–27, 1930. Emphasis is mine.

76. See Broden, "Outline of Questionnaire"; "The Women and Girls Question"; "Poll of Boys' Work Committeemen"; "Proposals Making Possible Identical Status of the Sexes as Affecting Recognition, Rights, and Responsibilities in Associations' Affairs," proposed amendment to the standing rules of the International Constitution of the National Council of the U.S., August 10–11, 1931, p. 9.

77. See especially, Shenton, "Reconnaissance Study," p. 279. One response in particular, much like modern family values rhetoric, linked "preservation of the American Home" with "normal mingling of the sexes."

78. Memo, J. W. Ogg to Neil McMillan, Jr., June 19, 1928.

79. "The Women and Girls' Question."

80. See Kevin White, *The First Sexual Revolution: The Emergence of Male Heterosexuality in Modern America* (New York: New York University Press, 1993); Christina Simmons, "Modern Sexuality and the Myth of Victorian Repression," in Kathy Peiss, Christina Simmons, with Robert Padgug, eds., *Passion and Power: Sexuality in History* (Philadelphia: Temple University Press, 1989), pp. 157–177; Lisa Duggan, "The Social Enforcement of Heterosexuality and Lesbian Resistance in the 1920s," in Amy Swerdlow and Hanna Lessinger, eds., *Class, Race and Sex: The Dynamics of Control*, (Boston: G. K. Hall, 1983); Rayna Rapp and Ellen Ross, "The Twenties Backlash: Compulsory Heterosexuality, the Consumer Family, and the Waning of Feminism," in Ann Snitow, Christine Stansell, and Sharon Thompson, eds., *Powers of Desire: The Politics of Sexuality* (New York: Monthly Review Press, 1983); Christian Simmons, "Companionate Marriage and the Lesbian Threat," *Frontiers* 4 (1979); Nancy Sahli, "'Smashing': Women's Relationships before the Fall," *Chrysalis* 8 (1979): 17–27.

81. Chambers et al., "Activities That Unite," p. 33.

82. Not surprisingly, this view was more often promoted by women than by men. See Irma Voight, "Co-operation with This Generation," *Intercollegian* 41, no. 8 (May 1924): 13–14.

83. Reports on mixed work as well as activities jointly sponsored by the YMCA and the YWCA included descriptions of mixed sex education work and curricula. Apparently an issue of some concern was whether it was appropriate to discuss sex matters in front of mixed groups. It was unanimously agreed, however, that mixed sex education was not only appropriate but essential. See "Description of YMCA-YWCA Activities, Jointly Planned and Executed," September 1932, for Omaha, Nebraska; Syracuse, New York; Minneapolis, Minnesota; New Haven, Connecticut; Toledo, Ohio; Rochester, New York; Westfield, New Jersey; and Hackensack, New Jersey; James F. Bunty, "Should Mixed Groups Discuss Questions of Sex? An

Account of One Group Project in This Area," typescript, Rochester, NY: YM-YW Council, 1932. See also "The Problem of Marriage," *Association Men* 52, no. 10 (June 1927): 446.

84. "Descriptions of YMCA-YWCA Activities, p. 9.

Chapter Six

1. Paula Lupkin, "Buildings for Building Men: The Architectural Development of the Young Men's Christian Association, 1870–1915," paper presented at the Society of Architectural Historians, Philadelphia, PA, 1994.

2. Louis E. Jallade, *The Association Building: Supervision and Circulation* (New York: Association Press, 1913), p. 13.

3. See, for instance, a lecture of S. W. Dean, in "The Operation and Maintenance of Association Buildings," Lake Geneva Summer School of City Association Administration, 1915, p. 4. "All of us will agree that environment has a very important part in the moulding of the ideals of men and boys. . . . Our buildings furnish stimuli which will create impulses in the men and boys who come to our buildings,— impulses which will be either for good or for bad depending on the kind of environment."

4. H. S. Ninde, J. T. Bowne, and Erskine Uhl, eds. *A Hand-Book of the History, Organization, and Methods of Work of Young Men's Christian Associations* (New York: International Committee of Young Men's Christian Associations, 1892), p. 8.

5. See also ibid., which basically reprinted the 1891 advice book; *Hints about the Construction of Young Men's Christian Association Buildings* (New York: International Committee of the YMCA's of North America, 1909); Jallade, *The Association Building;* "The Operation and Maintenance of Association Buildings"; *The Building Enterprise of a City Young Men's Christian Association* (New York: Building Bureau of the International Committee of Young Men's Christian Associations, 1919); H. T. Friermood, Lectures, "Association Science: Buildings," c. 1923.

6. *The Association Building* (N.p., 1919), p. 6.

7. Dexter A. Rau, "The Dormitory Question" (Graduating thesis, George Williams College, 1913), pp. 33–34. Apparently wanting to protect the Portland YMCA from any more negative attention than it had already received, Rau referred to the scandal in the main body of the text only as a "report . . . concerning one of our Western Associations." Only in a footnote did he specify that he was talking about Portland.

8. *Suggestions Regarding a Young Men's Christian Association Building*, p. 14; Jallade, *The Association Building*, p. 45.

9. H. T. Friermood, Lectures, pp. 1–2.

10. YMCAs did not, however, lose buildings as a result of the Great Depression. It appears that heroic budget cuts were made in other areas specifically to preserve physical plant. See C. Howard Hopkins's discussion of the effects of the Great Depression on the YMCA, *History of the YMCA in North America* (New York: Association Press, 1951), pp. 586–590.

11. See YMCA *Yearbooks* for 1890, 1901, 1905, 1910, 1915, 1920, 1925, and 1930.

12. In the 1920s, YMCA leaders began to devote increasing attention to the dormitory problem, though there had been some discussion of the dilemmas posed by dormitory work from around the turn of the century. See John S. Schroeder, "Economic Features in Association Work," *Association Seminar* 11, no. 8 (May 1903): 292–309; *The Dormitory Problem in the Young Men's Christian Association* (Asilomar, CA: General Secretaries, 1915); George W. Miller, "The True Purpose in Operating a YMCA Dormitory" (manuscript, c. 1925); T. W. Merriam, "The Dormitory Project" (manuscript, c. 1925); and Chester D. Barr (Assistant to the General Executive, Columbus YMCA), "YMCA Dormitories: Theory and Practice" (Master's thesis in Social Administration, Ohio State University, 1927). Starting in the mid-1920s, the *Bulletin of the Dormitory Secretaries Association of the YMCA's of Ohio* came into being as a means of disseminating advice about how to handle dormitory problems and providing support for the small but growing number of dormitory secretaries.

13. *Suggestions Regarding a Young Men's Christian Association Building*, p. 6.

14. Hopkins, *History of the YMCA*, p. 154.

15. For a discussion of the lengths to which police went to harass urban "tearooms," see, for instance, Steven Maynard, "Through a Hole in the Lavatory Wall: Homosexual Subcultures, Police Surveillance, and the Dialectics of Discovery, Toronto, 1890–1930," *Journal of the History of Sexuality* 5, no. 2 (1994): 207–242.

16. Laurence L. Doggett, *History of the Boston YMCA* (Boston: YMCA, 1901), pp. 50–52.

17. Ibid., p. 76.

18. "Editorials," *Triangle* 1, no. 2 (March 1891): 30–31.

19. Laurence L. Doggett, *A Man and a School: Pioneering in Higher Education at Springfield College* (New York: Association Press, 1943), p. 160.

20. Cited in Doggett, *Man and a School*, p. 48.

21. Ethel J. Dorgan, *Luther Halsey Gulick, 1865–1918* (New York: Bureau of Publications, Teachers College, Columbia University, 1934), p. 43.

22. Ibid., pp. 26, 31.

23. *Young Men's Era* 28 (1892): 182–184.

24. Luther H. Gulick, "Robert J. Roberts and His Work" (typescript, n.d.).

25. William Blaikie, "Physical Training in the Young Men's Christian Association," *Association Men* 27 (March 1902): 233.

26. Robert J. Roberts, "The Home Dumb Bell Drill," *Physical Education* 11, no. 10 (1893): 154–160; and no. 11 (1894): 174–178.

27. Ibid. Emphasis in original.

28. George M. Martin, "Does the Size of the Muscle Indicate Health?" *Association Men* 38 (October 1912): 5.

29. Letter, L. W. Messer to Fred S. Goodman, August 5, 1897, Messer Papers, Chicago YMCA Archives, Chicago Historical Society, Chicago, IL.

30. R. C. Morse, Address at the Bible Teachers' Training School, New York City, February 14, 1910, R. C. Morse Papers.

31. Martin, "Size," p. 6.

32. John Brown, Jr., M.D., "Rural Health and Recreation," *Association Men* 38 (October 1912): 10.

33. R. C. Cubbon, "The Physical Department's Religious Opportunity," *Association Men* 38 (October 1912): 28. Emphasis in original.

34. Blaikie, "Physical Training," p. 236.

35. See Harry Oosterhuis and Hubert Kennedy, *Homosexuality and Male Bonding in Pre-Nazi Germany* (New York: Harrington Park Press, 1991).

36. Every major history of YMCA physical education and the North American physical culture movement acknowledges the heavy influence of German physical culture philosophy. See Hopkins, *History of the YMCA,* pp. 245–270; Elmer L. Johnson, *The History of YMCA Physical Education* (Chicago: Follett Publishing Co., 1979); Emmett A. Rice, *A Brief History of Physical Education* (New York: A. S. Barnes and Co., 1969; orig. publ. 1926); Fred Eugene Leonard, *A Guide to the History of Physical Education* (Philadelphia: Lea and Febiger, 1947); Physical Directors' Society of the Young Men's Christian Associations of North America, *Physical Education in the Young Men's Christian Associations of North America* (New York: Association Press, 1920); see also Mabel Lee, *A History of Physical Education and Sports in the U.S.A.* (New York: Wiley, 1983); Betty Mary Spears, *History of Sport and Physical Activity in the United States* (Dubuque, IA: William C. Brown Co., 1978); and Earle E. Zeigler, *A History of Physical Education and Sport in the United States and Canada* (Champaign, IL: Stipes Publishing Co., 1975).

37. See John Preston, "My Life with Pornography," in John Preston, ed., *Flesh and the Word: An Anthology of Erotic Writing* (New York: Dutton, 1992); Emmanuel Cooper, *Fully Exposed: The Male Nude in Photography* (New York: Routledge, 1995); Emmanuel Cooper, *The Sexual Perspective: Homosexuality and Art in the Last 100 Years in the West* (New York: Routledge, 1994). The connection between physical culture and early gay porn was vividly brought to my attention in 1992 when, perusing a stack of 1950s and 1960s "physique" magazines, I ran across images of Arnold Schwartzenegger. Although none of the poses were overtly sexual, and none of the models were completely nude, these magazines were deliberately titillating, and they were almost uniquely consumed by gay men as pornography. (In *Sexual Perspective* Emmanuel Cooper discusses Schwartzenegger's role in removing the aura of sexual dubiousness under which the bodybuilding profession had fallen by the 1960s.)

38. Greg Mullins, "Nudes, Prudes, and Pigmies: The Desirability of Disavowal in *Physical Culture,*" *Discourse: Journal for Theoretical Studies in Media and Culture* 15, no. 1 (Fall 1992): 27–48.

39. Doggett, *Man and a School*, p. 137.

40. See Luther Gulick, "Gymnasium Exhibitions," *Young Men's Era* 16 (May 22, 1890): 330.

41. Luther Gulick, "The Physical Department," in Ninde, Bowne, and Uhl, eds. *A Hand-Book of the History,* pp. 304–305.

42. *Physical Training* 19, no. 3 (January 1922): 115.

43. Robert Weidensall, *Man's Needs and Their Supplies* (New York: Association Press, 1919), p. 198. Emphasis is mine.

44. The only account of John reclining on Jesus's breast is found in John 13: 23–25.

45. See Luke 7:36–50.

Chapter Seven

1. Interview, Jim Kepner, August 20, 1992. The phenomenon of homosexual cruising in YMCA locker rooms, shower rooms, gymnasiums, swimming pools, and dormitories has been observed and acknowledged at least since the turn of the century. It has been mentioned by sex researchers from Magnus Hirschfeld to Alfred Kinsey and Evelyn Hooker. In fact, Kinsey's research included an extensive section on cruising at the YMCA. YMCA cruising has not only become a part of modern American gay folklore, but it has been celebrated in song, painting, and erotic literature by gay artists and writers. The 1920s gay novel *Scarlet Pansy* was set in the Baltimore YMCA. Many other gay erotic writers since the twenties have set their stories in YMCAs. Gay artist Paul Cadmus painted a canvas in 1933 called "YMCA Locker Room" which features a sexy locker room ambiance where young, naked bodies weave past each other and several older men proposition young men. The Village People song "YMCA" has long been recognized within the gay community as a campy (if coded) description of the YMCA as a gay sexual arena, but there have been other songs about YMCA cruising as well, like Rae Bourbon's "Queen of the YMCA." By the early 1970s, gay guidebooks like Francis Hunter's *The Gay Insider* listed and described YMCAs, with hints about what kind of action could be expected in particular locales, and which YMCAs required more discretion. For a certain generation of gay men, YMCA memorabilia became very popular. In an interview I conducted in Los Angeles with Paul McGuinness, September 11, 1992, he recalled men who kept and even framed YMCA towels. In 1964, the cruising scene at the YMCA was brought with embarrassing force to public attention when Walter Jenkins, a high-ranking Johnson administration official, was arrested at the Lafayette YMCA near the White House for soliciting sex.

2. Xavier Mayne, *The Intersexes: A History of Similisexualism as a Problem in Social Life* (New York: Arno Press, 1975), p. 639. The Arno Press edition is a reprint of the privately published original of 1908.

3. Emmett Dedmon, *Great Enterprises: 100 Years of the YMCA of Metropolitan Chicago* (New York: Rand McNally, 1957), p. 93.

4. George Chauncey, Jr., "Christian Brotherhood or Sexual Perversion? Homosexual Identities and the Construction of Sexual Boundaries in the World War I Era," *Journal of Social History* 19 (1985): 189–212.

5. For a more detailed account of the Newport, Rhode Island, scandal, see Chauncey, "Christian Brotherhood or Sexual Perversion?"; and Lawrence R. Murphy, *Perverts by Official Order: The Campaign against Homosexuals by the United States Navy* (New York: Haworth Press, 1988).

6. For most of the material in this section I am deeply indebted to Tom Cook of Portland, Oregon, who made me aware of the scandal, and who kindly photocopied

and sent me relevant articles from the Portland press, courtroom transcripts from the Oregon State Archives, and judicial reports.

7. "Rotten Scandal Reaches into the YMCA," *Portland News*, November 15, 1912, vol. 13, no. 45; "Forty Men and Boys in Big YMCA Scandal," *Portland News*, November 16, 1912, vol. 13, no. 46.

8. "Mayor Puts Police on Job for Decency," *Portland News*, November 21, 1912, vol. 13, no. 50.

9. Cited in the *Oregon Journal*, November 25, 1912.

10. See "The News—Also Degenerates and Their Allies," *Portland News*, November 17, 1912, vol. 13, no. 46; *Oregon Journal*, November 25, 1912.

11. Dr. Winfield S. Hall, M.D., "Slumming," *Association Men* 38 (December 1912): 122.

12. Ibid., p. 138.

13. *Portland News*, November 15–December 4, 1912, vol. 13, nos. 44–63; *McAlister vs. State of Oregon,* transcript of proceedings, Oregon State Archives; *Start vs. State of Oregon,* transcript of proceedings, Oregon State Archives.

14. "One Attempts Suicide—Eleven under Arrest," *Oregon Journal*, November 17, 1912.

15. "Grand Jury Will Investigate Charges," *Oregon Journal*, November 19, 1912.

16. "Rotten Scandal," *Portland News*, November 15, 1912, vol. 13, no. 44.

17. See Jonathan Ned Katz, *Gay American History: Lesbians and Gay Men in the U.S.A.* (New York: Meridian, 1992); John D'Emilio, *Sexual Politics, Sexual Communities: The Making of a Homosexual Minority in the United States, 1940–1970* (Chicago: University of Chicago Press, 1983); George Chauncey, *Gay New York: Gender, Urban Culture, and the Making of the Gay Male World, 1890–1940* (New York: Basic Books, 1994).

18. The main character in *Scarlet Pansy* was Fay Etrange (French for "strange fairy"). In an attempt to avoid censorship, the author, Robert Scully (a pen name), cast the main character as a woman but then used gay code to indicate to knowing readers that he was really writing about a gay man. To avoid confusion, I am using masculine personal pronouns to describe the protagonist of this novel even though the actual novel refers to Fay as a woman.

19. Telephone interview, Martin Block, August 27, 1992.

20. Interview, Harry Hay, Los Angeles, August 29, 1992.

21. Interview, William Billings, Los Angeles, August 31, 1992.

22. Interview, Paul Hardman, Los Angeles, August 31, 1992.

23. Pierre Foreau, "The White Peacock," *One* 8, no. 1 (January 1960): 13, relying on Edward H. Maisel, *Charles T. Griffes: The Life of an American Composer* (New York: 1943).

24. Telephone interview, Dorr Legg, August 21, 1992.

25. Interview, Paul Hardman, Los Angeles, August 31, 1992.

26. See the *Portland News*, 1912–1913; *Oregon Reports*, 1912.

27. Telephone interview, Martin Block, August 27, 1992.

28. Hardman interview.

29. Billings interview.

30. Ibid.

31. Hay interview.

32. Hardman interview.

33. Billings interview.

34. Allan Bérubé, *Coming Out under Fire: Gay Americans and the Military in World War II* (New York: Free Press, 1989).

35. Laud Humphreys's *Tearoom Trade: Impersonal Sex in Public Spaces* (Chicago: Aldine Publishing Co., 1970) was severely criticized for relying on unethical research methods. Humphries followed a number of men without their consent, took their license plate numbers, and tracked them to their homes, where he conducted surveys about their sexual attitudes and essentially spied on their household situations and family lives under false pretenses. Humphries defended his actions on the grounds that this was the only way to get the information that he sought, and suggested that the ends might justify the means if he could, through the study, win greater tolerance for homosexuality and put an end to police harassment. Other studies of the cruising phenomenon include: Martin Weinberg, "Gay Baths and the Social Organization of Impersonal Sex," *Social Problems* 22 (1975): 124–136; and Richard Troiden, "Homosexual Encounters in a Highway Rest Stop," in E. Goode and R. Troiden, eds., *Sexual Deviance and Sexual Deviants* (New York: Morrow, 1974).

36. *Association Men* 31 (March 1906): 259.

37. Donald Vining, *A Gay Diary* (New York: Pepys Press, 1979).

38. "Statement by the Committee on Counseling of the Program Services Department concerning the Homosexual and the YMCA," National Council of YMCAs, New York, January 1966, Bob Harlan File.

39. Hay interview.

40. Block interview.

41. Kepner interview.

42. Interview, George Mendenhall, San Francisco, September 2, 1992.

43. Interview, Jim Dawson, Los Angeles, August 25, 1992.

44. Interview, Hal Call, San Francisco, September 2, 1992.

45. Telephone interview, Larry Littlejohn, August 31, 1992.

46. Vining, *Gay Diary*, vol. 1, p. 395.

47. Mendenhall interview.

48. Telephone interview, Sam Steward, September 2, 1992.

49. Vining, *Gay Diary*, vol. 1, pp. 274, 372, 381, 434, 436.

50. Ibid., pp. 274, 404, 424, 433.

51. Kepner interview.

52. McGuinness interview.

53. Mendenhall interview.

54. Telephone interview, Bob Basker, September 3, 1993.

55. Block interview.

56. Telephone interview, Dorr Legg, August 21, 1992.

57. Telephone interview, August 21, 1992.

58. Chauncey, "Christian Brotherhood or Sexual Perversion," 189–212.

59. *Association Men* 38 (October 1912).

60. "There Is Just One Paper in This Town That Dares Stand for Decency," *Portland News*, November 19, 1912, vol. 13, no. 48.

61. "Committee Will Investigate Vice Scandal Report," *Oregon Journal*, November 21, 1912.

62. Luther H. Gulick, *The Dynamic of Manhood* (New York: Association Press, 1917).

63. "Vice Ulcer Spreads," *Portland News*, November 26, 1912, vol. 13, no. 54.

64. For a discussion of Symonds's life and work, and an account of his relationship with Walt Whitman, see Jeffrey Weeks, *Coming Out: Homosexual Politics in Britain from the Nineteenth Century to the Present*, rev. ed. (New York: Quartet Books, 1990), pp. 47–56.

65. "Walt Whitman as an Army Man," *Association Men* 45, no. 5 (April 1920): 484.

66. See Justin Kaplan, *Walt Whitman: A Life* (New York: Simon and Schuster, 1980); Charley Shively, *Drum Beats: Walt Whitman's Civil War Boy Lovers* (San Francisco: Gay Sunshine Press, 1989); Charley Shively, *Calamus Lovers: Walt Whitman's Working-Class Camerados* (San Francisco: Gay Sunshine Press, 1987); Jimmie Killingsworth, *Whitman's Poetry of the Body: Sexuality, Politics, and the Text* (Chapel Hill: University of North Carolina Press, 1989); Betsy Erkkila and Jay Grossman, eds., *Breaking Bounds: Whitman and American Cultural Studies* (New York: Oxford University Press, 1996).

Epilogue

1. Interview, Wayne Flottman, Los Angeles, August 25, 1992.

2. Interview, Paul McGuinness, Los Angeles, September 11, 1992.

3. Interview, Paul Hardman, Los Angeles, August 31, 1992.

4. McGuinness interview.

5. Interview, Jim Dawson, Los Angeles, August 25, 1992.

6. Interview, William Billings, Los Angeles, August 31, 1992.

7. McGuinness interview.

8. "Statement by the Committee on Counseling of the Program Services Department concerning the Homosexual and the YMCA," National Council of YMCAs, New York, January 1966. Bob Harlan File.

9. Telephone interview, Dorr Legg, August 21, 1992.

10. Laud Humphreys mentions in a footnote a "confidential" report by the Central YMCA of Philadelphia, entitled "The Use of Closed Circuit TV for the Study and Elimination of Homosexual Activity in the YMCA." Laud Humphreys, *Tearoom Trade: Impersonal Sex in Public Places* (Chicago: Aldine Publishing Co., 1970), p. 83.

11. Memo, Charlotte Himber to Bob Harlan, May 11, 1971; see also Robert Harlan File on Homosexuality, which contains numerous magazine and newspaper articles

documenting gay dissatisfaction with the YMCA, and a speech Harlan gave to the National Council urging implementation of the 1966 report.

Appendix One

1. Roster of Paid Secretaries, 1879–1900.

2. For this statistical analysis technique, I am indebted to Steven Ruggles of the University of Minnesota. All errors in its application are of course my own.

Appendix Two

1. For discussions of the concept of the spirit/body split, see Mary Daly, *Beyond God the Father: Toward a Philosophy of Women's Liberation* (Boston: Beacon, 1973); John Y. Fenton, ed., *Theology and Body* (Philadelphia: Westminster, 1974); Rosemary Radford Ruether, *New Woman, New Earth: Sexist Ideologies and Human Liberation* (New York: Seabury, 1975); and James B. Nelson, *Embodiment: An Approach to Sexuality and Christian Theology* (Minneapolis: Augsburg Publishing House, 1978).

2. Letter to the editor, Pearl M. Campbell, *L.A. Times*, October 24, 1964.

3. Grinker's speech and the question-and-answer session that followed were reported in a YMCA newsletter, *Counseling* 20, no. 2 (March–April 1962): 3.

SELECTED BIBLIOGRAPHY

Manuscript Collections

YMCA of the USA Archives, St. Paul, MN. Applications for the position of Secretary, 1879–1880. Bio B Files. Cephas Brainerd Papers. India Files. "Kansas Sudan Mission Movement" Papers. William Chauncy Langdon Papers. Robert R. McBurney Papers. Richard Cary Morse Papers. Charles K. Ober Papers. Roster of Paid Secretaries, 1879–1900. Samuel M. Sayford Papers. Glenn K. Shurtleff Papers. Robert Weidensall Papers. Luther D. Wishard Papers. YMCA-YWCA Relations Papers.

Chicago Historical Society, Chicago, IL. Chicago YMCA Archives. Loring Wilbur Messer Papers.

Periodicals

Association Forum, 1953–1959.
Association Men, 1899–1959.
Association Monthly, Executive Committee, 1870–1873.
Association Monthly, National Board, 1907–1922.
Association Outlook, 1892–1900.
The Companion, 1855–1883.
Kansas Pilgrim, 1891.
Open Door, 1944–1949.
One Magazine, 1953–1961.

Physical Education, 1892–1896.

Physical Training, 1901–1928.

Proceedings of the Convention of Young Men's Christian Associations, 1854–1877.

Triangle, 1891–92.

The Watchman, 1875–1889.

Year Book of the Young Men's Christian Associations, 1878-present.

YMCA Weekly Bulletin, 1878–1884.

Young Men's Christian Journal, 1859–1860.

Young Men's Era, 1890–1896.

Young Men's Magazine, 1857–1859; 1875–1879; 1889–1898.

Manuscripts

Barnett, Eugene E. "As I Look Back: Recollections of Growing Up in America's South-land and of Twenty-six Years in Pre-Communist China, 1888–1936." Typescript. 1963. YMCA of the USA Archives, St. Paul, MN.

————. "Memoirs of Eugene Epperson Barnett." Typescript, edited by Committee on YMCA Historical Resources, National Board of Young Men's Christian Associations of the U.S., 1968. YMCA of the USA Archives, St. Paul, MN.

Barr, Chester D. "YMCA Dormitories: Theory and Practice." Master's thesis in Social Administration, Ohio State University, 1927. YMCA of the USA Archives, St. Paul, MN.

Brainerd, Cephas, "The Work of the Army Committee of the New York YMCA, Which Led to the Organization of the U.S. Christian Commission." Typescript. 1866. YMCA of the USA Archives, St. Paul, MN.

Brainerd, Ira H., and E. W. "Cephas Brainerd Biography." Typescript. 1947. YMCA of the USA Archives, St. Paul, MN.

Bunty, James F. "Should Mixed Groups Discuss Questions of Sex? An Account of One Group Project in This Area." Typescript. Rochester, New York: YM-YW Council, 1932. YMCA of the USA Archives, St. Paul, MN.

Davidann, Jon Thares. "The American YMCA in Meiji Japan: God's Work Gone Awry." Seminar Paper, University of Minnesota. 1990.

Dean, S. W. "The Operation and Maintenance of Association Buildings." Typescript. Lecture, Lake Geneva Summer School of City Association Administration, 1915. YMCA of the USA Archives, St. Paul, MN.

Fels, G. L. "History of the Louisville YMCA" Typescript. 1945. YMCA of the USA Archives, St. Paul, MN.

"Forty Years of the YMCA of Portland, Oregon, 1868–1909." Typescript. N.d. YMCA of the USA Archives, St. Paul, MN.

Gulick, Luther. "Robert J. Roberts and His Work." Typescript. N.d. YMCA of the USA Archives, St. Paul, MN.

Hamilton, Charles Conrad. "Journal." Manuscript. 1892–1893. YMCA of the USA Archives, St. Paul, MN.

Hantover, Jeff. "Sex Role, Sexuality, and Social Status in the Early Years of the Boy Scouts of America." Ph.D. diss., University of Chicago. 1976.

"Highlights in the History of the YMCA of Chicago 1858–1944." Typescript. 1944. YMCA of the USA Archives, St. Paul, MN.

"History of the Indianapolis YMCA 1854–1948." Typescript. 1948. YMCA of the USA Archives, St. Paul, MN.

King, Miriam L., Steven Ruggles, and Russell R. Menard, eds. "America at 1880: A View from the Census." Typescript. Department of History, University of Minnesota, 1994.

Lupkin, Paula. "Buildings for Building Men: The Architectural Development of the Young Men's Christian Association, 1870–1915." Paper presented at the Society of Architectural Historians, Philadelphia, PA, 1994.

McBurney, Robert R. "Business Management in the Association." Typescript. 1892. YMCA of the USA Archives, St. Paul, MN.

"Outline for History of San Antonio YMCA." Typescript. 1949. YMCA of the USA Archives, St. Paul, MN.

Rau, Dexter A. "The Dormitory Question." Graduating thesis, George Williams College. 1913. YMCA of the USA Archives, St. Paul, MN.

Rhodes, I. B. "The Development of Dormitories in the YMCA's in the U.S." Typescript. International Committee, ca. 1935. YMCA of the USA Archives, St. Paul, MN.

Shenton, Herbert. "Reconnaissance Study: YMCA-YWCA Relations in the Field in the United States of America." Report. 1930. YMCA of the USA Archives, St. Paul, MN.

Simmons, Christina. "Marriage in the Modern Manner: Sexual Radicalism and Reform in America, 1914–1941." Ph.D. diss., Brown University, 1982.

Steinmetz, Cheryl. "Christian Manhood: YMCA Literature and Libraries, 1850–1885." Seminar Paper, University of Minnesota, 1990.

Subcommittee on Methods and Procedure in Connection with Immediate Situations, Appointed by YMCA Commission and YWCA Commission, "Synopsis of Case Histories of YMCA and YWCA Relationships." Report. 1926. YMCA of the USA Archives, St. Paul, MN.

Weidensall, Robert. "Early History of the College Work of Young Men's Christian Associations." Typescript. 1911. YMCA of the USA Archives, St. Paul, MN.

———. "The Origin of the Association of General Secretaries of YMCAs and the Early History of the Training Schools of YMCAs." Typescript. 1911. YMCA of the USA Archives, St. Paul, MN.

———, comp. "Letters: Cephas Brainerd to Robert Weidensall, 1868–1893." Typescript. 1911. YMCA of the USA Archives, St. Paul, MN.

Wells, M. C. "History of the First Seventy Years of the YMCA of Hartford, Connecticut." Typescript. 1949. YMCA of the USA Archives, St. Paul, MN.

Wishard, Luther D. "The Beginning of the Students' Era in Christian History." Typescript. 1917. YMCA of the USA Archives, St. Paul, MN.

Worman, E. C. "History of Brooklyn and Queens YMCA, 1853–1949." Typescript. 1949. YMCA of the USA Archives, St. Paul, MN.

Wrathall, John D. "American Manhood and the YMCA, 1869–1920." Ph.D. diss., University of Minnesota, 1994.

Articles

Banner, Lois. "Religious Benevolence as Social Control: A Critique of an Interpretation." *Journal of American History* 60 (1973): 23–41.

Bloch, Ruth H. "Untangling the Roots of Modern Sex Roles: A Survey of Four Centuries of Change." *Signs* 4 (1978): 237–252.

Blount, Jackie M. "Manly Men and Womanly Women: Deviance, Gender Role Polarization, and the Shift in Women's School Employment, 1900–1976." *Harvard Educational Review* 66:2 (1996): 318–338.

Brissett, Dennis, and Lionel Lewis. "Guidelines for Marital Sex: An Analysis of Fifteen Popular Marriage Manuals." *Family Coordinator* 19 (January 1970): 41–48.

Bullough, Vern, and Martha Vogt. "Homosexuality and Its Confusion with the 'Secret Sin' in Pre-Freudian America." *Journal of the History of Medicine* 28 (1973): 143–154.

Burnham, John C. "Early References to Homosexual Communities in American Medical Writings." *Human Sexuality* 7 (1973): 34–49.

———. "The Progressive Era Revolution in American Attitudes toward Sex." *Journal of American History* 59 (1973): 885–908.

Chapman, Terry L. "'An Oscar Wilde Type': 'The Abominable Crime of Buggery' in Western Canada, 1890–1920." *Criminal Justice History* 4 (1983): 97–118.

Chauncey, George, Jr. "Christian Brotherhood or Sexual Perversion? Homosexual Identities and the Construction of Sexual Boundaries in the World War I Era." *Journal of Social History* 19 (1985): 189–212.

Clark, Clifford. "The Changing Nature of Protestantism in Mid-Nineteenth-Century America: Henry Ward Beecher's Seven Lectures to Young Men." *Journal of American History*, 57 (1971): 832–846.

Coburn, C. A. "The Great General Secretary." *Association Forum* 8 (1928): 8–9.

Cook, Blanche Wiesen. "The Historical Denial of Lesbianism." *Radical History Review* (1979): 60–65.

Cott, Nancy. "Passionlessness: An Interpretation of Victorian Sexual Ideology, 1790–1850." *Signs* 15 (1978): 219–236.

Dunn, F. R. "Formative Years of the Chicago YMCA: A Study in Urban History." *Journal of the Illinois State Historical Society* 37 (1944): 329–350.

Gadlin, Howard. "Private Lives and Public Order: A Critical View of the History of Intimate Relations in the U.S." *Massachusetts Review* 17 (Summer 1976): 304–330.

Gordon, Michael. "From an Unfortunate Necessity to a Cult of Mutual Orgasm: Sex in American Marital Education Literature, 1830–1940." In James Henslin and

Edward Sagarin, eds., *The Sociology of Sex: An Introductory Reader*, rev. ed. New York: Schocken,1978.

Gullette, Margaret Morganroth. "Male Midlife Sexuality in a Gerontocratic Economy: The Privileged Stage of the Long Midlife in Nineteenth-Century Age-Ideology." *Journal of the History of Sexuality* 5 (1994): 58–89.

Gutman, Herbert. "Protestantism and the American Labor Movement: The Christian Spirit in the Gilded Age." *American Historical Review* 72 (1966):74–101.

Hall, Lesley A. "Forbidden by God, Despised by Men: Masturbation, Medical Warnings, Moral Panic, and Manhood in Great Britain, 1850–1950." *Journal of the History of Sexuality* 2 (1992): 365–387.

Handy, Robert T. "The Protestant Quest for a Christian America 1830–1930," *Church History* 21–22 (1952–1953): 8–20.

Hansen, Bert. "American Physicians' Earliest Writings about Homosexuals, 1880–1900." *Milbank Quarterly* 67 (1989): 92–108.

Hilliard, David. "UnEnglish and Unmanly: Anglo-Catholicism and Homosexuality." *Victorian Studies* 25 (1982): 181–210.

Lerner, Gerda. "Where Biographers Fear to Tread." *Women's Review of Books* 11 (1987): 11–12.

"Luther Halsey Gulick, 1865–1918: A Symposium." *American Educational Review* 23 (1918): 413–426.

Lynch, Michael. "'Here Is Adhesiveness': From Friendship to Homosexuality." *Victorian Studies* 29 (1985): 67–96.

Mahood, Linda, and Barbara Littlewood. "The 'Vicious' Girl and the 'Street-Corner' Boy: Sexuality and the Gendered Delinquent in the Scottish Child-Saving Movement, 1850–1940." *Journal of the History of Sexuality* 4 (1994): 549–578.

Maynard, Steven. "Through a Hole in the Lavatory Wall: Homosexual Subcultures, Police Surveillance, and the Dialectics of Discovery, Toronto, 1890–1930." *Journal of the History of Sexuality* 5 (1994): 207–242.

McIntosh, Mary. "The Homosexual Role." *Social Problems* 16 (1968): 182–192.

Minton, Henry L. "Femininity in Men and Masculinity in Women: American Psychiatry and Psychology Portray Homosexuality in the 1930s." *Journal of Homosexuality* 13 (1986): 1–21.

Moorland, Jesse E. "The YMCA among Negroes." *Journal of Negro History* 9 (1924): 127–138.

Mullins, Greg. "Nudes, Prudes, and Pigmies: The Desirability of Disavowal in *Physical Culture*." *Discourse: Journal for Theoretical Studies in Media and Culture* 15, no. 1 (Fall 1992): 27–48.

Newton, Esther. "The Mythic Mannish Lesbian: Radclyffe Hall and the New Woman." *Signs* 9 (1984): 557–578.

Ober, C. K. "Robert R. McBurney, Master Secretary." *Association Men* 38 (1913): 619–620.

Rich, Adrienne. "Compulsory Heterosexuality and Lesbian Existence." *Signs* 5 (1980): 631–660.

Roberts, Robert J. "The Home Dumb Bell Drill." *Physical Education* 11, no. 10 (1893): 154–160; and no. 11 (1894): 174–178.

Rotundo, E. Anthony. "Romantic Friendship: Male Intimacy and Middle-Class Youth in the Northern United States, 1802–1900." *Journal of Social History* 23 (1989): 1–25.

Rupp, Leila J. "'Imagine My Surprise': Women's Relationships in Mid-Twentieth Century America." *Frontiers: A Journal of Women's Studies* 5 (1980): 61–70.

Sahli, Nancy. "'Smashing': Women's Relationships before the Fall." *Chrysalis* 8 (1979): 17–27.

Schlesinger, Arthur. "A Critical Period in American Protestantism, 1875–1900." *Massachusetts Historical Society Proceedings* 64 (1930–1932): 523–48.

Schroeder, John S. "Economic Features in Association Work." *Association Seminar* 11, no. 8 (May 1903): 292–309.

Simmons, Christina. "Companionate Marriage and the Lesbian Threat." *Frontiers* 4 (1979): 54–59.

———. "African Americans and Sexual Victorianism in the Social Hygiene Movement, 1910–40." *Journal of the History of Sexuality* 4 (1993): 51–75.

Smith-Rosenberg, Carroll. "Beauty, the Beast, and the Militant Woman: A Case Study in Sex Roles and Social Stress in Jacksonian America." *American Quarterly* 23 (1971): 562–584.

———. "The Female World of Love and Ritual: Relations between Women in Nineteenth-Century America." *Signs* 1 (1975): 1–29.

Sprague, Gregory. "Male Homosexuality in Western Culture: The Dilemma of Identity and Subculture in Historical Research." *Journal of Homosexuality* 10 (1984): 29–44.

Strong, Bryan. "Ideas of the Early Sex Education Movement in America, 1890–1920." *History of Education Quarterly* (1972).

Thompson, Gilbert. F. "History of the Physical Work in the YMCA of America." *Association Seminar* 12, no. 11 (1904): 301–315; no. 12 (1904): 380–389; 13, no. 1 (1905): 13–39; no. 2 (1905): 47–67; no. 3 (1905): 95–104; no. 4 (1905): 127–147, 156.

Vandenberg-Daves, Jodi. "The Manly Pursuit of a Partnership between the Sexes: The Debate over YMCA Programs for Women and Girls, 1914–1933." *Journal of American History* 78 (March 1992): 1324–1346.

Weinberg, Jonathan. "Cruising with Paul Cadmus." *Art in America* (November 1992): 102–109.

Weinberg, Martin. "Gay Baths and the Social Organization of Impersonal Sex." *Social Problems* 23 (1975): 124–136.

Warburton, G. A. "A Study in Secretarial Personality." *Association Forum* 1 (1920): 1–3.

———. "The Tower Room." *Association Forum* 9 (1928): 9.

Welter, Barbara. "The Cult of True Womanhood, 1820–1860." *American Quarterly* 18, no. 2, pt. 1 (1966): 151–74.

———. "The Feminization of American Religion 1800–1860." In Mary S. Harman and Lois Banner, eds., *Clio's Consciousness Raised,* pp. 137–157. New York: Harper and Row, 1974.

Wrathall, John D. "Provenance as Text: Reading the Silences around Sexuality in Manuscript Collections." *Journal of American History* 79, no. 1 (June 1992): 165–178.

Zald, Mayer N., and Patricia Denton. "From Evangelism to General Service: The Transformation of the YMCA." *Administrative Science Quarterly* 8 (1963): 214–234.

Books

Abell, Aaron Ignatius. *The Urban Impact on American Protestantism, 1865–1900.* Cambridge: Harvard University Press, 1943.

Abelove, Henry. *The Evangelist of Desire: John Wesley and the Methodists.* Stanford: Stanford University Press, 1990.

Adair, Ward. *Memories of George Warburton.* New York: J. J. Little and Ives Co., n.d.

———. *The Road to New York.* New York: Association Press, 1936.

Adams, James Eli. *Dandies and Desert Saints: Styles of Victorian Masculinity.* Ithaca, NY: Cornell University Press, 1995.

Addresses and Papers of John R. Mott. Vol. 4. New York: Association Press, 1946–1947.

Ahlstrom, Sydney. *A Religious History of the American People.* New Haven: Yale University Press, 1972.

Allan, Graham A. *Friendship: Developing a Sociological Perspective.* New York: Harvester Wheatsheaf, 1989.

Appel, Joseph H. *The Business Biography of John Wanamaker.* New York: Macmillan, 1930.

Barker-Benfield, G. J. *Horrors of the Half-Known Life: Male Attitudes toward Women and Sexuality in Nineteenth-Century America.* New York: Harper and Row, 1976.

Bartlett, Lester W., and Alden W. Boyd. *The YMCA Physical Director: An Analysis of the Activities of the Secretary Who Is Responsible for Physical Education in a Local YMCA.* Chicago: University of Chicago Press, 1929.

Bartlett, Lester W., Ralph M. Hogan, and Alden W. Boyd. *The YMCA Executive Secretary.* Chicago: University of Chicago Press, 1929.

Bederman, Gail. *Manliness and Civilization: A Cultural History of Gender and Race in the United States, 1880–1917.* Chicago: University of Chicago Press, 1995.

Beisel, Nicola Kay. *Imperiled Innocents: Anthony Comstock and Family Reproduction in Victorian America.* Princeton, NJ: Princeton University Press, 1997.

Berger, Peter L. *The Sacred Canopy: Elements of a Sociological Theory of Religion.* Garden City: Doubleday, 1967.

Berger, Peter L., and Thomas Luckmann. *The Social Construction of Reality.* Garden City: Doubleday, 1966.

Bérubé, Allan. *Coming Out under Fire: Gay Americans and the Military in World War II.* New York: Free Press, 1989.

Best, Nolan Rice. *Two Y Men: David A. Sinclair and Edwin L. Shuey.* New York: Association Press, 1925.

Better Than a Fortune. Pamphlet, 1918.

Bishop, C. S. *L. Wilbur Messer, An Appreciation.* New York: Association Press, 1931.

Boegner, Marc. *The Long Road to Unity.* London: Collins, 1970.

Bowman, Louis A. *The Life of Isaac Eddy Brown.* New York: Association Press, 1926.

Boyer, Paul S. *Purity in Print: The Vice-Society Movement and Book Censorship in America.* New York: Scribner's, 1968.

——. *Urban Masses and Moral Order in America, 1820–1920.* Cambridge: Harvard University Press, 1978.

Braisted, Ruth Wilder. *In This Generation: The Story of Robert P. Wilder.* New York: Association Press, 1941.

Bray, Alan. *Homosexuality in Renaissance England.* London: Gay Men's Press, 1982.

Bremner, Robert H., and David Brody, eds., *Change and Continuity in Twentieth Century America: The 1920s.* Columbus: Ohio State University Press, 1968.

Brockman, Fletcher S. *I Discover the Orient.* New York: Harper and Brothers, 1935.

Brod, Harry, ed. *The Making of Masculinities: The New Men's Studies.* Boston: Allen and Unwin, 1987.

Brown, William Adams. *Morris Ketchum Jesup: A Character Sketch.* New York: Charles Scribner's Sons, 1910.

The Building Enterprise of a City Young Men's Christian Association. New York: Building Bureau of the International Committee of Young Men's Christian Associations, 1919.

Bullock, R. W. *Survey of the Work of YMCA's Among Colored Men and Boys.* Pamphlet, National Council of the Young Men's Christian Associations, 1938.

Butler, Jon. *Awash in a Sea of Faith: Christianizing the American People.* Cambridge: Harvard University Press, 1990.

Cahn, Susan. *Coming On Strong: Gender and Sexuality in Twentieth-Century Women's Sport.* New York: Free Press, 1994.

Chapman, J. Wilbur, D.D. *The Life and Work of Dwight C. Moody.* Philadelphia: International Publishing Co., 1900.

Carnes, Mark C. *Secret Ritual and Manhood in Victorian America.* New Haven: Yale University Press, 1989.

Carnes, Mark C., and Clyde Griffen, eds. *Meanings for Manhood: Constructions of Masculinity in Victorian America.* Chicago: University of Chicago Press, 1990.

Charleston, South Carolina, YMCA. *Half a Century in Charleston 1854–1904.* N.p., 1904.

Chauncey, George. *Gay New York: Gender, Urban Culture, and the Making of the Gay Male World, 1890–1940.* New York: Basic Books, 1994.

Clarke, Charles Walter. *Taboo: The Story of the Pioneers of Social Hygiene.* Washington: Public Affairs, 1961.

Clawson, Mary Ann. *Constructing Brotherhood: Class, Gender, and Fraternalism.* Princeton, NJ: Princeton University Press, 1989.

Cleveland YMCA. *G. K. Shurtleff Memorial.* N.p., 1909.

Cocks, Orrin G. *Engagement and Marriage: Talks with Young Men.* Sex Education Series Study no. 4. New York: Association Press, 1913.

Cole, Charles C. *The Social Ideas of the Northern Evangelicals 1820–1860.* New York: Columbia University Press, 1954.

Cole, Steward G. *The History of Fundamentalism.* New York: R. R. Smith, Inc., 1931.

Colton, Ethan T. *Forty Years with Russians.* New York: Association Press, 1940.

Connelly, Mark Thomas. *The Response to Prostitution in the Progressive Era.* Chapel Hill: University of North Carolina Press, 1980.

Cook, Blanche Wiesen. *Eleanor Roosevelt.* New York: Viking, 1992.

Cooper, Emmanuel. *The Sexual Perspective: Homosexuality and Art in the last 100 Years in the West.* New York: Routledge, 1994.

———. *Fully Exposed: The Male Nude in Photography.* New York: Routledge, 1995.

Cory, Donald Webster. *The Homosexual in America: A Subjective Approach.* New York: Greenberg, 1951.

Cree, J. K. and H. S. Ninde, eds. *Thomas Kirby Cree, A Memorial.* New York: Association Press, 1914.

Cross, W. R. *The Burned-over District.* Ithaca, NY: Cornell University Press, 1965.

Crow, Duncan. *The Victorian Woman.* London: Allen and Unwin, 1971.

Daly, Mary. *Beyond God the Father: Toward a Philosophy of Women's Liberation.* Boston: Beacon, 1973.

DeBerg, Betty A. *Ungodly Women: Gender and the First Wave of American Fundamentalism.* Minneapolis: Fortress Press, 1990.

Dedmon, Emmett. *Great Enterprises: 100 Years of the YMCA of Metropolitan Chicago.* New York: Rand McNally, 1957.

Degler, Carl. *At Odds: Women and the Family in America from the Revolution to the Present.* New York: Oxford University Press, 1980.

D'Emilio, John. *Sexual Politics, Sexual Communities: The Making of a Homosexual Minority in the United States, 1940–1970.* Chicago: University of Chicago Press, 1983.

D'Emilio, John, and Estelle B. Freedman. *Intimate Matters: A History of Sexuality in America.* New York: Harper and Row, 1988.

Ditzion, Sidney. *Marriage Morals and Sex in America: A History of Ideas.* New York: Bookman, 1953.

Dobkin, Marjorie Housepian. *The Making of a Feminist: Early Journals and Letters of M. Carey Thomas.* Kent, Ohio: Kent State University Press, 1980.

Doggett, Laurence L. *History of the YMCA.* New York: Association Press, 1896.

———. *History of the Boston Young Men's Christian Association.* Boston: YMCA, 1901.

———. *Life of Robert R. McBurney.* Cleveland, Ohio: F. M. Barton, 1902.

———. *A Man and a School: Pioneering in Higher Education at Springfield College.* New York: Association Press, 1943.

Doggett, L. L., William H. Ball, H. M. Burr, and William Knowles Cooper. *Life Prob-*

lems: Studies in the Native Interests of Young Men. New York: International Committee, 1905.

Dollar, Robert. *Memoirs of Robert Dollar.* San Francisco: Privately published, 1925.

Dorgan, Ethel J. *Luther Halsey Gulick, 1865–1918.* New York: Bureau of Publications, Teachers College, Columbia University, 1934.

The Dormitory Problem in the Young Men's Christian Association. Asilomar, CA: General Secretaries, 1915.

Douglas, Ann. *The Feminization of American Culture.* New York: Knopf, 1977.

Drummond, Henry. *Natural Law in the Spiritual World.* New York: J. Pott and Co., 1897.

Drury, Clifford M. *San Francisco YMCA: 100 Years by the Golden Gate, 1853–1953.* Glendale, CA: Arthur H. Clark Co., 1963.

Duberman, Martin. *About Time: Exploring the Gay Past.* New York: Gay Presses of New York, 1986.

Duberman, Martin Bauml, Martha Vicinius, and George Chauncey, Jr., eds. *Hidden from History: Reclaiming the Gay and Lesbian Past.* New York: Meridian, 1989.

Eddy, Sherwood. *A Pilgrimage of Ideas, or The Re-education of Sherwood Eddy.* New York: Farrar and Rinehart, 1934.

Elliott, Grace Loucks, and Harry Bone. *The Sex Life of Youth.* New York: Association Press, 1929.

Ellis, Michael J. *The Business of Physical Education.* Champaign, IL: Human Kinetics Books, 1988.

Erkkila, Betsy, and Jay Grossman, eds. *Breaking Bounds: Whitman and American Cultural Studies.* New York: Oxford University Press, 1996.

Exner, Max J. *The Rational Sex Life for Men.* New York: Association Press, 1914.

————. *Friend or Enemy.* N.p., 1918.

————. *Physician's Answer.* N.p., n.d.

Faber, Doris. *The Life of Lorena Hickok: E. R.'s Friend.* New York: William Morrow, 1980.

Faderman, Lillian. *Surpassing the Love of Men: Romantic Friendship and Love between Women from the Renaissance to the Present.* New York: Morrow, 1981.

————. *Odd Girls and Twilight Lovers: A History of Lesbian Life in Twentieth-Century America.* New York: Columbia University Press, 1991.

Farwell, John V. *Early Recollections of Dwight L. Moody.* Chicago: Winona Publishing Co., 1907.

Farwell, John V., Jr. *Some Recollections of John V. Farwell.* N.p., 1911.

Fass, Paula. *The Damned and the Beautiful: American Youth in the 1920s.* Oxford: Oxford University Press, 1977.

Fenton, John Y., ed. *Theology and Body.* Philadelphia: Westminster, 1974.

Filene, Peter. *Him/Her/Self.* New York: Harcourt Brace Jovanovich, 1975.

Findlay, James F. *Dwight L. Moody.* Chicago: University of Chicago Press, 1969.

Fisher, Galen M. *Public Affairs and the YMCA, 1844–1944.* New York: Association Press, 1948.

Folger, Allen. *Twenty-five Years as an Evangelist.* Boston: James H. Earle and Co., 1905.

Foucault, Michel. *History of Sexuality.* 3 vols. Translated by Robert Hurley. New York: Vintage Books, 1978–1988.

Franzen, Trisha. *Spinsters and Lesbians: Independent Womanhood in the United States.* New York: New York University Press, 1996.

Frye, Marilyn. *Politics of Reality: Essays in Feminist Theory.* Freedom, CA: Crossing Press, 1983.

Furniss, Norman F. *The Fundamentalist Controversy, 1918–1931.* New Haven: Yale University Press, 1954.

Gay, Peter. *The Bourgeois Experience: Victoria to Freud.* Vol. 1, *Education of the Senses.* New York: Oxford University Press, 1984.

———. *The Bourgeois Experience: Victoria to Freud.* Vol. 2, *The Tender Passion.* New York: Oxford University Press, 1986.

General Board of the Young Men's Christian Associations. *Men Working: The YMCA Program and the Present Needs of Youth.* New York: Association Press, 1936.

Gibbons, Herbert Adam. *John Wanamaker.* 2 vols. New York: Harper and Brothers, 1926.

Glazer-Malbin, N. *Old Family/New Family: Interpersonal Relationships.* New York: Van Nostrand, 1976.

Goode, E., and R. Troiden, eds. *Sexual Deviance and Sexual Deviants.* New York: Morrow, 1974.

Goodspeed, C. T. B., et al. *Loring Wilbur Messer, Metropolitan General Secretary.* Chicago: Young Men's Christian Association, 1934.

Gray, A. Herbert. *Men, Women, and God: A Discussion of Sex Questions from the Christian Point of View.* New York: Association Press, 1923.

Greenberg, David F. *The Construction of Homosexuality.* Chicago: University of Chicago Press, 1988.

Griffin, Clifford S. *Their Brothers' Keepers: Moral Stewardship in the United States 1800–1865.* New Brunswick, NJ: Rutgers University Press, 1960.

Gulick, Luther H. *The Dynamic of Manhood.* New York: Association Press, 1917.

Haley, Bruce. *The Healthy Body and Victorian Culture.* Cambridge: Harvard University Press, 1978.

Hall, Lesley A. *Hidden Anxieties: Male Sexuality 1900–1950.* Cambridge: Polity, 1991.

Hall, Mary Ross, and Helen Firman Sweet. *Women in the YMCA Record.* New York: Association Press, 1947.

Hall, Winfield S. *Reproduction and Sex Hygiene.* New York: Association Press, 1907.

———. *Youth: Its Education, Regimen, and Hygiene.* New York: Association Press, 1907.

———. *Developing into Manhood.* New York: Association Press, 1911.

———. *Life's Beginnings.* New York: Association Press, 1912.

Haller, John S., Jr., and Robin M. Haller. *The Physician and Sexuality in Victorian America.* Urbana: University of Illinois Press, 1974.

Halperin, David M. *One Hundred Years of Homosexuality and Other Essays on Greek Love*. New York: Routledge, 1990.

Handy, Robert T. *A Christian America: Protestant Hopes and Historical Realities*. New York: Oxford University Press, 1971.

Hargreaves, Jennifer. *Sporting Females: Critical Issues in the History and Sociology of Women's Sports*. New York: Routledge, 1994.

Hartmann, Mary S., and Lois Banner, eds. *Clio's Consciousness Raised*. New York: Harper and Row, 1974.

[Harris, Mrs. Frederick Morgan], ed. *Frederick Morgan Harris: A Little of His Life and Some of His Letters*. Chicago: Privately printed, 1929.

Hicks, Clarence J. *My Life in Industrial Relations: Fifty Years in the Growth of a Profession*. New York: Harper and Brothers, 1941.

Hints about the Construction of Young Men's Christian Association Buildings. New York: International Committee of the YMCA's of North America, 1909.

Hopkins, C. Howard. *The Rise of the Social Gospel in American Protestantism, 1865–1900*. Cambridge: Harvard University Press, 1943.

———. *History of the YMCA in North America*. New York: Association Press, 1951.

———. *John R. Mott, 1865–1955: A Biography*. Grand Rapids, MI: William B. Eerdmans Publishing Co., 1979.

Hudson, Winthrop S. *American Protestantism*. Chicago: University of Chicago Press, 1961.

———. *Religion in America*. 2d ed. New York: Charles Scribner's Sons, 1973.

Hughes, Thomas. *The Manliness of Christ*. Boston: Houghton Mifflin and Co., 1879.

Hull, Gloria T. *Color, Sex, and Poetry: Three Women Writers of the Harlem Renaissance*. Bloomington: Indiana University Press, 1987.

Humphreys, Laud. *Tearoom Trade: Impersonal Sex in Public Places*. Chicago: Aldine Publishing Co., 1970.

Hunter, James Davison. *American Evangelicalism: Conservative Religion and the Quandary of Modernity*. New Brunswick, NJ: Rutgers University Press, 1983.

Hunter, John Francis. *The Gay Insider U.S.A.* New York: Stonehill, 1972.

Hunton, Addie W. *William Alphaeus Hunton: A Pioneer Prophet of Young Men*. New York: Association Press, 1938.

Jallade, Louis E. *The Association Building: Supervision and Circulation*. New York: Association Press, 1913.

James, William. *The Varieties of Religious Experience*. New York: Modern Library, 1902.

Jeal, Tim. *The Boy-Man: The Life of Lord Baden-Powell*. New York: William Morrow, 1990.

Johnson, Elmer. *The History of YMCA Physical Education*. Chicago: Follett Publishing Co., 1979.

Kaplan, Justin. *Walt Whitman: A Life*. New York: Simon and Schuster, 1980.

Katz, Jonathan Ned. *Gay American History: Lesbians and Gay Men in the U.S.A.* New York: Meridian, 1992. Originally published 1976.

———. *Gay/Lesbian Almanac: A New Documentary*. New York: Harper and Row, 1983.

———. *The Invention of Heterosexuality*. New York: Dutton, 1995.

Kennedy, Elizabeth Lapovsky, and Madeline D. Davis. *Boots of Leather, Slippers of Gold: The History of a Lesbian Community*. New York: Routledge, 1993.

Kerber, Linda. *Women of the Republic: Intellect and Ideology in Revolutionary America*. Chapel Hill: University of North Carolina Press, 1980.

Killingsworth, Jimmie. *Whitman's Poetry of the Body: Sexuality, Politics, and the Text*. Chapel Hill: University of North Carolina Press, 1989.

Kinsey, Alfred C., Wardell B. Pomeroy, and Clyde E. Martin. *Sexual Behavior in the Human Male*. Philadelphia: W. B. Saunders, 1948.

Kirstein, Lincoln. *Paul Cadmus*. New York: Imago Print, 1984.

Knebel, Aaron G. *Four Decades with Men and Boys*. New York: Association Press, 1936.

Kohn, George C. *Encyclopedia of American Scandal*. New York: Facts on File, 1989.

Latourette, Kenneth S. *The Great Century,* A.D. *1800–*A.D. *1914: Europe and the U.S.A.* Vol. 4, *A History of the Expansion of Christianity*. New York: Harper, 1953.

Lee, Mabel. *A History of Physical Education and Sports in the U.S.A.* New York: Wiley, 1983.

Leonard, Fred Eugene. *A Guide to the History of Physical Education*. Philadelphia: Lea and Febiger, 1947.

Leuba, J. H. *Psychological Study of Religion*. New York: Macmillan, 1912.

Leverenz, David. *Manhood and the American Renaissance*. Ithaca: Cornell University Press, 1989.

Limbert, Paul M. *Christian Emphasis in YMCA Program*. New York: Association Press, 1944.

Luckmann, Thomas. *The Invisible Religion: The Problem of Religion in Modern Society*. New York: Macmillan, 1967.

Lystra, Karen. *Searching the Heart: Women, Men, and Romantic Love in Nineteenth-Century America*. New York: Oxford University Press, 1989.

Marcus, Steven. *The Other Victorians: A Study of Sexuality and Pornography in Mid-Nineteenth-Century England*. New York: Basic Books, 1964.

Marsden, George M. *Fundamentalism and American Culture: The Shaping of Twentieth-Century Evangelicalism, 1870–1*. New York: Oxford University Press, 1980.

Marty, Martin E. *Righteous Empire: The Protestant Experience in America*. New York: Dial Press, 1970.

———. *Pilgrims in Their Own Land*. Boston: Little, Brown, 1984.

———. *Modern American Religion*. Vol. 1, *The Irony of It All*. Chicago: University of Chicago Press, 1986.

———. *Religion and Republic*. Boston: Beacon Press, 1987.

Mason, Michael. *The Making of Victorian Sexual Attitudes*. New York: Oxford University Press, 1994.

May, Henry F. *Protestant Churches and Industrial America*. New York: Harper, 1949.

Maynard, John. *Victorian Discourses on Sexuality and Religion*. Cambridge: Cambridge University Press, 1993.

Mayne, Xavier. *The Intersexes: A History of Similisexualism as a Problem in Social Life*. New York: Arno Press, 1975. Originally published 1908.

McBurney, Robert R. *Historical Sketch of the YMCA*. Pamphlet, St. Louis: State Executive Committee, 1884.

———. *Secretarialism*. New York: Association Press, 1908.

McCandless, James W. *Association Administration: A Study of the Professional Task of Operating a Young Men's Christian Association*. New York: Association Press, 1925.

McCleod, David I. *Building Character in the American Boy: The Boy Scouts, YMCA, and Their Forerunners, 1870–1920*. Madison: University of Wisconsin Press, 1983.

McCoy, Henry J., et al. *San Francisco, Five Decades: 1853–1903 Historical Record*. San Francisco: YMCA, 1903.

McKim, Judson J. *The Operation and Management of the Local Young Men's Christian Association*. New York: Association Press, 1927.

McLoughlin, William G. *Revivals, Awakenings, and Reform: An Essay on Religion and Social Change in America, 1607–1977*. Chicago: University of Chicago Press, 1978.

Memorandum respecting New York as a Field for Moral and Christian Effort among Young Men. Pamphlet, New York YMCA, 1866.

Messerer, Michael A., and Donald F. Sabo, eds. *Sport, Men, and the Gender Order: Critical Feminist Perspectives*. Champaign, IL: Human Kinetics, 1990.

Mintz, Steven. *A Prison of Expectations: The Family in Victorian Culture*. New York: New York University Press, 1983.

Mintz, Steven, and Susan Kellogg. *Domestic Revolutions: A Social History of American Family Life*. New York: Free Press, 1988.

Mjagkij, Nina. *Light in the Darkness: African Americans and the YMCA, 1852–1946*. Lexington: University of Kentucky Press, 1994.

Mjagkij, Nina, and Margaret Spratt, eds. *Men and Women Adrift: The YMCA and the YWCA in the City*. New York: New York University Press, 1997.

Moberg, David O. *The Great Reversal*. Philadelphia: Lippincott, 1977.

Morse, Richard Cary. *Fifty Years of Federation of the YMCA's of North America*. New York: International Committee of the Young Men's Christian Associations, 1905.

———. *My Life with Young Men*. New York: Association Press, 1918.

Murphy, Lawrence R. *Perverts by Official Order: The Campaign against Homosexuals by the United States Navy*. New York: Haworth Press, 1988.

Nelson, James B. *Embodiment: An Approach to Sexuality and Christian Theology*. Minneapolis: Augsburg Publishing House, 1978.

Ninde, H. S., J. T. Bowne, and Erskine Uhl, eds. *A Hand-Book of the History, Organization, and Methods of Work of Young Men's Christian Associations*. New York: International Committee of Young Men's Christian Associations, 1892.

Northcote, H. *Christianity and the Sex Problem.* New York, 1907.

Nurse and the Knight. Pamphlet, 1918.

Ober, C. K. *Luther D. Wishard: Projector of World Movements.* New York: Association Press, 1927.

———. *Exploring a Continent: Personal and Associational Reminiscences.* New York: Association Press, 1929.

Ober, Frank W., ed. *James Stokes: Pioneer of Young Men's Christian Associations.* New York: Association Press, 1921.

Oosterhuis, Harry, and Hubert Kennedy, *Homosexuality and Male Bonding in Pre-Nazi Germany.* New York: Harrington Park Press, 1991.

Pearsall, Ronald. *Public Purity, Private Shame: Victorian Sexual Hypocrisy Exposed.* London: Weidenfeld and Nicolson, 1976.

Peiss, Kathy. *Cheap Amusements: Working Women and Leisure in Turn-of-the-Century New York.* Philadelphia: Temple University Press, 1986.

Peiss, Kathy, and Christina Simmons, with Robert Padgug, eds. *Passion and Power: Sexuality in History.* Philadelphia: Temple University Press, 1989.

Pence, Owen E. *The YMCA and Social Need: A Study of Institutional Adaptation.* New York: Association Press, 1946.

———. *Present-Day YMCA Church Relations in the United States.* New York: Association Press, 1948.

Physical Directors' Society of the Young Men's Christian Associations of North America. *Physical Education in the Young Men's Christian Associations of North America.* New York: Association Press, 1920.

Pivar, David J. *Purity Crusade: Sexual Morality and Social Control, 1868–1900.* Westport, CT: Greenwood Press, 1973.

Preston, John, ed. *Flesh and the Word: An Anthology of Erotic Writing.* New York: Dutton, 1992.

Proceedings of the First Conference of Wives of Secretaries of the Young Men's Christian Associations of North America. New York, 1900.

Quinn, D. Michael. *Mormonism and the Magic World View.* Salt Lake City: Signature Books, 1987.

———. *Same-Sex Dynamics among Nineteenth-Century Americans: A Mormon Example.* Urbana: University of Illinois Press, 1996.

Rice, Emmett A. *A Brief History of Physical Education.* New York: A. S. Barnes and Co., 1969; originally published 1926.

Robson, John M. *Marriage or Celibacy? The "Daily Telegraph" on a Victorian Dilemma.* Toronto: University of Toronto Press, 1995.

Roper, Michael, and John Tosh, eds. *Manful Assertions: Masculinities in Britain since 1800.* New York: Routledge, 1991.

Rothblum, Esther D., and Kathleen A. Brehony, eds. *Boston Marriages: Romantic but Asexual Relationships among Contemporary Lesbians.* Amherst: University of Massachusetts Press, 1994.

Rothman, Ellen K. *Hands and Hearts: A History of Courtship in America.* New York: Basic Books, 1984.

Rubin, Lillian. *Intimate Strangers: Men and Women Together*. New York: Harper and Row, 1983.

Ruether, Rosemary Radford. *New Woman, New Earth: Sexist Ideologies and Human Liberation*. New York: Seabury, 1975.

Ryan, Mary P. *Cradle of the Middle Class*. New York: Cambridge University Press, 1981.

Sanday, Peggy. *Female Power and Male Dominance: On the Origins of Sexual Inequality*. Cambridge: Cambridge University Press, 1981.

Sandeen, Ernest R. *The Roots of Fundamentalism: British and American Millenarianism, 1800–1930*. Chicago: University of Chicago Press, 1970.

Sayford, Samuel M. *Personal Work*. New York: International Committee, 1899.

Schlesinger, Arthur M. *The Rise of the City, 1878–1898*. Vol. 10, *A History of American Life*. New York: Macmillan, 1933.

Scudder, Charles D. *A Handbook for Young Men on Personal Purity*. New York: New York YMCA, White Cross Committee, n.d.

Scully, Robert. *The Scarlet Pansy*. New York: Royal Publishers, n.d. [ca. 1925]

Sedgwick, Eve Kosofsky. *Between Men: English Literature and Male Homosocial Desire*. New York: Columbia University Press, 1985.

———. *Epistemology of the Closet*. Berkeley: University of California Press, 1990.

Seerley, F. N. *Suggested Methods for Instruction in Sexual Hygiene*. N.p., 1913.

Seidman, Steven. *Romantic Longings: Love in America, 1830–1980*. New York: Routledge, 1991.

———. *Embattled Eros: Sexual Politics and Ethics in Contemporary America*. New York: Routledge, 1992.

Shedd, Clarence P. *Two Centuries of Student Christian Movements: Their Origin and Intercollegiate Life*. New York: Association Press, 1934.

Shires, Linda M., ed. *Rewriting the Victorians: Theory, History, and the Politics of Gender*. New York: Routledge, 1992.

Shively, Charley. *Calamus Lovers: Walt Whitman's Working-Class Camerados*. San Francisco: Gay Sunshine Press, 1987.

———. *Drum Beats: Walt Whitman's Civil War Boy Lovers*. San Francisco: Gay Sunshine Press, 1989.

Sickels, F. E. *Fifty Years of the YMCA of Buffalo*. Buffalo, NY: Association, 1902.

Smith, Edwin Burritt, et al. *Historical Sketch of the YMCA of Chicago 1858–1898*. Chicago: Association, 1898.

Smith, Michael, ed. *Black Men/White Men*. San Francisco: Gay Sunshine Press, 1983.

Smith, Timothy L. *Revivalism and Social Reform in Mid-Nineteenth-Century America*. Baltimore: Johns Hopkins University Press, 1980.

Smith, W. H. H., et al. *The Record of Fifty Years and a Look Ahead*. N.p., 1902.

Smith-Rosenberg, Carroll. *Disorderly Conduct: Visions of Gender in Victorian America*. New York: Knopf, 1985.

Spears, Betty Mary. *History of Sport and Physical Activity in the United States*. Dubuque, IA: William C. Brown Co., 1978.

Sperry, Lyman E. *Confidential Talks with Young Men*. New York, 1907.

Spurlock, John. *Free Love: Marriage and Middle-Class Radicalism in America, 1820–1860*. New York: New York University Press, 1988.

Stall, Sylvanus. *What a Young Boy Ought to Know*. Philadelphia: Vir Publishing Co., 1897.

———. *What a Young Man Ought to Know*. Philadelphia: Vir Publishing Co., 1897.

———. *What a Young Husband Ought to Know*. Philadelphia: Vir Publishing Co., 1899.

———. *What a Man of Forty-five Ought to Know*. Philadelphia, Vir Publishing Co., 1901.

Starbuck, E. D. *Psychology of Religion*. New York: Scribner's Sons, 1901.

Stearns, Peter N. *Be A Man! Males in Modern Society*. New York: Holmes and Meier, 1979.

The Story of Twenty Years in the Life of the YMCA of Dayton, Ohio. Dayton: Association, 1890.

Super, Paul. *Outline Studies of Some Fundamental Principles and Tested Policies of the North American YMCAs*. New York: Association Press, 1920.

———. *Training a Staff: A Manual For Young Men's Christian Association Executives*. New York: Association Press, 1920.

———. *Formative Ideas in the YMCA*. New York: Association Press, 1929.

Sweet, William Warren. *Revivalism in America: Its Origin, Growth, and Decline*. New York: Scribner's Sons, 1944.

———. *The Story of Religion in America*. New York: Harper, 1950.

Swerdlow, Amy, and Hanna Lessinger, eds. *Class, Race, and Sex: The Dynamics of Control*. Boston: G. K. Hall, 1983.

Tejirian, Edward J. *Sexuality and the Devil: Symbols of Love, Power, and Fear in Male Psychology*. New York: Routledge, 1990.

The Test of Active Membership in YMCA's. Pamphlet, International Committee, 1870.

Then and Now, 1881–1891: The Progress of a Decade of Years in the YMCA, Newburgh, N.Y. Newburgh, NY: Association, 1891.

Thompson, Robert Ellis, ed. *The Life of George H. Stuart, Written by Himself*. Philadelphia: J. M. Stoddard and Co., 1890.

Thompson, Russell. *The YMCA of Cleveland*. Cleveland: Association, 1901.

Turner, E. S. *What Advantages Have Accrued to Work for Young Men as a Result of Securing Association Buildings?* Pamphlet, International Committee, 1883.

U.S. Department of Commerce, Bureau of the Census. *Historical Statistics of the United States*. Part I. Washington, DC: U.S. Bureau of the Census, 1975.

Urice, J. A. *Committees and Boards in the Early History of the NYC YMCA 1852–70*. New York: Association Press, 1928.

The Verdict of Time: Fifty Years—Philadelphia YMCA. Philadelphia: YMCA, 1905.

Vining, Donald. *A Gay Diary*. Vol. 1, *1933–1946*. New York: Pepys Press, 1979.

Wade, Richard C. *The Urban Frontier*. Chicago: University of Chicago Press, 1964.

Walkowitz, Judith R. *Prostitution and Victorian Society: Women, Class, and the State*. New York, Cambridge University Press, 1980.

Walters, Ronald G. *Primers for Prudery: Sexual Advice to Victorian America*. Englewood Cliffs, NJ: Prentice-Hall, 1974.

Warburton, George A. *George Alonzo Hall: A Tribute to a Consecrated Personality*. New York: International Committee of the Young Men's Christian Associations, 1905.

————. *A Typical General Secretary: The Life of Edwin F. See*. New York: Association Press, 1908.

Warner, Lucien Calvin. *Personal Memoirs of Lucien Calvin Warner, During Seventy-three Eventful Years, 1841–1914*. New York: Association Press, 1915.

Weber, Max. *Sociology of Religion*. Boston: Beacon Press, 1964.

Weeks, Jeffrey. *Coming Out: Homosexual Politics in Britain from the Nineteenth Century to the Present*. rev. ed. New York: Quartet Books, 1990.

Weidensall, Robert. *Man's Needs and Their Supplies*. New York: Association Press, 1919.

Wells, Anna Mary. *Miss Marks and Miss Woolley*. Boston: Houghton Mifflin, 1978.

Welter, Barbara, ed. *Dimity Convictions: The American Woman in the Nineteenth Century*. Athens: Ohio University Press, 1976.

White, Kevin. *The First Sexual Revolution: The Emergence of Male Heterosexuality in Modern America*. New York: New York University Press, 1993.

Whiteside, William B. *The Boston YMCA and Community Need*. New York: Association Press, 1951.

Wiley, S. Wirt. *History of YMCA-Church Relations in the United States*. New York: Association Press, 1944.

Wiley, S. Wirt, and Florence Lehman. *Builders of Men: A History of the Minneapolis YMCA, 1866–1936*. Minneapolis, MN: Association, 1938.

Williams, Walter L. *The Spirit and the Flesh: Sexual Diversity in American Indian Culture*. Boston: Beacon Press, 1992.

Williams, Wayne C. *Sweet of Colorado*. New York: Association Press, 1943.

Wishard, Luther D. *The Intercollegiate YMCA Movement*. Pamphlet, International Committee, 1885.

————. *A New Program of Missions*. New York: F. H. Revell Co., 1895.

————. *The Students' Challenge to the Churches*. Chicago: F. H. Revell Co., 1900.

Woodhull, Victoria. *The Scare Crows of Sexual Slavery*. New York: Woodhull and Claflin, 1874.

YMCA Buildings. Pamphlet, International Committee, 1885, 1886, 1887.

Zald, Mayer N. *Organizational Change: The Political Economy of the YMCA*. Chicago: University of Chicago Press, 1970.

Zeigler, Earle E. *A History of Physical Education and Sport in the United States and Canada*. Champaign, IL: Stipes Publishing Co., 1975.

INDEX